W9-CAH-780

faith first

Legacy Edition
PARISH

Grade Four

RESOURCES FOR CHRISTIAN LIVING®

www.FaithFirst.com

"The Ad Hoc Committee to Oversee the Use of the Catechism, United States Conference of Catholic Bishops, has found this catechetical series, copyright 2006, to be in conformity with the *Catechism of the Catholic Church.*"

NIHIL OBSTAT
Reverend Robert M. Coerver
Censor Librorum

IMPRIMATUR
† Most Rev. Charles V. Grahmann
Bishop of Dallas

September 15, 2004

The Nihil Obstat and Imprimatur are official declarations that the material reviewed is free of doctrinal or moral error. No implication is contained therein that those granting the Nihil Obstat and Imprimatur agree with the contents, opinions, or statements expressed.

Copyright © 2006
by RCL • Resources for Christian Living®

All rights reserved. No part of this book shall be reproduced or transmitted in any form or by any means, electronic or mechanical, including photocopying, recording, or by any information or retrieval system, without written permission from the Publisher.

Send all inquiries to:
RCL • Resources for Christian Living
200 East Bethany Drive
Allen, Texas 75002-3804

Toll Free 877-275-4725
Fax 800-688-8356

Visit us at **www.RCLweb.com**
www.FaithFirst.com

Printed in the United States of America

20374 ISBN 0-7829-1066-1 (Student Book)
20384 ISBN 0-7829-1078-5 (Teacher Guide)

1 2 3 4 5 6 7 8 9 10
05 06 07 08 09 10 11

ACKNOWLEDGMENTS

Scripture excerpts are taken or adapted from the *New American Bible with Revised New Testament and Psalms* Copyright © 1991, 1986, 1970, Confraternity of Christian Doctrine, Washington, DC. Used with permission. All rights reserved. No part of the *New American Bible* may be reproduced by any means without the permission of the copyright owner.

Excerpts are taken or adapted from the English translation of the *Roman Missal* © 1973, International Committee on English in the Liturgy, Inc. (ICEL); the English translation of Act of Contrition from *Rite of Penance* © 1974, ICEL; excerpts from the English translation of *Rite of Confirmation, Second Edition* © 1975, ICEL; excerpts from the English translation of *A Book of Prayers* © 1982, ICEL; excerpts from the English translation of *Book of Blessings* © 1988, ICEL. All rights reserved.

Excerpts from the English translation of The Nicene Creed, The Apostles' Creed, *Sanctus, Agnus Dei,* and *Gloria Patri* by the International Consultation on English Texts.

Faith First Legacy Edition Development Team

Developing a religion program requires the gifts and talents of many individuals working together as a team. RCL is proud to acknowledge the contributions of these dedicated people.

Program Theology Consultants
Reverend Louis J. Cameli, S.T.D.
Reverend Robert D. Duggan, S.T.D.

Advisory Board
Judith Deckers, M.Ed.
Elaine McCarron, SCN, M.Div.
Marina Herrera, Ph.D.
Reverend Frank McNulty, S.T.D.
Reverend Ronald J. Nuzzi, Ph.D.

National Catechetical Advisor
Jacquie Jambor

Catechetical Specialist
Jo Rotunno

Contributing Writers
Student Book and Catechist Guide
Christina DeCamp
Judith Deckers
Mary Beth Jambor
Michele Norfleet

Art & Design Director
Lisa Brent

Electronic Page Makeup
Laura Fremder

Production Director
Jenna Nelson

Designers/Photo Research
Pat Bracken
Kristy O. Howard
Susan Smith

Project Editors
Patricia A. Classick
Steven M. Ellair
Ronald C. Lamping

Web Site Producers
Joseph Crisalli
Demere Henson

General Editor
Ed DeStefano

President/Publisher
Maryann Nead

Contents

We Celebrate: The Liturgical Seasons

Welcome to Faith First!

We Pray

Happy are those
who walk in
the ways of
the LORD.

PSALM 128:1

**Dear God,
Help us to learn more this year about being good followers of your Son, Jesus. Help us to make good choices, to treat others with care and respect, and to grow in love for you. Amen.**

Thoughts About Me

My name is ______________________.

I like to be called ______________________.

A hero of mine is ______________________.

A movie I enjoyed is ______________________.

My favorite meal is ______________________.

The hardest thing I ever had to do was

______________________.

My Favorite Day

Tell a partner about a favorite time you have had with your family.

Making Good Choices

Every day we use the gift of our minds to discover good choices. The Church guides us to make the best decisions. This year you will learn four ways the Church helps us. You will learn:

- what Catholics believe about our relationship with God.
- how the sacraments help us celebrate our good choices.
- rules that guide us in making good decisions.
- ways to pray when we need God's help and the guidance of the Holy Spirit.

Figure It Out!

Follow this path to make good choices. At each stop along the way, discover a way God helps us to make a right decision. A clue in each box will help you know the answer. Unscramble the letters and write the answer. Move along the path to the next choice box.

We Believe

Write who guides us to live as children of God. Tell a partner one other thing you know about this answer. Check your answer on page 72.

L H Y O   T S R I P I

____

We Worship

Write the sacrament that helps us begin anew. Tell a partner one thing that happens at this celebration. Check your answer on page 123.

N O T E L R I C A I C N O I

____

We Live

Write the name of the eight guides to happiness Jesus gave us. Tell a partner one kind of person who is blessed by God. Check your answer on pages 159 and 160.

A S E U T D I B T E

____

We Pray

Write the name of the the prayer that teaches us how Jesus tells us to live. Tell a partner one thing this prayer teaches. Check your answer on page 228.

R U O H F T R E A

____

Summing Up

Tell how Jesus asks us to live. All the letters you need are in the unscrambled words you wrote on these pages. Seven letters are filled in to help you.

_ _ V _ Y _ U _

_ _ _ G _ _ _ _ _ S

_ _ _ R _ _ L _.

The Law of the Lord

LEADER: O Lord, we gather to thank you for speaking to us through the Holy Bible.

ALL: **Your word is truth and life.**

LEADER: A reading from the holy gospel according to Saint Matthew.

ALL: **Glory to you, O Lord.**

LEADER: A Pharisee came up to Jesus to trick him and asked, "Teacher, which commandment in the law is the greatest?" Jesus said to him,

"You shall love the Lord, your God,
with all your heart,
with all your soul,
and with all your mind.

This is the greatest and the first commandment.
The second is like it:

You shall love your neighbor
as yourself.

The whole law and the prophets depend on these two commandments." MATTHEW 22:36–40

The gospel of the Lord.

ALL: **Praise to you,
Lord Jesus Christ.**

*Come and bow
before the Bible.*

Unit 1 • We Believe

What are some ways we express our faith?

Getting Ready

What I Have Learned

What is something you already know about these three faith terms?

Faith

____

____

The Incarnation

____

____

The Last Supper

____

____

Words to Know

Put an X next to the faith terms you know. Put a ? next to faith terms you need to know more about.

Faith Vocabulary

______ divine Revelation
______ Sacred Scripture
______ YHWH
______ original sin
______ public ministry of Jesus
______ Passover
______ Corporal Works of Mercy
______ Body of Christ

Questions I Have

What questions would you like to ask about the public ministry of Jesus?

____

____

____

____

A Scripture Story

Shepherd and his sheep

Why is Jesus called the Good Shepherd?

I Will Be Your God

We Pray

**Praise the LORD;
the LORD is good!**
PSALM 135:3

God our loving Father, we give you thanks and praise. Amen.

What are some of the ways you spend time with your friends?

Friends get to know each other by talking and doing things together. The same is true about our friendship with God.

How do you come to know God?

God Has Revealed Himself

Faith Focus

How does God make himself known to us?

Faith Vocabulary

divine Revelation. God making known both himself and his plan of creation and salvation for the world and all people.

faith. The gift from God that helps us know him and believe in him and all that he has revealed.

Our Friendship with God

God created us to live in friendship with him. God wants everyone to be totally happy with him on earth and in heaven. He invites all people to believe in him and trust him more than anyone else.

God has revealed himself, or made himself known, to help us grow in friendship with him. We call this **divine Revelation.** Little by little and over a long period of time God has revealed himself and his plan of creation and salvation. But we can never fully know God or explain the mystery of God in words.

The story of God's revelation was first written down in the Old Testament. There we read the story of creation and God's first promise of friendship with people. We read the story of God's promises to Noah and to Abraham. We learn about his promises to Moses and David and to the other great leaders of God's people. We call this promise of friendship between God and the People of God the Covenant.

Tell why the Covenant is a promise of friendship.

Jesus Most Fully Reveals God

Jesus is at the center of our life and of our covenant with God. Everything Jesus said and did on earth tells us about God. God has revealed himself most fully in Jesus Christ. Everything Jesus said and did invites us to believe in God and place our trust in him. There will be no further revelation after Jesus.

The New Testament tells the story of the new Covenant that God made in Jesus Christ. Jesus is the Son of God. We believe in Jesus Christ and all that he has revealed about God. Jesus Christ is the new and everlasting Covenant that God has made with people. We live and deepen our friendship with God and our belief in Jesus Christ with the help of the Holy Spirit.

Faith-Filled People

The Israelites

The Israelites were the descendants of Abraham chosen by God to be his people. The name *Israelites* comes from the name of one of Abraham's sons, Israel. Israel's name was Jacob before he wrestled with the angel. This story can be found in chapter 32 of the Book of Genesis.

Write five words that tell about God or our relationship with God.

Coming to Know God

T **R** ust

E

V

E

A

L

God Gives Us the Gift of Faith

God gives us the gift of **faith** to help us come to know and believe in him and all that he has revealed. Faith is a gift from God. It is God's invitation to believe in him and our acceptance of that invitation. Faith is not something we can earn.

The Bible has many stories about people of faith. One of these stories tells about the faith of Thomas the Apostle.

> Jesus appeared to the disciples after he was raised from the dead. When the disciples told Thomas that they had seen the Risen Jesus, he refused to believe. A week later the Risen Jesus again appeared to the disciples. This time Thomas was there. He saw Jesus and believed. Jesus said, "Have you come to believe because you have seen me? Blessed are those who have not seen and have believed."
>
> BASED ON JOHN 20:24, 25, 26, 28–29

Faith is giving ourselves to God whom we do not see. It is believing in God simply because God has revealed himself.

The Doubting of Saint Thomas
by Duccio di Buoinsegna (c. 1225–1319)

Create a faith banner.

Our Church Makes a Difference

We Profess Our Faith

Each Sunday at Mass we profess our faith in God and all that God has revealed. We pray one of the creeds of the Church. The creeds are symbols of faith. They are brief summaries of the faith of the Church.

The creeds of the Church are also called professions of faith. We profess there is one God in three divine Persons—God the Father, God the Son, and God the Holy Spirit. We profess the faith of the Church in God the Holy Trinity.

Praying the creeds of the Church reminds us of who we are. We are followers of Jesus Christ. We are the Church. We are to live our faith. We are to love God and others as Jesus taught. We are to profess our faith in actions and not just in words.

Look at the pictures on this page. How are the people professing and living their faith in God?

Our Catholic Identity

The Apostles' Creed

The Apostles' Creed is one of the earliest summaries of the faith of the Church. We call it the Apostles' Creed because it tells the main beliefs the Church has professed from the time of the Apostles.

What Difference Does Faith Make in My Life?

You are a person of faith. The Holy Spirit invites you to give yourself to God. You are invited to come to know God more and more and to live your faith.

Praying together is one way we profess our faith in God. Write a prayer that is a summary of what you believe about God. Share your prayer with others.

Sharing My Faith

My Faith Choice

This week I will profess my faith in God by what I say and what I do. I will

____

____.

We Pray

Our Faith

We first profess our faith in God and what God has revealed at Baptism. Pray this creed which is taken from the rite of Baptism.

Leader: Let us profess our faith.
Do you believe in God the Father?

All: **I do.**

Leader: Do you believe in Jesus Christ,
his only Son, our Lord?

All: **I do.**

Leader: Do you believe in the Holy Spirit?

All: **I do.**

We Remember

Write the term on the line that best completes each statement.

creed **revealed** **community**
Faith **Covenant**

1. God has ___revealed___ his love for us in many ways.
2. The special friendship between God and the Israelites is called the ___Covenant___.
3. ___Faith___ is both God's invitation to believe in him and also our acceptance of that invitation.
4. A ___creed___ is a brief summary of what the Church believes.

To Help You Remember

1. God has revealed himself through the Bible.
2. God has revealed himself most fully in his own Son, Jesus Christ. Jesus Christ is the fullness of Revelation.
3. God gives us the gift of faith to help us know and believe in him.

1 With My Family

This Week . . .

In chapter 1, "I Will Be Your God," your child learned about the mystery of God. God has created us to know, love, and serve him and to be happy with him on earth and in heaven. God has revealed himself and his plan of creation and salvation. God has revealed himself most fully in his Son, Jesus Christ. We call this divine Revelation. We can never fully comprehend the mystery of God. God gives us the gift of faith to help us come to know and believe in him and all that he has revealed.

For more on the teachings of the Catholic Church on the mysteries of faith and divine Revelation, see *Catechism of the Catholic Church* paragraph numbers 27–43, 50–67, and 142–197.

Sharing God's Word

Read together the Bible story about Jesus appearing to Thomas the Apostle and the other disciples after Jesus was raised from the dead. You can read this Gospel story in John 20:26–29 or read an adaptation of the story on page 16. Emphasize that faith is believing in God even though we do not see God.

Praying

In this chapter your child prayed a profession of faith that is taken from the rite of Baptism. Read and pray together the act of faith on page 19.

Making a Difference

Choose one of the following activities to do as a family or design a similar activity of your own.

- Read Jeremiah 7:23. Then pray together, asking God to strengthen your faith.
- God created us to live in friendship with him. Share with each other ways in which God is part of your everyday lives.
- Invite each person to share a Bible story of Jesus that tells, or reveals, something about God.

For more ideas on ways your family can live your faith, visit the "Faith First for Families" page at **www.FaithFirst.com.** You will find the "About Your Child" page helpful as your child begins a new year.

God's Word to Us

2

We Pray

[LORD God,] your word is a lamp for my feet.

PSALM 119:105

Lord God, open our hearts and minds to listen to your word. Amen.

What is your favorite story about your family?

Each family has favorite stories about the people and events of their family. The Bible tells us the faith stories of the Church.

What is your favorite Bible story? Why is it your favorite?

The Faith Story of God's People

Faith Focus

Why do we call the writings collected in the Bible "holy writings"?

Faith Vocabulary

Sacred Scripture. The holy writings of the people of God inspired by the Holy Spirit and collected in the Bible.

YHWH. The four letters of the Hebrew alphabet for the name for God that God revealed to Moses.

Sacred Scripture

At first God's people passed on the faith stories of God's friendship and life with them by word of mouth. Years later scribes, or writers, wrote down these faith stories. Eventually, God's people gathered the stories together.

Sacred Scripture is the collection of these holy writings. The words *sacred scriptures* mean "holy writings." God is the real author of Sacred Scripture. The Holy Spirit inspired, or guided, the human writers of the Bible to write God's word for his people. The Bible is the book in which the Church has collected the holy writings of God's people.

Here is part of one of the most important faith stories in the Bible. In it God reveals his name to Moses. God said, "[T]ell the Israelites: I AM sent me to you" (Exodus 3:14).

The English words *I AM* are the same as the Hebrew word *YHWH.* YHWH are the four letters of the Hebrew alphabet for the name for God that God revealed to Moses.

What are other names the Bible uses for God? Talk about your favorite.

The Old Testament

The Bible is divided into the Old Testament and the New Testament. The forty-six books of the Old Testament begin with the story of creation and Adam and Eve. We read that God created Adam and Eve to live in friendship with him, but Adam and Eve turned away from God. We also read that God promised to send someone to renew that friendship. All the writings of the Bible after that tell the story of God fulfilling that promise.

God's people also made a promise. They promised to worship God alone and to obey his commands, or the laws that he gave them. These laws are summarized in the Ten Commandments. God's people promised, "Everything the LORD has said, we will do" (Exodus 19:8).

Faith-Filled People

Moses

God chose Moses to lead the Israelites out of slavery in Egypt and to live in freedom in a land God promised them. The journey from slavery to freedom is called the Exodus. During the Exodus God made the Covenant with the Israelites and gave them the Ten Commandments.

Find and circle the words about the Old Testament hidden in the puzzle. Use some of the words to tell others what God reveals to us in the Old Testament.

The New Testament

The twenty-seven books of the New Testament tell about the fulfillment of God's promises in Jesus Christ. The Gospel is the heart of the New Testament. The word *gospel* means "good news." There are four Gospels, or written accounts, of the good news of Jesus Christ in the New Testament. They are named after four followers of Jesus: Matthew, Mark, Luke, and John. These four writers are called the Evangelists, or the four writers of the Good News.

The Holy Spirit inspired the Evangelists and other writers of the Bible to write down all God revealed. The four Gospels share the good news of Jesus' life from the announcement of his birth by the angel to his Ascension to his Father. Each shares the good news of God's love for us. Through the Gospels God speaks to us and invites us to believe and trust in him.

Mosaic of the four Evangelists

Look at the Bible page. Review how you look up a Bible passage.

Ezekiel = *name of book in Bible*

32 = *chapter of book*

2 = *verse of chapter*

Our Church Makes a Difference

Reading the Bible

Christians come to grow in their love for God by reading and praying the Bible. From the very beginning of the Church, sharing the stories about Jesus and his teachings was important to the Church. At first the Church shared these stories and teachings by word of mouth. About the year A.D. 50, they began writing the New Testament, which was completed around the year A.D. 100.

For the next 1,300 years scribes made copies of the Bible by hand. After the first Bible was printed in 1456 by John Gutenberg, it became easier to make copies of the Bible. Today the Bible is available in almost every language. It is one of the most widely read and studied books in the world.

The Church tells us to read and pray the Bible often. When we pray Sacred Scripture, we listen and speak to God.

Why do you think the Bible is still one of the most widely read books today?

Our Catholic Identity

The Homily

At Mass the priest or deacon preaches the homily. The homily helps us understand God's word and put it into action in our lives each day. It helps us live faithfully our covenant with God and with one another.

Reading a Bible story online

What Difference Does Faith Make in My Life?

Reading the Bible will help you learn more about God's love for you. The more you hear and tell the faith stories of God's people, the more you will grow in your friendship with God.

The Church community listens to the Bible every Sunday at Mass. What story from the Bible do you remember? Draw or write how it helps you grow in your friendship with God.

Listening to God's Word

My Faith Choice

This week I will prayerfully read the Bible. To help me put this decision into action I will

____

______________________________________.

We Pray

Lord, Open Our Hearts

We pray with gestures. Signing our forehead, lips, and chest over our heart is one prayer gesture the Church uses.

Leader: Let us prepare ourselves to listen to God's word by signing our forehead, lips, and chest over our heart with a small sign of the cross.

All: *Trace a cross on your forehead.*

Leader: May we remember your word when we speak.

All: *Trace a cross on your lips.*

Leader: May we keep your word in our heart and lives.

All: *Trace a cross over your heart. Silently read your favorite Gospel story.*

We Remember

Write a sentence about the Bible. Use three or more of these words.

YHWH **Moses** **Jesus Christ** **Covenant**
Old Testament **New Testament** **Gospel**

____

____

____

____

____

To Help You Remember

1. The Bible is the inspired, written word of God.
2. God entered into the Covenant with his people. The story of the first Covenant is told in the Old Testament.
3. The Gospel is the center of our Bible. It shares the Church's faith in Jesus Christ, who is the new and everlasting Covenant.

2 With My Family

This Week . . .

In chapter 2, "God's Word to Us," your child learned more about the Bible, or Sacred Scripture. The Bible is the inspired, written word of God. God is the real author of the Bible. The Holy Spirit inspired the human writers of the Bible to assure that God's word would be faithfully and accurately communicated. The two main parts of the Bible are the forty-six books of the Old Testament and the twenty-seven books of the New Testament. The Gospel is at the center of the whole Bible because God has revealed himself fully in his Son, Jesus Christ. In Jesus, the new and everlasting Covenant, God has established his covenant forever.

For more on the teachings of the Catholic Church on the Sacred Scripture, see *Catechism of the Catholic Church* paragraph numbers 101–133.

Sharing God's Word

Ask each person in your family to share what they know about the Bible. Read and talk about a favorite Bible story. Emphasize that the Bible is God's word to us.

Praying

In this chapter your child learned to pray with gestures. These are the same gestures we use before we listen to the Gospel at Mass. Read and pray together the prayer on page 27.

Making a Difference

Choose one of the following activities to do as a family or design a similar activity of your own.

- Create and decorate a special place for the Bible in your home. Open the Bible to a favorite story. Read the story and talk about it.
- Make bookmarks that say "God's Word to Us." Use these bookmarks in your Bibles.
- Review with each other how to look up Scripture references. This is an important skill for all children to develop. Use the information on page 24.

For more ideas on ways your family can live your faith, visit the "Faith First for Families" page at **www.FaithFirst.com**. Click on "Bible Stories" and discuss the story with your child this week.

Listening to God
A Scripture Story

We Pray

Listen and obey
the word of God!
Based on Isaiah 66:5

Lord, our God,
send the Holy Spirit
to help us listen
and respond
to your every word.
Amen.

Name some times when it is especially important to listen.

Listening attentively helps us learn. When we listen to the faith stories of our Church, we learn about God and what he has revealed to us.

What are some things you have learned by listening to Bible stories?

Samuel helping in the shrine at Shiloh

Bible Background

Faith Focus

What does Samuel teach us about listening attentively to the word of God?

Faith Vocabulary

judges of Israel. The leaders of the Israelites before they had kings.

Ark of the Covenant. The decorated chest in which the Israelites kept the stone tablets on which the Ten Commandments were written.

3,000-year-old pottery stand found at Shiloh

The Books of Samuel

The two Old Testament Books of Samuel share memories about the role of Samuel in God's plan for his people. Samuel was one of the **judges of Israel.** God chose Samuel to anoint Saul to be the first king of the Israelites.

The First Book of Samuel begins with the story of Hannah, the mother of Samuel. She prayed to God with great faith and trust to have a child. God heard and answered her prayer. Hannah gave birth to a son whom she named Samuel. The name *Samuel* means "one who hears God."

When Samuel was a young boy, Hannah brought him to the shrine at Shiloh to serve God. Eli was the head priest of all the Jewish priests who lived at the shrine. Eli taught Samuel about God and God's covenant of friendship with the Israelites.

Describe the places or times when you try to listen attentively to God.

Reading the Word of God

Samuel Listens to God

One night when he was getting ready for bed, Samuel thought he heard Eli calling him. He went to Eli, but Eli said, "I did not call you. Go back to bed." Two more times Samuel heard the voice, and two more times he went to Eli.

> After Samuel came to him three times, Eli understood that it was God calling Samuel. So he told Samuel if he heard the voice again to say, "Speak, LORD, for your servant is listening." Samuel heard his name called out as before. This time Samuel answered, "Speak, LORD. Your servant is listening."
>
> BASED ON 1 SAMUEL 3:8–10

Years later God chose Samuel to be the last of the judges of Israel. As a judge, Samuel helped God's people listen to God's word and faithfully live the Covenant.

Describe how Samuel showed his faith in God.

Samuel Serves God

Samuel served God by helping the priests and the pilgrims who visited the shrine at Shiloh. While he lived in the shrine, Samuel slept near the **Ark of the Covenant.** An ark is a decorated chest used to carry something.

The Israelites built and first used the Ark of the Covenant during the Exodus to carry the tablets on which the Ten Commandments were written. Later, when they settled in the land God promised them, the Israelites kept the Ark in shrines like the shrine at Shiloh. Finally, they kept the Ark in the Temple of Jerusalem.

The Ark of the Covenant was a sign for the Israelites that God was always with them. Seeing the Ark reminded the Israelites to keep their part of the Covenant and to obey God's Law.

Describe things in your church that are signs God is always present with the Church. Tell how they help you listen to God.

Signs of God's Presence

____

____

____

____

King David leading the Ark of the Covenant into Jerusalem, from a painting by L. Ademollo (1764–1849), Italian artist

Our Church Makes a Difference

Vocation

Eli and the other priests lived at the shrine at Shiloh. They were always there to help the people worship God and to learn to live the Covenant.

God calls people to serve our Church community. He gives these members of the Church the vocation to lead and serve the community of the Church. The word *vocation* means "a call from God to do a special work."

Your pastor and other parish priests listened to God and answered God's call to be a priest. Priests work with the bishop to lead and serve the people of your parish community. They work with the bishop to lead the people in worship, preach the Gospel, and teach the community to live the Gospel as Jesus taught.

Together, the priests and all the other people of your parish live the Gospel. The Holy Spirit helps them live "God's commandments as Christ taught us, by loving God and our neighbor" *(Rite of Baptism of Children)*.

Our Catholic Identity

The Tabernacle

The tabernacle is the place in our church in which the Blessed Sacrament is kept for bringing Holy Communion to the sick and for the devotion of the people. A lighted candle near the tabernacle is a sign that the Blessed Sacrament is in the tabernacle.

How does your parish work together to live the Gospel? Clue: Check your parish bulletin and web site.

What Difference Does Faith Make in My Life?

God is always with you. The Holy Spirit guides, teaches, and gives you the grace to live as a child of God.

Read this story about Saint Francis of Assisi. How did listening to the word of God help Francis make his decision to live the Gospel?

Speak, Lord, I Am Listening

Francis of Assisi wanted to know how he could best live as a follower of Jesus. One day he read these words of Jesus: "Sell everything you own, give the money to the poor, and follow me" (based on Mark 10:21). Francis listened and did just that. Many people, such as Saint Clare of Assisi, saw what Francis did and did the same. Today there are thousands of men and women living all over the world who are followers of Francis. They are known as Franciscans.

How can this story help you live as a follower of Jesus?

My Faith Choice

It is important to spend time alone with God. This week I will

____

______________________________________.

We Pray

Speak, Lord, I Am Listening

Spending quiet time with God and listening to God is called a prayer of meditation. In a prayer of meditation we try to understand God's word and how it should be lived.

1. Sit quietly. Close your eyes. Breathe slowly.
2. Picture yourself someplace where you can talk and listen to God.
3. Think about the Bible story of Samuel.
4. Take time to talk and listen to God. Say, "Speak, Lord, I am listening."
5. Reflect for a moment, then ask, "What is God saying to me?"
6. Write key words or phrases that you remember.

We Remember

Match the faith words in the left column with the meanings in the right column.

FAITH WORDS

c 1. Eli

b 2. Samuel

a 3. shrine

d 4. Ark of the Covenant

MEANINGS

a. a holy place of worship for the Israelites

b. one of the judges of Israel

c. one of the priests of Israel

d. chest containing the tablets of the Ten Commandments

To Help You Remember

1. Samuel showed his faith in God by listening to God.
2. Samuel listened to God and learned how God wanted him to serve God's people.
3. Samuel helped God's people keep their part of the Covenant and obey God's Law.

3 With My Family

This Week . . .

In chapter 3, "Listening to God: A Scripture Story," your child learned the importance of listening and responding to the word of God. Your child heard the Bible story of Samuel being called by God and how Samuel listened attentively and learned from Eli how to respond to God's call. This Old Testament story reminds us that God is ever present to us and dwells within and among us, calling us by name. We, too, need to listen attentively and reverently to God's word and to respond to God in faith as Samuel did.

For more on the teachings of the Catholic Church on the mystery of God's living word and our faith response to that word, see *Catechism of the Catholic Church* paragraph numbers 54–61, 121–130, 157–165, and 1373–1381.

Sharing God's Word

Read together the Bible story about Samuel in 1 Samuel 3:3–5, 8–10 or read the adaptation of the story on page 31. Emphasize that Samuel showed his faith in God by listening and responding to God.

Praying

In this chapter your child learned to pray a meditation. Read and follow together this prayer on page 35.

Making a Difference

Choose one of the following activities to do as a family or design a similar activity of your own.

- Read again the Bible story about Samuel on page 31. Talk about how you can help each other listen to God.
- Ask each person to share where and when they listen to God. Explain why these times and places are important to you.
- During Samuel's time, the Israelites carried the Ark of the Covenant with them to remind them that God was always with them. This week after Mass make a visit to the Blessed Sacrament present in the tabernacle in your parish church. Talk about how we remember that Jesus is always present with us.

For more ideas on ways your family can live your faith, visit the "Faith First for Families" page at **www.FaithFirst.com**. This week pay special attention to "Questions Kids Ask."

Our Father in Heaven

We Pray

Praise God, all creation.
All creation praise the name of God.

BASED ON PSALM 148:5, 13

Abba, Father, we give you thanks and praise, for you love us. Amen.

What are some ways you get to know a new person or place?

Think of the many ways we come to know people. God has told us about himself. We come to know God in many ways. One way we can come to know God is by looking at the wonderful world of creation.

What do your favorite parts of creation tell you about God?

God the Father Almighty

Faith Focus

What does it mean to call God Abba, Father?

Faith Vocabulary

Almighty. God's power to do everything and anything good.

Creator. God, who created everything and everyone, seen and unseen, out of love and without any help.

God Reveals Himself

We believe God tells us about himself in many ways. Just by looking at and thinking about creation, we can come to know something about God. Here are some of the things God tells us about himself in the Bible.

1. **God is the Father, the Almighty.** Every Sunday at Mass we stand and profess our faith in one God who is the Father, the **Almighty.**
2. **God is the Creator.** There was nothing besides God before God created. God made everyone and everything, seen and unseen, out of love and without any help.
3. **God is always with us.** More than anyone else, God is always there for us. Placing our trust in God is the best thing we can ever do.
4. **God is All-knowing.** We believe God knows us by name and always loves us. He is All-loving and All-knowing.
5. **God is Truth and Love.** God always loves us. His word is always true. He always keeps his promises. He is always faithful. Like King David, we say,

"Lord GOD, you are God
and your words are truth."

2 SAMUEL 7:28

What have you come to know about God from the Bible?

God Cares for All Creation

Best of all, God told us about himself through Jesus Christ. Jesus called his Father "Abba." *Abba* means "Father." This shows us Jesus' love for his Father and the trust he had in his Father. Jesus showed his trust in the Father in everything he said and did. Jesus invites us to trust God the Father as he did. One day he told his disciples,

> "Look at the birds in the sky and the wild flowers. Your heavenly Father takes care of them. You are more important to God than they are. God will provide much more for you."
>
> BASED ON MATTHEW 6:26, 28, 30

Faith-Filled People

Julian of Norwich

Blessed Julian saw creation as a great sign of God's love. She believed that people are the greatest part of creation because Jesus, the Son of God, became a man. Because of Jesus people are the heart of the universe. People are the greatest sign of God's love.

Jesus invited his listeners to trust that God delights in providing for us. Every moment of every day of our lives, God, our Almighty Father, cares for us and his creation. We call this truth about God divine Providence.

One way we show that we believe this about God is by being good stewards of creation. Good stewards faithfully care for someone or something that belongs to someone else. Most importantly, good stewards share the gifts of God's creation with other people, especially with people in need.

Use words or pictures to describe one way you can work with others to care for creation.

God Our Creator

In the Nicene Creed we profess our faith in God, who is the creator of all that is, seen and unseen. God is the creator of all living and nonliving creatures. He is the creator of people and angels. Angels are spiritual creatures who do not have a body as humans do. They give glory to God without stopping.

All God's creation is good. But God loves people more than any other part of his creation. Here is the reason.

> God created man in his image; . . .
> male and female he created them.
>
> GENESIS 1:27

God created people with a body and a soul. Our soul is that spiritual part of us that lives forever.

God created people to share in the life of the Holy Trinity now and forever in heaven. The Holy Trinity is the mystery of one God in three divine Persons—God the Father, God the Son, and God the Holy Spirit.

Blessed

be

God.

Decorate this prayer card. Bless and thank God for creating you.

Our Church Makes a Difference

Saints Isidore and Maria

Christians have always followed God's command to care for creation. Farmers have always been and continue to be special stewards of creation.

Saint Isidore and his wife, Saint Maria de la Cabeza, were farmers who worked for a wealthy landowner in Spain many years ago. Isidore and Maria loved the land. It was God's gift to them. Like good stewards, they cared for the land. Today Isidore is known to Christians as Saint Isidore the Farmer. We honor him as the patron saint of farmers.

What are some of the ways you can care for creation?

Our Catholic Identity

Rogation Days

The Church celebrates rogation days. The term *rogation days* means "days of asking." On the three days before the feast of the Ascension, some Christian farmers ask God for his blessing on their work and for a good harvest. Some parishes have processions and bless the farmlands.

What Difference Does Faith Make in My Life?

God is your Abba. He is your loving Father and Creator. He is always with you and always caring for you. You show your love for God and for all people when you live as a good steward of God's creation.

Pretend your parish is planning a "Good Stewardship" project. Create an announcement for the home page of your parish web site.

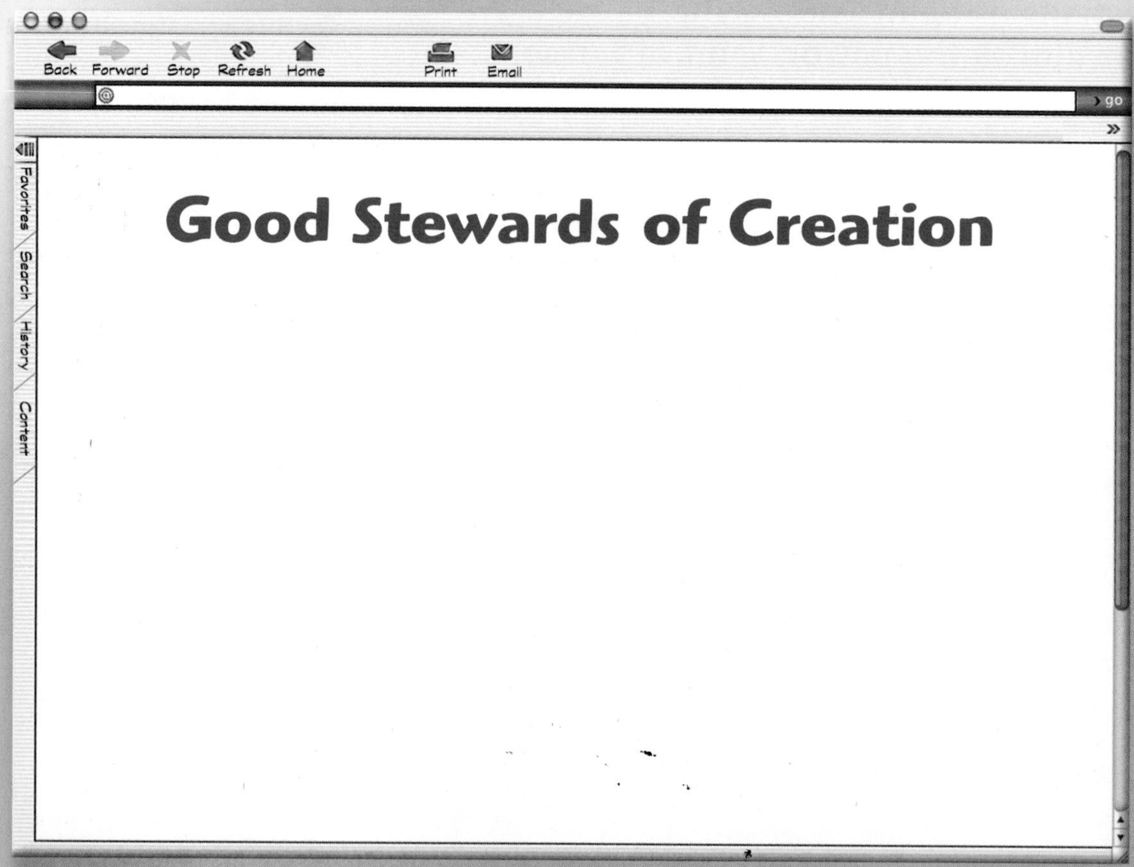

My Faith Choice

This week I will be a good steward of God's creation. I will

____

______________________________________.

We Pray

Praying a Psalm

The Church prays the Psalms each day. One way we pray the Psalms is by alternately praying the verses aloud.

All: **God, the Creator,**
how great is your name.

Group 1: Your love for us is so great.
Group 2: You always care for us.

Group 1: You have made us your greatest creation.
Group 2: You have given us a place of honor among all your creation.

All: **God, the Creator,**
how great is your name.

BASED ON PSALM 8:2, 5–7, 10

We Remember

Complete the sentences. Use the words in the word bank.

Creator	**Abba**
Providence	**Holy Trinity**

Jesus called God the Father Abba.

God the Father is the first Person of the Holy TRINITY. God the Father is the Creator of all that is, both seen and unseen. He always loves us and provides for us. We call this truth about God divine Providence.

To Help You Remember

1. God is our Father, the Almighty, who is All-knowing, All-loving, Love, and Truth.
2. God is the Creator of all that is, seen and unseen.
3. God always cares and provides for all of his creation.

4 With My Family

This Week . . .

In chapter 4, "Our Father in Heaven," your child discovered more about God the Father, the first Person of the Holy Trinity. We profess our faith in God, the Father, the Almighty, the Creator of all that is, both seen and unseen. God is Love and Truth. He is All-knowing and All-good. He delights in providing for us and all of his creation. One way we respond to God's love and providence is by caring for and wisely using creation, especially by sharing the gifts of creation with people in need.

For more on the teachings of the Catholic Church on the mysteries of God and creation, see *Catechism of the Catholic Church* paragraph numbers 199–379.

Sharing God's Word

Read together the Bible story in Matthew 6:26–31 about how God cares for all creation or read the adaptation of the story on page 39. Emphasize that Jesus was teaching people to trust in God.

Praying

In this chapter your child prayed a psalm. Read and pray together Psalm 8 on page 43.

Making a Difference

Choose one of the following activities to do as a family or design a similar activity of your own.

- Talk about how your family can care for God's creation. Then choose one thing you will do this week together to care for creation.
- Find pictures in magazines of good stewards of creation. Make a stewardship collage. Tell stories about the pictures. If you do not have magazines, draw the pictures.
- Research together the recycling rules in your community. Choose one way to improve your family's recycling efforts.

For more ideas on ways your family can live your faith, visit the "Faith First for Families" page at **www.FaithFirst.com.** The "Make a Difference" page goes especially well with this chapter.

The Promise of Isaiah
A Scripture Story

We Pray

[M]ay the LORD bless his people with peace! PSALM 29:11

Father of our Lord Jesus Christ, you always keep your promises. Fill our hearts with joy and hope. Amen.

Who has kept a promise to you?

We trust people who keep their promises. God always keeps his promises. The accounts of these promises are found in the Bible.

What do you remember about God's promises to us?

Jesus, the Messiah promised by Isaiah the Prophet

Bible Background

Faith Focus

What did God promise his people through the prophet Isaiah?

Faith Vocabulary

original sin. The sin the first humans committed that lost original holiness not only for themselves but for all human beings.

hope. A gift from God that enables us to trust in him and in his promises.

God's Plan of Salvation

God created us to know, love, and serve him. He created us to be happy with him here on earth and forever in heaven. Yet we know people suffer. Have you ever asked, "Why are people treated unjustly? Why do so many children go hungry each day?" God's people in the Old Testament asked God questions like that. They wrote the answer God revealed to them in the Book of Genesis.

Adam and Eve, the names the Bible gives to the first humans, rejected God's original plan of happiness. They freely chose to turn away from God and God's plan of happiness for people and for all creation. The Church calls this choice of Adam and Eve and its effect on all people **original sin.**

By his sin Adam lost the gift of original holiness, or friendship with God, not only for himself but for all human beings. Suffering, unhappiness, sin, and evil of all kinds came into the world.

God's love refused to let evil and suffering destroy his original plan. He set a new plan in motion—God's plan of salvation. The person at the center of that plan was a savior who would free all people from sin and suffering.

In the space name and describe someone you know who helps people who are suffering.

Reading the Word of God

The New Leader Promised by Isaiah

About six hundred years before the birth of Jesus, the Israelites were suffering in many ways. Many of their kings were unjust. Things got especially bad when many of the Israelites were forced to move out of their homeland and live in Babylon. This period of suffering is known as the Exile.

God's people prayed for a savior to free them. God sent the prophet Isaiah to speak to the Israelites in his name. In the Book of the Prophet Isaiah we read,

> Upon those who dwelt in the land of gloom
> a light has shone.
> For a child is born to us, a son is
> given us. . . .
> They name him Wonder-Counselor,
> God-Hero, . . .
> Prince of Peace. ISAIAH 9:1, 5

These words filled the hearts of the Israelites with **hope.** God would one day send to them the savior they prayed for. This savior came to be called the Messiah, or God's Anointed One. The Israelites kept on trusting that God's promise would come true.

When did God's promise to the Israelites come true?

Jesus Christ Is the Messiah

Each year at Christmas, Catholics listen to the message of hope in the Book of the Prophet Isaiah. We hear the names, or titles, that Isaiah used to describe this new leader.

Wonder-Counselor

He is wise and clearly knows God's plan for all people.

God-Hero

He brings blessings on people because he follows God's commands.

Prince of Peace

He establishes the peace God had always promised to his people.

These titles Isaiah gave to the Messiah help Christians understand the identity of Jesus Christ and his work. The name *Christ* means "Anointed One." Jesus' birth and his life, Passion, death, Resurrection, and Ascension established the beginning of the kingdom of God. The kingdom of God is a kingdom of mercy and love, peace, and justice that will last forever. It will finally come about when Jesus Christ returns in glory at the end of time.

Create a coat of arms for the Messiah.

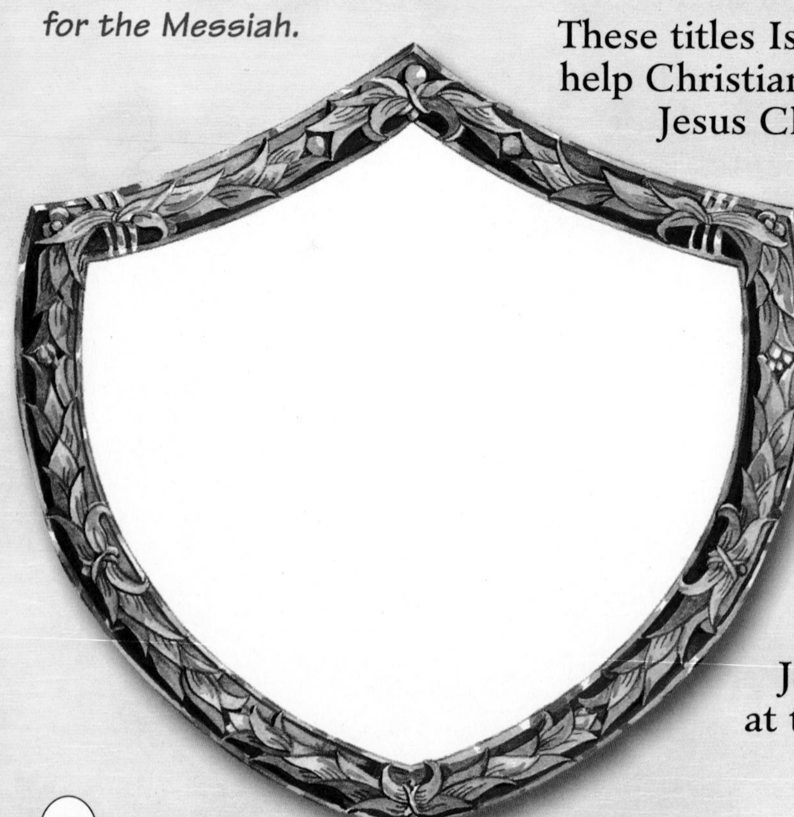

Our Church Makes a Difference

Dorothy Day and her daughter

Our Catholic Identity

Works of Mercy

The Corporal Works of Mercy and the Spiritual Works of Mercy help prepare for the coming of the kingdom that Jesus, the Messiah and Savior, began to build. When we live the works of mercy, we share the gift of hope with people.

Building a Just World

Dorothy Day shared God's message of hope with people. Dorothy was a writer who reported on the sufferings of the poor. In 1932 Dorothy prayed that she could find a way to change things for the poor and not just report on them. That was the beginning of a new kind of work for Dorothy that the Holy Spirit was calling her to do.

Dorothy Day and her friend Peter Maurin began the Catholic Worker movement. They chose to live in poverty with the poor. They set up Catholic Worker houses where people who were homeless could live. Because of her work, some have called Dorothy Day a modern-day prophet.

The Church has named Dorothy a Servant of God and calls her Venerable Dorothy Day. We honor Dorothy best when we live the Gospel as she did. Then we too are prophets of hope who build a just world.

Dorothy Day (center) with Catholic Worker volunteers

Find out how your parish works with people who are suffering. How does that give hope to people?

What Difference Does Faith Make in My Life?

The Holy Spirit helps you be a messenger of hope to others. You can learn from Dorothy Day and other faithful followers of Jesus how to be a messenger of hope.

Pretend you are a news reporter. You are reporting a story about young people who are bringing hope to suffering people. Write the details of your report.

Messengers of Hope

1. Who are the people who bring hope to other people?

2. What are they doing for others?

3. How does their work bring hope?

My Faith Choice

This week I will bring hope to someone. I will

____

____.

We Pray

Praising the Savior

Prayers of praise give glory to God. Pray this prayer, praising God for Jesus, the Savior of the world.

All: **Lord Jesus, you are the Savior.**

Group 1: Lord Jesus, you are the Messiah.

Group 2: Lord Jesus, you are the Prince of Peace.

All: **Lord Jesus, you are the Savior.**

We Remember

Complete this crossword puzzle.

Across

1. A prophet speaks in the name of ___ .
3. ___ was a prophet.
5. The ___ is the Anointed One, the Savior, promised by God.

Down

2. ___ sin is the name we give to the first sin committed by Adam and Eve.
4. ___ is the Savior promised by God.

To Help You Remember

1. Adam and Eve lost the gift of original holiness, or friendship with God, by their sin.
2. The Book of the Prophet Isaiah describes the Messiah whom God would send to save his people.
3. Jesus Christ is the Messiah whom God promised to send.

5 With My Family

This Week . . .

In chapter 5, "The Promise of Isaiah: A Scripture Story," your child learned more about God's promise to send the world a savior and messiah. Suffering, evil, sin, and death entered the world as a result of original sin. It became difficult for the people of God to faithfully live the Covenant. In a time of great suffering, Isaiah the Prophet brought a message of hope to God's people. God would send a messiah who would establish a kingdom of righteousness, justice, and peace. Jesus Christ is the Messiah, God's Promised One, the Savior and Redeemer.

For more on the teachings of the Catholic Church on the mysteries of evil and the Savior promised by God, see *Catechism of the Catholic Church* paragraph numbers 385–412.

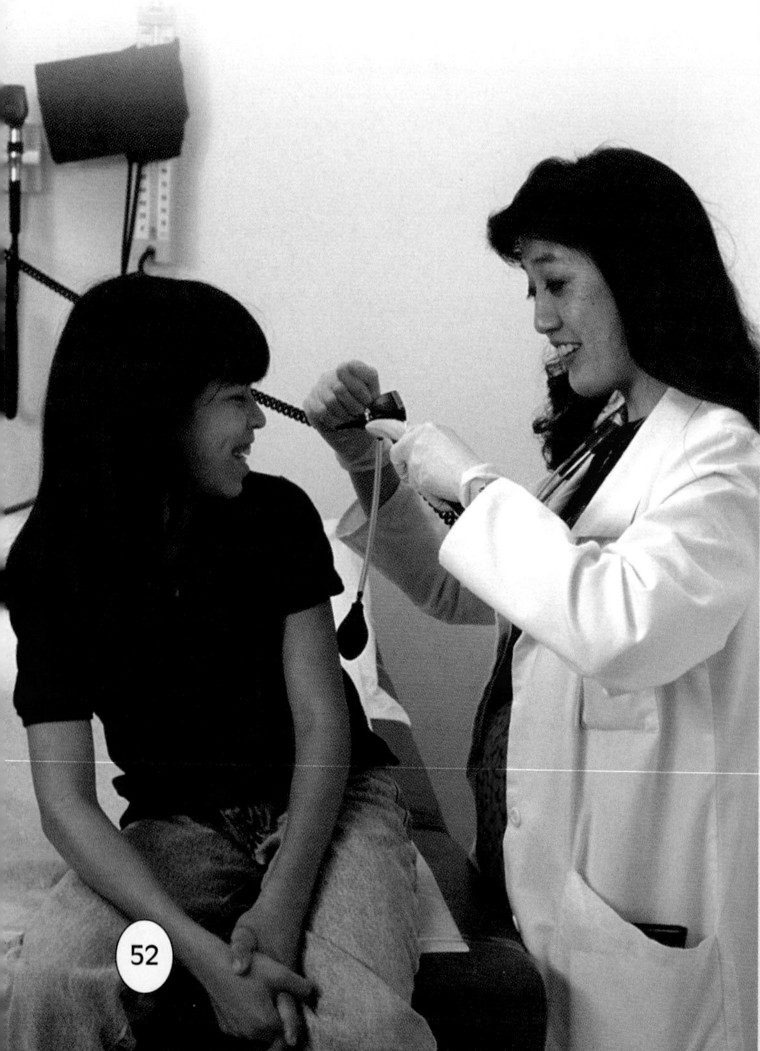

Sharing God's Word

Read together the Bible story in Isaiah 9:1, 5 about Isaiah's message to the Israelites or read the adaptation of the story on page 47. Emphasize that Jesus is the Messiah God promised to send.

Praying

In this chapter your child prayed a short prayer of praise. Read and pray together the prayer on page 51.

Making a Difference

Choose one of the following activities to do as a family or design a similar activity of your own.

- Ask each family member to share a story about a time when they were hurting or sad. Tell about a person who helped them and what that person did to help.
- Isaiah was a powerful leader. Talk about what qualities make a good leader.
- Like Isaiah, Dorothy Day shared God's message of hope with people. Talk about all the ways your parish shares God's message of hope with those in need.
- Use the Internet to learn more about the Catholic Worker community closest to where you live. Choose a way to support this community.

For more ideas on ways your family can live your faith, visit the "Faith First for Families" page at **www.FaithFirst.com**. You will find the "Contemporary Issues" page helpful this week.

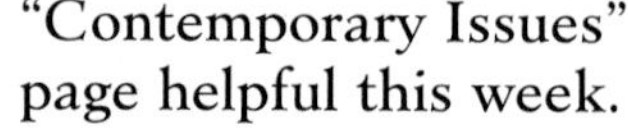

Jesus Christ, the Son of God

We Pray

"The blessing of
the LORD
be upon you!"
PSALM 129:8

God our Father, we rejoice in the birth of our Savior. May the Holy Spirit help us live as Jesus taught. Amen.

What do you think the saying "Seeing is believing" means?

God wanted his people to see very clearly how to live in love. He sent his only Son, Jesus, to be a model for us of how we are to live as children of God.

In what ways is Jesus a good model, showing us how to love God and our neighbor?

Jesus blessing the children

God's Promise Fulfilled

Faith Focus

What did Jesus do to show us who God is?

Faith Vocabulary

Incarnation. The mystery of the Son of God, the second Person of the Trinity, becoming truly human while not giving up being divine, or God.

public ministry of Jesus. The saving work that God the Father sent Jesus to do, beginning with the baptism of Jesus and his announcement of that work in the synagogue in Nazareth.

The Promised Savior Is Born

The birth of the Savior promised by God begins with another promise. The angel Gabriel announced to the Virgin Mary,

> "[Mary,] the holy Spirit will come upon you. . . . [Your child] will be called holy, the Son of God." LUKE 1:35

In a dream, an angel also told Joseph that the Virgin Mary would give birth to a son. The angel said,

> "You are to name him Jesus, because he will save his people from their sins." MATTHEW 1:21

Mary's son, Jesus, is the only Son of God. *Jesus* is a Hebrew name that means "God saves." The only Son of God the Father took on flesh, became human without giving up being God, and lived among us. We call this mystery of faith the **Incarnation.** The word *incarnation* means "putting on flesh." Jesus is true God and true man.

Jesus, the only Son of God, is the Savior of the world. Because Mary is the mother of Jesus, who is truly God, Mary is truly the Mother of God.

Write a sentence telling why Christmas is a celebration of hope.

____

____

____

____

Jesus Begins His Ministry

Jesus grew up in the town of Nazareth in Galilee. When it became time for Jesus to begin the work the Father sent him to do, he left his home. We call this work the **public ministry of Jesus.**

Jesus went to the synagogue in Nazareth. He took a scroll containing the writings of the prophet Isaiah, unrolled it, stood up, and read aloud,

"The Spirit of the Lord is upon me,
because he has anointed me
to bring glad tidings to the poor.
He has sent me to proclaim liberty
to captives
and recovery of sight to the blind,
to let the oppressed go free,
and to proclaim a year acceptable
to the Lord." LUKE 4:18–19

With these words, Jesus announced the work the Father sent him to do. He was the Messiah who had been sent to them by God.

Describe one person you have read about or know who has continued the work of Jesus.

Faith-Filled People

John the Baptist

Saint John the Baptist is the last of the prophets and the herald of Jesus. John prepared the people for the coming of Jesus and announced Jesus to be the Messiah, the Lamb of God. The Church celebrates the birth of Saint John the Baptist on June 24.

Signs of God's Love

Jesus' whole life on earth was a sign of his Father's love for all people. Miracles were some of the most amazing things Jesus did that were signs of God's love. The word *miracle* means "wonder, something amazing and marvelous." The miracles of Jesus were amazing signs of God's love at work in the world. This is the Good News announced by the Gospel.

Read about the miracle of Jesus giving sight to the two blind men in Matthew 9:27–31. See how it changed the lives of the two blind men. This miracle invited the two blind men and the other people who were there to believe and trust in God. They believed. They began to see not only with their eyes but also with "eyes of faith."

On the clock, write the things you do during the day to be a sign of God's love.

We are called to be people of faith. We are called to live our faith. We are to be signs of God's love for others to see.

Our Church Makes a Difference

Patron Saints

Saints lived lives of faith, hope, and love. In their lives they put into practice the values Jesus lived while he was on earth. Some of the saints of the Church are patron saints. Patron saints are role models for groups of people, such as lawyers, students, parishes, and nations.

Saint Anthony of Padua is the patron saint of travelers and children. He had a great love for the child Jesus. He was also a great preacher and missionary who traveled to tell others about Jesus Christ.

Learning about Saint Anthony of Padua and the other saints helps us live our faith in Jesus. It helps us be signs of God's love for others to see.

Share something you have learned about a patron saint.

Our Catholic Identity

Signs of God's Love

All the people of the Church are called to be signs of God's love. People in your parish do this in many ways. Priests and deacons, laypeople and religious, married and single people all work together to put into practice the values Jesus lived on earth.

What Difference Does Faith Make in My Life?

You are a sign of God's love. The things you do and the things you say announce to others the Good News of Jesus Christ. The Holy Spirit is always helping you learn, more and more, how to be a sign of God's love.

Design a message that invites people to love and serve others as Jesus taught us to do.

My Faith Choice

This week I will live my faith in Jesus Christ and be a sign of God's love. I will

____

_______________________________________.

We Pray

We Believe in Jesus Christ

We profess our faith in Jesus Christ when we pray the creeds of the Church. Pray this part of the Nicene Creed. We pray the Nicene Creed each Sunday at Mass.

Group 1: We believe in one Lord, Jesus Christ,
the only Son of God,
Group 2: eternally begotten of the Father,
God from God, Light from Light,

Group 1: true God from true God,
begotten, not made, one in Being with
the Father.
Group 2: Through him all things were made.

Group 1: For us men and for our salvation
he came down from heaven:
Group 2: by the power of the Holy Spirit
he was born of the Virgin Mary,
and became man.

We Remember

Circle the faith words hidden in the puzzle. Share the meaning of each word with a partner.

Incarnation **public ministry**
miracles **Nazareth**

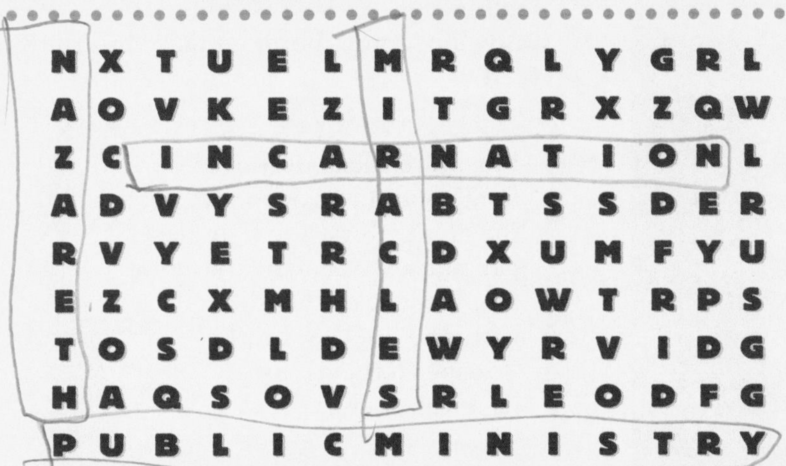

To Help You Remember

1. Jesus is the only Son of God who became one of us and did not give up being God.
2. When Jesus began his public ministry, he announced that he was the Promised One of God.
3. Everything Jesus said and did was a sign of God's love for people.

6 With My Family

This Week . . .

In chapter 6, "Jesus Christ, the Son of God," your child discovered more about the fulfillment of God's promise to send the Messiah, the Savior and Redeemer of the world. When it became time for God to send the promised Savior, he announced to the Blessed Virgin Mary that she would give birth to the Son of God and name him Jesus. Jesus is true God and true man. This mystery of faith is called the Incarnation. When Jesus began his public ministry, he announced that he was the Messiah, God's Promised One. Jesus' whole life was a sign of God's saving love for all people. The miracles of Jesus were unique signs of God's saving presence in the world, inviting people to faith in God.

For more on the teachings of the Catholic Church on the mystery of the Incarnation and the public ministry of Jesus, see *Catechism of the Catholic Church* paragraph numbers 422–507 and 512–560.

Sharing God's Word

Read together the Bible story in Luke 4:18–19 about Jesus reading from the writings of the prophet Isaiah in the synagogue in Nazareth or read the adaptation of the story on page 55. Emphasize that this is how Jesus announced what God had sent him to do.

Praying

In this chapter your child prayed part of the Nicene Creed. Read and pray together the prayer on page 59.

Making a Difference

Choose one of the following activities to do as a family or design a similar activity of your own.

- Read the story of Jesus' baptism in Matthew 3:13–17. Talk about how John the Baptist prepared the people for the coming of Jesus.
- Talk about people you know in your parish who are continuing the work of Jesus. Then choose one thing to do as a family this week to continue the work of Jesus.
- Make puzzles of the Nicene Creed (see page 284). Write the words of this creed on a piece of paper. Cut the paper into small pieces. As you assemble the puzzle, you will become more familiar with the creed.

For more ideas on ways your family can live your faith, visit the "Faith First for Families" page at **www.FaithFirst.com**. Share some of the ideas with one another on the "Gospel Reflections" page this week.

Ff

The Death and Resurrection of Jesus

We Pray

**Lord, by your cross
and resurrection you
have set us free.
You are the Savior
of the world.**

MEMORIAL ACCLAMATION

**Lord God,
may the death and
Resurrection of
your Son strengthen
our hope in your
promise of life
everlasting. Amen.**

When have you made a sacrifice?

People are willing to make sacrifices for people they love. The Passion of Jesus was the greatest sacrifice of all. Jesus' Passion and Resurrection are the greatest signs of God's love for us.

What do you remember about these events?

The Last Days of Jesus on Earth

Faith Focus

What were the main events of Jesus' last days on earth?

Faith Vocabulary

Passover. The Jewish feast celebrating God's freeing the Israelites from suffering and slavery in Egypt and leading them to freedom in the land he had promised them.

Last Supper. The last meal Jesus celebrated with the disciples at which he gave the Church the gift of his Body and Blood, the Eucharist.

The Celebration of Passover

Jesus went up to Jerusalem with his disciples to celebrate **Passover** one last time before he completed his work on earth. As Jesus entered Jerusalem, a crowd welcomed him as the One who God promised would set them free. They cheered, "Hosanna to the Son of David" (Matthew 21:9).

Later that week Jesus ate a special meal with his disciples. Christians call this meal the **Last Supper.** At the Last Supper, Jesus gave us the gift of his Body and Blood, the Eucharist. He told his disciples to celebrate and share the Eucharist in memory of him. The Church does what Jesus did at the Last Supper at every celebration of the Mass.

Read Matthew 26:26–28. Compare what you read here with what you see and hear at Mass.

Matthew's Gospel	Mass

Jesus' Trial, Death, and Burial

After the Last Supper, Jesus went to the Garden of Gethsemane to pray. While Jesus and his disciples were there, soldiers came and arrested Jesus. They took him to Pontius Pilate, the Roman governor, and put him on trial.

Pilate could not find Jesus guilty of any crime and wanted to release him. But the religious leaders who plotted against Jesus shouted, "Crucify him! Crucify him!" (Luke 23:21). So Pilate sentenced Jesus to be crucified.

The Roman soldiers led Jesus to Calvary, the place the Romans crucified criminals. They fastened Jesus to the cross he was carrying. As he was dying on the cross, Jesus prayed,

> "Father, forgive them, they know not what they do." LUKE 23:34

Around three o'clock in the afternoon, Jesus cried out,

> "Father, into your hands I commend my spirit." LUKE 23:46

After speaking these words, Jesus died. Joseph of Arimathea, a disciple of Jesus, asked Pilate's permission to bury Jesus' body. Jesus' disciples wrapped Jesus' body in a linen cloth and placed it in a tomb carved out of rock.

Faith-Filled People

Joanna

Joanna, a follower of Jesus, Mary, the wife of Clopas, and Mary Magdalene were at the Crucifixion along with Jesus' mother. Women disciples also prepared Jesus' body for burial and were the first disciples to learn about the Resurrection.

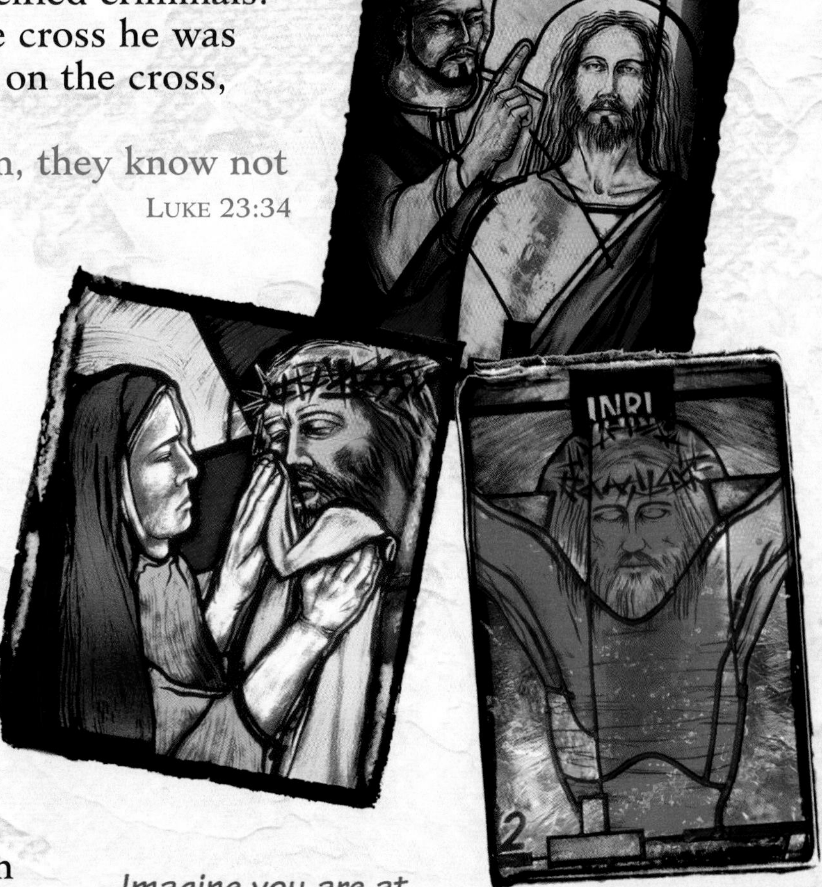

Imagine you are at Jesus' trial and Crucifixion. Describe your thoughts and feelings.

The Resurrection and Ascension

On the morning of the third day after Jesus' death and burial, Mary Magdalene and another disciple of Jesus named Mary went to Jesus' tomb. They discovered the stone in front of the tomb was rolled away and saw that Jesus' body was gone. Two angels announced to them that God had raised Jesus to new life.

For forty days after the Resurrection, the Risen Jesus appeared to his disciples on many occasions. Then the Risen Lord took his disciples to a mountain in Galilee. He commanded them to teach everyone what he had taught them. They were to go into the whole world and baptize people and make them his disciples. Then Jesus blessed his disciples and returned to his Father.

In your own words, rewrite these chapter titles.

Announcing the Good News

1. The Tomb of Jesus Is Empty

2. Jesus Returns to His Father

Our Church Makes a Difference

Saint Helena and the Cross

Christians use symbols to help us remember Jesus and the meaning of his life and work for the world. The most common of all Christian symbols is the cross. The cross is a symbol of Jesus' death and God's great love for us.

Almost three hundred years after Jesus died and was raised from the dead, a woman traveled from Rome to Jerusalem. The woman was Helena, the mother of Constantine who was the emperor of Rome.

According to legend, Helena dug at Calvary and found the true cross of Jesus. If you ever visit the Church of the Holy Sepulchre in Jerusalem, you can see a relic, or piece, of the cross she found.

As a Christian the cross reminded Helena to follow Jesus and love others as he did. Helena served the poor and homeless and the needy. The Church has named Helena a saint and celebrates her feast day on August 18.

Our Catholic Identity

Stations of the Cross

The Stations, or the Way, of the Cross is a prayer journey we take with Jesus. The Stations represent fourteen events of the Passion and death of Jesus. We walk from station to station, stopping at each for a moment of prayer. Some churches add a station to remember the Resurrection.

Describe someone who serves the poor, homeless, and needy as Saint Helena did.

Church of the Holy Sepulchre, Jerusalem

What Difference Does Faith Make in My Life?

The events of Jesus' suffering, death, Resurrection, and Ascension are part of your faith story. Each time you generously help others and bring them hope, you are doing what Jesus did.

Use words or pictures and tell about the Crucifixion, Resurrection, and Ascension. Think about how important they are for you and for all people.

My Faith Story

My Faith Choice

This week I will show my thanks for Jesus' great gift of love. I will

____

____.

We Pray

Adoration of the Cross

This prayer is from the liturgy of the Church for Good Friday. Come forward one by one and show reverence for the crucifix. Say these words:

We adore you, O Christ,

and we bless you.

By your holy cross

you have redeemed the world.

We Remember

Place these events of the last days in the life of Jesus in their proper order. Mark the first event with the number 1 and the last event with the number 7.

__6__ The Resurrection

__7__ The Ascension

__1__ The Last Supper

__4__ The Crucifixion

__2__ The arrest in the garden

__3__ The trial before Pontius Pilate

__5__ The burial in the tomb

To Help You Remember

1. Jesus celebrated the Last Supper during Passover before he was crucified.
2. Jesus suffered and died on the cross for us.
3. Jesus was raised from the dead and forty days later returned, or ascended, to his Father in heaven.

7 With My Family

This Week . . .

In chapter 7, "The Death and Resurrection of Jesus," your child deepened his or her understanding of the meaning of the saving events of the last days of Jesus on earth. At the Last Supper, Jesus gave us the gift of his Body and Blood, the Eucharist. On that night he was betrayed, arrested, and handed over to Pilate for trial. Although not found guilty of any crime, Jesus was put to death on the cross as a common criminal. On the third day after his death and burial, Jesus was raised to new life and, for forty days, appeared to the disciples on many occasions. After commanding them to make disciples of all nations by baptizing and teaching others what he had taught them, Jesus ascended to his Father in heaven.

For more on the teachings of the Catholic Church on the mystery of the Passion, death, Resurrection, and Ascension, see *Catechism of the Catholic Church* paragraph numbers 595–667.

Sharing God's Word

Invite each family member to share what they know about the Gospel stories of Jesus' Passion, death, Resurrection, and Ascension. Explain that there were many people who witnessed both the death and Resurrection. Talk about how these people might have felt.

Praying

In this chapter your child prayed a prayer of adoration. Read and pray together the prayer on page 67.

Making a Difference

Choose one of the following activities to do as a family or design a similar activity of your own.

- There are many movies that depict Jesus' Passion, death, and Resurrection. Rent one and watch it together. Afterward, discuss the movie.
- Read Matthew 21:1–11. What was Matthew saying about Jesus when he wrote that the whole city was shaken?
- This week take time after Mass to walk the Stations of the Cross. Imagine what it might have been like to have been with Jesus.

For more ideas on ways your family can live your faith, visit the "Faith First for Families" page at **www.FaithFirst.com.** Click on "Family Prayer" to find a special prayer to pray together this week.

Receive the Holy Spirit

We Pray

We cannot say "Jesus is Lord" unless the Holy Spirit helps us.
Based on 1 Corinthians 12:3

**Lord,
send your Holy Spirit to show your salvation to all the world. Amen.**

Who helps you when you need help?

It is good to know that we have people we can turn to when we need help. Jesus promised that God the Holy Spirit is always with us to help us.

In what ways might the Holy Spirit help you live as a follower of Jesus Christ?

The dove, a symbol for the Holy Spirit

The Gift of the Holy Spirit

Faith Focus

Why is the Holy Spirit important to the Church?

Faith Vocabulary

Pentecost. The day that the Holy Spirit came to the disciples as Jesus had promised, fifty days after the Resurrection.

Jesus Promises the Holy Spirit

God sent Jesus into the world so that "the world might be saved through him" (based on John 3:17). For three years Jesus traveled with his disciples doing the work he was sent to do.

Jesus knew his disciples would be afraid and feel left alone when he died and returned to his Father. He made this promise to them,

> "I will ask the Father, and he will give you another Advocate to be with you always, the Spirit of truth. . . . I will not leave you orphans." JOHN 14:16–17, 18

With these words, Jesus promised that God the Father would send the Advocate, the Holy Spirit, to them. The disciples would never be alone. The Holy Spirit would help and teach them as Jesus did.

Pretend you are one of the disciples listening to Jesus. What might you ask him about the Holy Spirit?

____

____

____

The Coming of the Holy Spirit

Fifty days after Jesus' Resurrection, the city of Jerusalem was crowded. It was the feast of **Pentecost.** Jewish pilgrims had come from all over the world to thank God for the harvest.

> At that time Mary, Jesus' mother, and the disciples of Jesus were in Jerusalem. Out of nowhere, a loud wind filled the room in which they had locked themselves. Then there appeared tongues that looked like flames of fire that came and rested on each of them. They were all filled with the Holy Spirit. BASED ON ACTS OF THE APOSTLES 2:1–4

Jesus' promise came true. The Holy Spirit came to the disciples. Filled with the gift of the Holy Spirit, Peter and the other disciples unlocked the door and went into the street. Peter preached about Jesus' death and Resurrection. Many people came to believe in Jesus Christ and asked to be baptized. On this first Christian Pentecost, God fully revealed himself to be one God, who is Father, Son, and Holy Spirit.

Faith-Filled People

Paul the Apostle

Saint Paul traveled by land and sea to preach the Gospel. He was not always welcomed by the people. He was arrested, put in prison, and finally put to death because of his faith in Jesus. The Church celebrates the feast of the Conversion of Saint Paul on January 25, and the feast of Peter and Paul, Apostles, on June 29.

With the class, choose gestures to use as you pray The Glory Prayer. Then pray it together.

The Glory Prayer

Glory to the Father,
and to the Son,
and to the Holy Spirit,
as it was in the
beginning, is now,
and will be for ever.
Amen.

The Work of the Holy Spirit

At first, Peter and the other Apostles preached the Gospel in Jerusalem. Then, remembering Jesus' command, they traveled by land and sea to make disciples of all nations. Everywhere they went, the Apostles invited everyone to change their lives and become followers of Jesus. This was their message.

> "Repent and be baptized . . . in the name of Jesus Christ for the forgiveness of your sins; and you will receive the gift of the holy Spirit." ACTS OF THE APOSTLES 2:38

This is the work of the Holy Spirit. It is the same as the work the Father sent his Son, Jesus Christ, to do. It is the work of forgiving our sins and making us friends with God again. It is the work of restoring the life of God in us. It is the work of teaching and helping all people to live as children of God and followers of Jesus Christ.

Design a cover for this book that tells about the work of the Holy Spirit.

Our Church Makes a Difference

Maryknoll priest in Guatemala

Missionaries

The Holy Spirit invites people to believe in Jesus through the lives of missionaries. Missionaries, like the Apostles, travel to places in their own countries and in other countries to live and preach the Gospel.

Father James Walsh and Father Thomas Price were missionaries. They founded the Catholic Foreign Mission Society of America, which is also known as Maryknoll. Maryknoll missionaries first lived and preached the Gospel in China. Today Maryknoll priests, brothers, sisters, and laypeople serve in twenty-nine countries.

Our Catholic Identity

Christian Symbols

Symbols help us understand what we cannot see. The Church uses the symbols of wind and fire for the Holy Spirit. Wind is a symbol of life. Fire is a symbol of energy. The Holy Spirit shares with us the life of God and fills missionaries and all the baptized with the energy to live the Gospel.

Tell about missionary work you can do now.

Maryknoll sister in East Timor

Maryknoll lay missioner in Cambodia

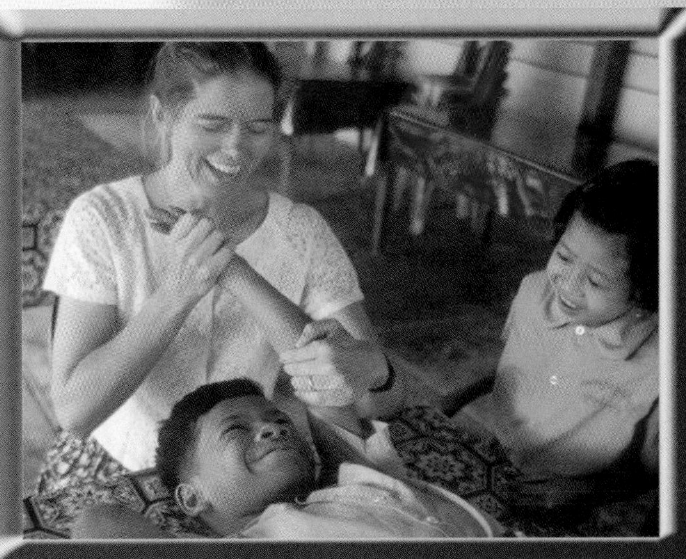

What Difference Does Faith Make in My Life?

The Holy Spirit is always with you. The Holy Spirit lives within you and shares God's life with you. The Holy Spirit gives you the energy to live as a follower of Jesus Christ.

Think about some of the activities you might take part in this week. Write a prayer to the Holy Spirit. Ask the Holy Spirit to help you take part in one of those activities in a way that shows you are a follower of Jesus Christ.

The Holy Spirit in My Life

____

____

____

____

____

____

Amen.

My Faith Choice

This week I will tell others about Jesus. I will

____

______________________________.

We Pray

Prayer to the Holy Spirit

This prayer to the Holy Spirit is from the liturgy of Pentecost.

Leader: Let us pray.

Group 1: Come, Holy Spirit,
fill the hearts of your faithful.
Group 2: And kindle in them
the fire of your love.

Group 1: Send forth your Spirit
and they shall be created.
Group 2: And you will renew
the face of the earth.

Leader: O God, on the first Pentecost you taught those who believed in you by the light of the Holy Spirit. By the same Spirit, teach us what is right and share with us your wisdom and joy. Amen.

We Remember

In the flames write or draw three things you learned about the Holy Spirit.

To Help You Remember

1. Jesus promised that he and the Father would send the Holy Spirit to help and teach the disciples as Jesus did.
2. The Holy Spirit came to the disciples on Pentecost.
3. The work of the Holy Spirit in the Church is the same work the Father sent Jesus to do.

8 With My Family

This Week . . .

In chapter 8, "Receive the Holy Spirit," your child deepened his or her understanding of and love for the Holy Spirit, the third Person of the Holy Trinity. The Holy Spirit, the Advocate, is God's gift to us. Jesus promised not to abandon his disciples. He said that he would ask the Father to send the Holy Spirit to always be with them. The Holy Spirit came to the disciples on Pentecost. The Holy Spirit gave the disciples the energy and courage to preach the Good News. The work of the Holy Spirit is the same work that the Father sent Jesus to do.

For more on the teachings of the Catholic Church on the mystery of the Holy Spirit, see *Catechism of the Catholic Church* paragraph numbers 683–741.

Sharing God's Word

Read together the Bible story in John 14:16–18 in which Jesus promises that God will send the Holy Spirit to his disciples or read the adaptation of the story on page 70. Emphasize that the Holy Spirit would help the disciples and teach them as Jesus did.

Praying

In this chapter your child prayed the Prayer to the Holy Spirit. Read and pray together the prayer on page 75.

Making a Difference

Choose one of the following activities to do as a family or design a similar activity of your own.

- Read John 14:15–30. Imagine that your family is listening to Jesus promising that God will send the Holy Spirit, the Advocate.
- Talk about how the Holy Spirit helps your family live as a Christian family.
- Make a poster of the Prayer to the Holy Spirit. Hang the poster where it can serve as a reminder to everyone in your family that the Holy Spirit is always with them.

For more ideas on ways your family can live your faith, visit the "Faith First for Families" page at **www.FaithFirst.com**. Click on "Games" and make learning fun for your child.

The Good Shepherd
A Scripture Story

We Pray

The LORD is my shepherd. PSALM 23:1

God, our Father, send us the Holy Spirit to give us the courage of Christ our shepherd. Amen.

Name people you think would give their life to protect someone.

Good shepherds would give their lives to protect their sheep. Jesus said he was a good shepherd.

Why do you think Jesus called himself a good shepherd?

Modern-day shepherd in land where Jesus lived

Bible Background

Faith Focus

Why is the image of a good shepherd a good image for Jesus?

Faith Vocabulary

sacrifice. To give up something of value out of love.

Corporal Works of Mercy. Seven ways we live Jesus' command to love others as he did by helping people care for their bodily, or corporal, needs.

Shepherds and Their Sheep

One of the ways that God tells us about himself in the Bible is through stories about shepherds and their sheep. Some of the stories describe God as the Shepherd of his people.

In Bible times shepherds roamed the valleys and mountains with their flocks. Holding a staff, a shepherd safely led the sheep on paths along the sides of mountains and across valleys. When wolves attacked the sheep, the shepherds would protect them with their own lives. If even one sheep strayed from the flock and got lost, the shepherd would search until he found the one lost sheep.

The sheep and the shepherd truly felt they belonged to one another. If a stranger called out to them, the sheep would stand still and refuse to move. Trusting the voice of their shepherd, sheep would follow wherever the shepherd led them.

Describe some of the "good shepherds" in your life.

Good Shepherds

____

____

____

____

____

____

Reading the Word of God

Jesus, the Good Shepherd

The Bible writers and the people of Jesus' time knew all about shepherds. They knew shepherds who really cared about their sheep and those shepherds who did not take good care of their sheep.

Jesus told his disciples he was the Good Shepherd. He said,

> "A good shepherd knows his sheep and gives up his life to protect them. I know my sheep, and my sheep know me. I will give up my life for my sheep."
>
> BASED ON JOHN 10:11, 14–15

Jesus' disciples and other listeners knew that the Scriptures used the image of the shepherd to describe God. God was the true Shepherd of his people who truly cared about them. Jesus was saying to the disciples that he was the Good Shepherd. He cared about people just as God did.

Describe one way a parent or a teacher or a coach might be a good shepherd.

We Follow the Good Shepherd

A good shepherd will do everything, even **sacrifice**, or give up, his life out of love for his sheep. Jesus Christ, our Savior, died for us. He is the Good Shepherd who sacrificed his life for us on the cross.

We show we belong to Jesus the Good Shepherd when we listen to him. The Church has named seven ways we can show we are listening to Jesus. When we do these things, we help people care for their bodily, or corporal, needs as he did. These seven actions or good deeds are called the **Corporal Works of Mercy.** They are:

1. Feed people who are hungry.
2. Give drink to people who are thirsty.
3. Clothe people who need clothing.
4. Visit people who are in prison.
5. Shelter people who do not have a place to live.
6. Visit people who are sick.
7. Bury people who have died.

Following the Good Shepherd

Design a full-page ad for your parish bulletin inviting people to live one of the Corporal Works of Mercy.

Our Church Makes a Difference

Honduras, Central America

Catholic Relief Services

The Church helps us live the Corporal Works of Mercy through the work of Catholic Relief Services. Catholic Relief Services works to end the suffering of people in more than eighty countries throughout the world.

Catholic Relief Services workers follow the command of Jesus the Good Shepherd. They make sacrifices to feed, clothe, and care for people in need. They develop programs to help people begin to meet these needs on their own.

Describe ways the people of your parish listen to the voice of the Good Shepherd and care for people.

Our Catholic Identity

Saint Joseph's Table

On the feast of Saint Joseph (March 19), many parishes live the Corporal Works of Mercy in a special way. They hold a banquet called Saint Joseph's Table. They open the doors of their parish and share food with people in the community who are having difficulty providing food for themselves and their families.

Guatemala, Central America

Colombia, South America

Ethiopia, Africa

What Difference Does Faith Make in My Life?

We need to take the time to help people as Jesus did. Helping people even in small ways is very important. You cannot imagine what your kindness and generosity mean to the people you help. When you do these things, you are living as a follower of Jesus the Good Shepherd.

Describe one of the small things you do each day to help others.

My Faith Choice

This week I will find one way to care for others as Jesus the Good Shepherd taught us. I will

____

______________________________.

We Pray

Praying a Psalm

The Church prays the Psalms every day. Pray this psalm to praise God.

All: **The LORD is my shepherd.**

Group 1: In green pastures you let me graze;
Group 2: to safe waters you lead me. . . .

Group 1: You guide me along the right path
Group 2: for the sake of your name.

Group 1: Only goodness and love will pursue me
Group 2: all the days of my life.

All: **The LORD is my shepherd.**

PSALM 23:1–2, 3, 6

We Remember

Use all these words in two or three sentences.

sacrifice shepherd trust Jesus command life good

____

____

____

____

____

____

To Help You Remember

1. The writers of the Bible use the image of a good shepherd to help us understand God's love for us.
2. Jesus said he was the Good Shepherd.
3. The Corporal Works of Mercy help us follow the command of Jesus the Good Shepherd to show our love for people as he did.

9 With My Family

This Week . . .

In chapter 9, "The Good Shepherd: A Scripture Story," your child learned that the writers of the Bible used images to help us understand the mystery of God's love. One of these images is that of the shepherd. Psalm 23 describes God as the Shepherd of Israel. In John's Gospel Jesus describes himself as the Good Shepherd. Joined to Christ at Baptism, all the baptized are called to put on the mind of the Good Shepherd and care for one another as Jesus revealed God cares for us. Living the Corporal Works of Mercy is one way we can follow Jesus the Good Shepherd.

For more on the teachings of the Catholic Church on the mystery of God's love and the call of the Church to serve others as Jesus did, see *Catechism of the Catholic Church* paragraph numbers 683–741.

Sharing God's Word

Read together the Bible story about Jesus the Good Shepherd. You can find this story in John 10:14–15 or an adaptation of the story on page 79. Emphasize that Jesus knew and cared about people just as a good shepherd knows and cares about his sheep.

Praying

In this chapter your child prayed Psalm 23. Read and pray together the prayer on page 83.

Making a Difference

Choose one of the following activities to do as a family or design a similar activity of your own.

- Make a list of all the ways your family cares for one another. Discuss how each of the things you do shows how much you love each other.
- Pretend that your family is going on vacation and you have asked someone to take care of the family pet. Write instructions explaining how this person should care for your pet. Help the person be a good shepherd to your pet just as you are.
- Review the Corporal Works of Mercy on page 80. Choose one thing you will do this week to put the Corporal Works of Mercy into practice.

For more ideas on ways your family can live your faith, visit the "Faith First for Families" page at **www.FaithFirst.com.** Click on "Family Prayer" and pray the prayer of the week.

The People of God

10

We Pray

We are God's people, the flock he always cares for.

Based on Psalm 100:3

Lord, look with kindness on the prayers and gifts of your Church. Amen.

What are some of the groups you belong to?

We belong to many different groups. We belong to the Catholic Church. The Church is the People of God.

What do members of the Catholic Church have in common?

People gathered to remember victims of September 11, 2001

Faith Focus

What does it mean to call the Church the new People of God?

Faith Vocabulary

People of God. A New Testament image for the Church that teaches that God has called together all people in Jesus Christ to be his people.

Body of Christ. A New Testament image for the Church that teaches that the members of the Church are made one in Christ, the Head of the Church.

Names for the Church

God the Father prepared for the Church from the beginning of time. Jesus, the Son of God, founded the Church. The Holy Spirit, the Advocate, is present with the Church as its guide and teacher. The Church can be described in many ways.

People of God. The New Testament describes the Church as

> a chosen race . . . a holy nation.
> 1 PETER 2:9

The Church is the people God has called together in Jesus Christ. We have been called to know, love, and serve God together. We are called to be God's people now and forever. God has created us to live in happiness with him forever. Christians have believed this about the Church from its very beginning.

Body of Christ. Baptism joins us to Jesus Christ. The Church is the Body of Christ. The Church is both human and divine. Christ is the Head of the Church, and the hierarchy, religious, and laypeople are its members. All the faithful followers of Christ who have died also belong to the Church family. There are parts you can see and parts you cannot see. The Church is spiritual and visible.

Describe the good works you see members of the Church doing in your parish.

The Work of the Church on Earth

Jesus founded the Church. He said to the Apostle Peter,

> "You are Peter, and upon this rock I will build my church."
>
> MATTHEW 16:18

Jesus gave Peter and the Apostles the authority and responsibility to baptize people, make all people his disciples, and to teach what he had taught. Jesus Christ continues to govern the Church today through the pope and the other bishops. The pope is the successor of Saint Peter and the bishops are the successors of the other Apostles. All the baptized are called to work with the Holy Spirit and continue the work of Christ on earth.

The work of Christ is described as the work of a priest, prophet, and king. That is the work of the Church too. We are to live holy lives. We are to tell others about God. We are to serve God, especially by serving people who are poor and suffering.

Faith-Filled People

The Apostles

The Apostles were the first shepherds of the Church. The Apostles Jesus first chose are named in Matthew 10:1–4. They are "Simon called Peter, and his brother Andrew; James, the son of Zebedee, and his brother John; Philip and Bartholomew, Thomas and Matthew the tax collector; James, the son of Alphaeus, and Thaddeus; Simon the Cananean, and Judas Iscariot who betrayed him." After Jesus' Ascension Paul and Barnabas were named Apostles.

Solve this code to discover what Jesus asked his followers to do.

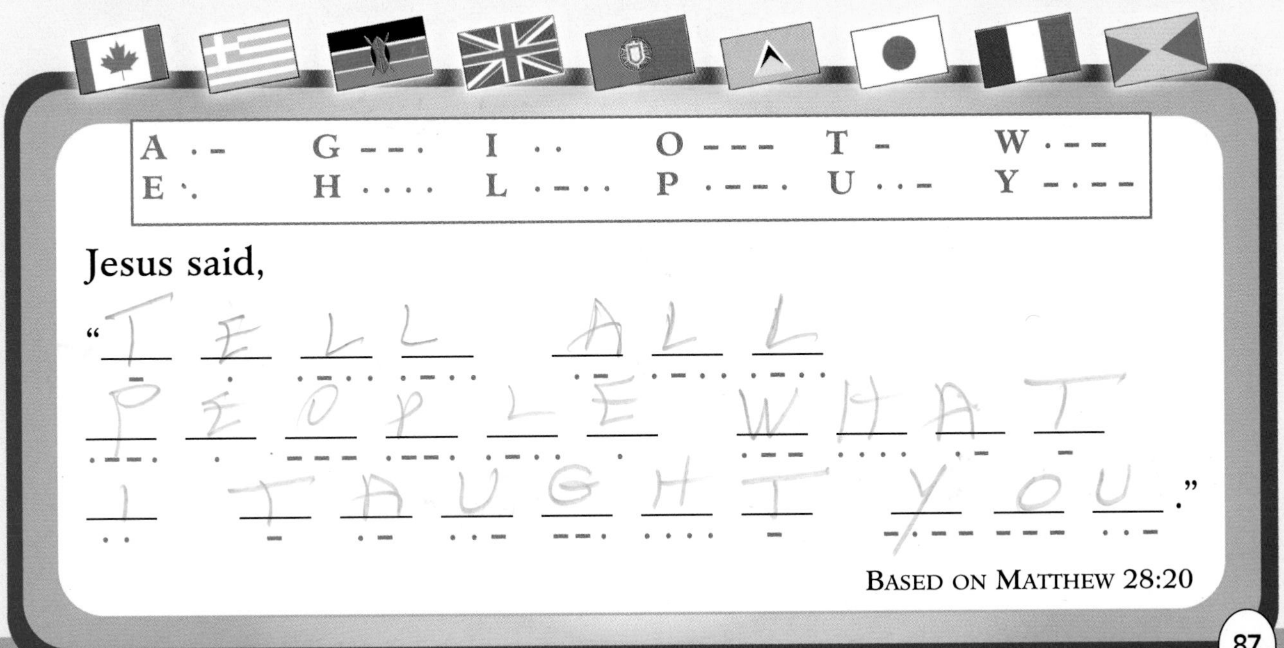

The Kingdom of God

FOOD
DRIVE

Jesus often taught about the kingdom, or reign, of God. Jesus said that the kingdom of God, or kingdom of heaven, is like a treasure. (Read Matthew 13:44.) It is something we all dream of and hope for. It is something we would be willing to sell everything we have to find and keep. It is something we pray for every time we pray "Thy kingdom come" in the Our Father.

MEALS ON
WHEELS

Together with the Holy Spirit, the Church works to prepare for the coming of God's kingdom. We work to build a world of love and peace, mercy and justice as Jesus did. This is good news for all people. It gives all people hope for the future. When this work of Christ is finished at the end of time, the kingdom of God will finally come about. God's loving plan of salvation will be finished.

Write six words to describe the kingdom of God.

Our Church Makes a Difference

The Communion of Saints

Christians have always believed that the members of the Church on earth belong to a bigger Church. We belong to the Communion of Saints.

The Communion of Saints includes all the baptized on earth and all the saints living in heaven with God. It also includes all those who have died in friendship with God but still must grow in holiness before they enjoy eternal happiness with God in heaven. We call these members of the Communion of Saints the souls in purgatory.

The Church's belief in the Communion of Saints helps us remember that we are all preparing for the coming of the kingdom of God. After we die, our life continues. We will live in heaven, which is the kingdom of everlasting happiness with God and all the saints.

Describe some of the ways your parish honors Mary and the other saints.

Our Catholic Identity

All Souls' Day

On November 2, the Church celebrates All Souls' Day. We pray for all the souls in purgatory. We believe that when we die our life is changed and not ended. We support one another by our prayers.

What Difference Does Faith Make in My Life?

You are a member of the Church. You are preparing for the coming of the kingdom of God. Each day you are helping to build a world in which all people will live together as brothers and sisters of Jesus.

Think about the acts of kindness you do each day. Describe what happens when you say a kind word to someone. Describe what happens when you treat others fairly.

Preparing for the Kingdom of God

My Faith Choice

This week I will continue the work of Christ and prepare for the kingdom of God. I will

____

____.

We Pray

A Prayer for All Souls

Jesus promised that all who believe in God and live as he taught will live forever in heaven. Let us pray for all who have died.

Leader: Merciful Father, you raised your Son, Jesus, from the dead. We gather to ask your mercy for all who have died believing in you.

Reader: A reading from the Book of Revelation.
Read Revelation 14:13.
The word of the Lord.

All: **Thanks be to God.**

Leader: Lord God, we believe that all who died trusting in you will live forever because of the death and Resurrection of your Son.

All: **We do believe! Amen!**

Use this code to decipher the message about the Church.

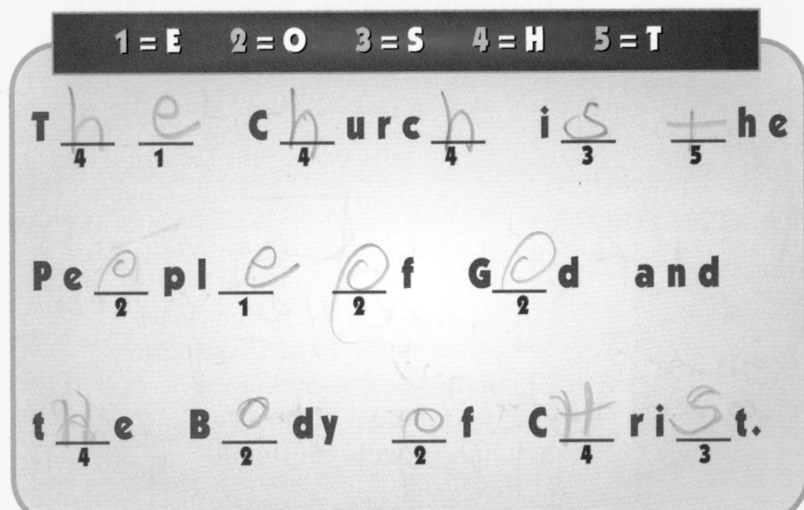

To Help You Remember

1. The Church is the Body of Christ, the People of God.
2. Jesus founded the Church on Saint Peter. All the members of the Church work with the Holy Spirit to continue the work of Christ the Priest, Prophet, and King.
3. Jesus announced the coming of the kingdom of God. The kingdom will come about in all its fullness at the end of time.

10 With My Family

This Week . . .

In chapter 10, "The Church," your child deepened his or her understanding of the mystery of the Church. God has called us together in Christ to be the new People of God. Christ is the Head of the Body of Christ, the Church. The hierarchy, religious, and laypeople are its members. Every member of the Church works together with the Holy Spirit to continue the work of Christ to prepare for the coming of the kingdom of God announced and promised by Jesus. The kingdom will finally come about in its fullness at the end of time.

For more on the teachings of the Catholic Church on the mystery of the Church, see *Catechism of the Catholic Church* paragraph numbers 748–959.

Sharing God's Word

Read together 1 Peter 2:9–10 and Matthew 16:13–19. Emphasize that the Church is the People of God and the Body of Christ.

Praying

In this chapter your child prayed a prayer for all the faithful who have died. Pray this prayer together on page 91.

Making a Difference

Choose one of the following activities to do as a family or design a similar activity of your own.

- Talk about what it means for your family to live as members of the Body of Christ.
- Choose one thing you will do this week to help prepare for the coming of God's kingdom.
- Make a banner of paper or cloth that says "We Are the Body of Christ." Ask each family member to include a symbol showing a way they can continue Christ's work. Hang the banner where it can serve as a reminder that your family is called to continue Christ's work in the world.

For more ideas on ways your family can live your faith, visit the "Faith First for Families" page at **www.FaithFirst.com.** You are only a click away from taking a "Tour of a Church" with your child this week.

Unit 1 Review

Name ______________________

A. The Best Word

Fill in the blanks, using the words from the word bank.

Faith	Passover	Ark of the Covenant
Divine Revelation	ministry	Original sin
Sacred Scripture	Incarnation	

1. ______________________ is God making himself and his plan for creation known over a long period of time.

2. ______________________ is both a gift from God to know and believe in him and our acceptance of that gift.

3. God is the real author of ______________________, or "Holy Writings" collected in the Bible.

4. The ______________________ is the chest the Israelites used to hold the tablets on which the Ten Commandments were written.

5. ______________________ is the choice that Adam and Eve freely made to turn away from God.

6. The ______________________ is the Son of God becoming human without giving up being God.

7. Jesus began his public ______________________ when he grew up and left home to begin the work God sent him to do.

8. ______________________ is the Jewish feast that celebrates God's freeing of the Israelites from slavery and leading them to the land he promised them.

B. Words and Phrases

Match the words or phrases in column A with the words or phrases in column B.

Column A

e 1. Feed the hungry; visit the sick

c 2. The day the Apostles received the Holy Spirit

d 3. The meal at which Jesus gave us the Eucharist

b 4. Isaiah's description of the Savior

a 5. The kingdom of God

f 6. Inspired by the Holy Spirit

Column B

a. place and time of lasting love and justice

b. Prince of Peace

c. Pentecost

d. Last Supper

e. Corporal Works of Mercy

f. writers of the Bible

C. What I Learned

1. *Name three things you learned in this unit. Share them with the group.*

____

____

____

2. *Look at the list of faith terms on page 12. Circle the ones you know now.*

D. From a Scripture Story

In the T chart compare Jesus to a good shepherd.

Good Shepherd	Jesus
Saved sheep from danger Sheep trusted	Saved us from sin We trust Jesus etc.

Unit 2 • We Worship

What signs of God's love do these pictures show?

Getting Ready

What I Have Learned

What is something you already know about these three faith terms?

The liturgy

____

____

The Paschal Mystery

____

____

The Sacraments at the Service of Communion

____

____

Words to Know

Put an X next to the faith terms you know. Put a ? next to faith terms you need to know more about.

Faith Vocabulary

______ liturgy
______ manna
______ Sacraments of Healing
______ Sacraments at the Service of Communion
______ holiness
______ Exodus
______ Paschal Mystery

Questions I Have

What questions would you like to ask about the Sacraments of Healing?

____

____

A Scripture Story

Jesus healing a young girl

Why did Jesus heal the young girl?

Celebrating God's Love for Us

We Pray

Give praise to the
LORD God.
Great are his works.

BASED ON PSALM 111:1, 2

Father, all life, all holiness comes from you through your Son, Jesus Christ, by the working of the Holy Spirit. Amen.

What are some ways you work together with others?

Families work together at home. Students and teachers work together. Members of the Church work together too. Celebrating the liturgy is one of the important works of the Church.

What are some of the ways you take part in the liturgy?

The blessing of the water used in Baptism at the Easter Vigil

Blessing and Thanking God

Faith Focus

Why does the Church gather to celebrate the liturgy?

Faith Vocabulary

liturgy. The work of the Church, the Body of Christ, of worshiping God.

Paschal Mystery. The mystery of Jesus' passing over from suffering and death to new and glorious life; Christ's work of salvation accomplished by his Passion, death, Resurrection, and Ascension.

The Liturgy of the Church

When the Church gathers to celebrate the **liturgy**, it is doing an important work. The word *liturgy* means "a public work," or "work of the people." The liturgy is the work of the Church, the Body of Christ.

The liturgy is also the work of God the Holy Trinity. God the Father blesses us with the gift of the Son. Jesus the Son of God blesses us with his Body and Blood. God the Holy Spirit blesses us with the gift of God's own life and love.

The priest leads the community of the Church gathered to worship God in the celebration of the liturgy. The priest acts together with and in the name and person of Christ, the Head of the Church. In the liturgy, the Catholic community gathers with Jesus Christ both to receive God's blessings and to bless and give thanks to the Father through the power of the Holy Spirit. The Church prays,

> "How wonderful are you,
> LORD God.
> Everyone on earth worships you
> and sings praises to you."
> BASED ON PSALM 66:3, 4

Tell about several blessings you and your family enjoy.

Praying the Eucharistic Prayer at Mass

Celebrating God's Work

The liturgy of the Church centers around the Eucharist and the other sacraments. Through the celebration of the liturgy, we become sharers in the saving work of Jesus Christ and in the life of God. We remember and celebrate and share in God's work among us today.

The Church joins with Jesus to celebrate the liturgy. We remember and share in the **Paschal Mystery.** The Paschal Mystery is the name we give to the good news of God's saving all people in Jesus. It is Christ's work of salvation accomplished by his Passion, death, Resurrection, and Ascension.

Faith-Filled People

John the Apostle

Saint John was the youngest of the Apostles chosen by Jesus. Jesus gave John and James, who was also an Apostle, the nickname "sons of thunder." John stood by the cross with Mary during the suffering and death of Jesus. The Church celebrates his feast day on December 27.

Describe what you can do to proclaim the good news of salvation to someone else.

The Liturgical Year

The Church celebrates the liturgy every day of the year. This is called the liturgical year. The liturgical year is made up of feasts and seasons that celebrate God's great plan of saving love in Christ. These are the seasons of the liturgical year.

Advent. We wait and prepare for the coming of Jesus. We prepare for our celebration of Christ's first coming and await his second coming at the end of time.

Christmas. We celebrate the birth of Jesus Christ, the Savior of all people whom God promised to send.

Lent. We prepare for Easter. Lent is a time to prepare to welcome new members into the Church and to renew our own baptismal promises.

Triduum. The word *triduum* means "three days." The Triduum is the center of the liturgical year. It is our three-day celebration on Holy Thursday, Good Friday, and the Easter Vigil/Easter Sunday of the Paschal Mystery of Jesus.

Easter. For fifty days, from Easter Sunday to Pentecost, we celebrate that Christ is risen and will come again.

Ordinary Time. The remaining weeks of the liturgical year are called Ordinary Time. We listen and respond to God's word. We grow in love for God and others.

Color the art next to your favorite time of the liturgical year. Tell why it is your favorite time.

Our Church Makes a Difference

Las Posadas

The people in Mexico celebrate Las Posadas each year during Advent. Las Posadas takes place during the eight days before Christmas. Celebrating Las Posadas helps the people get ready to celebrate the liturgy on Christmas.

Las Posadas acts out Mary and Joseph's looking for a place to stay in Bethlehem. In Mexico the people carry candles and walk in procession through the streets. Two people represent Mary and Joseph and sometimes ride on a donkey. They stop at homes and ask for a place to stay. They are turned away until a family finally welcomes them into their home.

Las Posadas reminds us that we always need to be ready to open our hearts to God's love. It is a wonderful, joyful celebration that shares with everyone the good news of God's love.

Our Catholic Identity

The Angelus

Some Catholic churches ring their church bells at 6:00 A.M., at 12:00 noon, and at 6:00 P.M. When they do, they are following the tradition of the Angelus. The ringing of the bells calls us to pray during the day. When we pray the Angelus, we thank and praise God for Jesus Christ, the Savior of the world.

What Christmas tradition does your family enjoy?

What Difference Does Faith Make in My Life?

Each day God shares his love with you. It is good to take the time to open your heart to God's love. Thank and bless God every day for his love.

Describe one way that you have come to know God's love. Create a prayer to thank God. Pray your prayer.

Thank You, God

____

____

____

____

____

____

My Faith Choice

This week I will thank God for his love for me. I will pray the prayer that I have written at least once a day.

We Pray

Holy, Holy, Holy Lord

God is the source of all our blessings. At Mass we begin our prayer of thanks, the Eucharistic Prayer, to God by praying this acclamation. An acclamation is a prayer that honors God.

Leader: Jesus suffered and died and was raised from the dead. Let us join with the angels and saints to give glory and thanks to God for the gift of Jesus, the Savior of the world.

All: **Holy, holy, holy Lord, God of power**
and might.
Heaven and earth are full of your glory.
Hosanna in the highest.
Blessed is he who comes in the
name of the Lord.
Hosanna in the highest.

FROM PREFACE, ROMAN MISSAL

We Remember

Write T next to the true statements. Write F next to the false statements. Make the false statements true.

____ **1.** The liturgy is the Church's work of worshiping God.

____ **2.** The liturgy is the work of the Holy Trinity.

____ **3.** The Paschal Mystery is the birth of Jesus.

____ **4.** Advent is the center of the liturgical year.

____ **5.** Lent is a time to prepare to welcome new members into the Church.

To Help You Remember

1. The Church gathers for liturgy, the work of worshiping God.
2. In the liturgy we are made sharers in the Paschal Mystery of Jesus Christ.
3. The Church celebrates and shares in God's plan of salvation all year long.

11 With My Family

This Week . . .

In chapter 11, "Celebrating God's Love for Us," your child learned that the liturgy is the Church's work of worshiping God. The liturgy of the Church centers around the Eucharist and the other sacraments. In the liturgy the members of the Church gather with Christ, the Head of the Church, to remember and share in the Paschal Mystery of Christ. The Paschal Mystery of Christ is his saving Passion, death, Resurrection, and Ascension. The Church gathers to receive God's blessing and to bless and give thanks to the Father. What Jesus did while he was on earth is made present here and now. We join with Christ all year long and share in his work of salvation. We call the Church's year of worship the liturgical year.

For more on the teachings of the Catholic Church on the liturgy, see *Catechism of the Catholic Church* paragraph numbers 1076–1109, 1136–1186, and 1200–1206.

Sharing God's Word

Read together Psalm 66:1–4. Emphasize that the word *liturgy* means "work of the people." The liturgy is the Church's work of worshiping God.

Praying

In this chapter your child prayed an acclamation. An acclamation is a prayer that honors God. Read and pray together the acclamation on page 103.

Making a Difference

Choose one of the following activities to do as a family or design a similar activity of your own.

- After your family participates in Mass this weekend, name all the people who assisted the priest, for example, the deacon, the readers, and the extraordinary ministers of Holy Communion. Then talk about the many ways that the assembly takes part in Mass.
- The word *eucharist* means "thanksgiving." Talk about how your family gives thanks to God.
- Invite each family member to share which of the liturgical seasons is their favorite. Ask each person to explain their answer.

For more ideas on ways your family can live your faith, visit the "Faith First for Families" page at **www.FaithFirst.com.** Click on "Contemporary Issues" this week to find an article on an especially interesting topic.

Sharing in Christ's Life and Work

We Pray

"Whoever drinks the water I shall give will never thirst."

JOHN 4:14

Father, may all the baptized rise with Jesus to newness of life through the power of the Holy Spirit. Amen.

Name and explain some of the signs you often see in the world around you.

We are surrounded by signs and symbols. The Church uses signs and symbols in the celebration of the liturgy and sacraments.

What are some of the signs and symbols you see being used by the Church in the sacraments?

Bread and wine, symbols for the Eucharist

God's Saving Work Among Us

Faith Focus

What do we celebrate in the three Sacraments of Initiation?

Faith Vocabulary

sacraments. The seven main liturgical signs of the Church, given to us by Jesus Christ, that make us sharers in the saving work of Christ and in the life of the Holy Trinity through the power of the Holy Spirit.

Sacraments of Initiation. The three sacraments of Baptism, Confirmation, and Eucharist, which are the foundation of the Christian life.

Baptism

Sharing in Christ's Life and Work

The liturgy of the Church centers around the Eucharist and the other **sacraments.** The sacraments are Baptism, Confirmation, Eucharist, Reconciliation, Anointing of the Sick, Holy Orders, and Matrimony.

The sacraments are celebrations of our faith. Given to us by Jesus, the sacraments through the power of the Holy Spirit make us sharers in the saving work of Christ and in the life of the Holy Trinity. That is why the Church teaches that for believers in Jesus Christ the sacraments are necessary for salvation.

Name one of the sacraments that you have received. Describe what you saw and heard.

The Sacraments of Initiation

Baptism, Confirmation, and Eucharist are the **Sacraments of Initiation.** These three sacraments are the foundation of the Christian life. Through the celebration of these sacraments a person is joined to Christ and becomes a full member of the Church.

Baptism is the first sacrament we receive. Through Baptism we are joined to Christ and become members of the Body of Christ, the Church. Saint Paul teaches,

> We have all been baptized into the one body of Christ. . . . We are all part of Christ's body. BASED ON 1 CORINTHIANS 12:13, 27

We receive the gift of the Holy Spirit. We are reborn as God's adopted children and begin our new life in Christ. Original sin and all personal sins are forgiven. Marked forever as belonging to Christ, we receive this sacrament only one time.

Confirmation strengthens the grace of Baptism. We are strengthened to share with others the good news of all God has done in Jesus Christ. In Confirmation as in Baptism, we receive a lasting character on our soul that marks us as belonging to Christ forever.

Describe what it means to be a disciple of Christ.

Faith-Filled People

Francis Xavier

Saint Francis Xavier was a member of the Society of Jesus, or Jesuits. He was a missionary to the people of India, where he lived and preached the Gospel. Many who listened to Francis Xavier asked for Baptism. Saint Francis Xavier is the patron of foreign missions. His feast day is December 3.

Man being confirmed at the Easter Vigil by a priest delegated by the bishop

Eucharist

The Eucharist is the third Sacrament of Initiation. In every celebration of the Eucharist, the whole Church on earth and in heaven joins with Christ, the Head of the Church. We give praise and thanksgiving to God the Father through the power of the Holy Spirit.

Jesus Christ is present and leads us in every celebration of the Eucharist. By the power of the Holy Spirit, Christ is present

- in the people gathered for worship,
- in the priest who leads the celebration,
- in the word of God proclaimed in Sacred Scripture, and, most especially,
- under the appearances of bread and wine, which have become his Body and Blood.

Through this sacrament we become sharers in God's life and the saving work of Christ's Paschal Mystery. We receive the Body and Blood of Christ in Holy Communion and are united more closely with Christ and one another.

What can you do to show that you are united to Christ? What will your actions show others?

What I Do	What It Shows
______________________	______________________
______________________	______________________
______________________	______________________

Our Church Makes a Difference

Bread for the World

The Holy Spirit teaches and helps the Church continue the work of Christ in the world. About forty years ago, a group of Catholics and other Christians had served food in church halls to families and people who lived on the streets. They worked in food pantries and had collected money to buy food for families on holidays.

This small group of Christians wanted to do more. They wanted to do things to stop hunger before it began. They talked and prayed about what they could do. In 1972 they began Bread for the World.

Today there are over 44,000 Bread for the World workers. They work with government leaders and Church leaders to set up programs that fight the things that cause hunger.

How has Bread for the World helped these African women? What can you do to help people who need food to feed their families?

Our Catholic Identity

Gifts of the Holy Spirit

The Holy Spirit teaches and helps all the members of the Church continue the work of Christ. The Holy Spirit shares with us the seven gifts of wisdom, understanding, right judgment, courage, knowledge, reverence, and wonder and awe. All these gifts help us continue the work of Christ in the world.

Young girl writing letter asking government leaders to help the hungry

African women grinding grain to make bread

What Difference Does Faith Make in My Life?

When you were baptized, you received the gift of the Holy Spirit. The Holy Spirit helps you live as a follower of Jesus and continue his work in the world.

Courage is one of the seven gifts of the Holy Spirit. Think about a time it took courage for you to be fair or to help someone or to do the right thing.

The Gift of Courage

What did you do?

____

____

____

____

Take a moment to thank the Holy Spirit.

My Faith Choice

This week I will do my best to live as a member of the Body of Christ, the Church. I will pray to the Holy Spirit each morning, afternoon, or night. *(Circle one.)*

We Pray

Anointing

Anointing with chrism is a sign that shows we belong to Christ. When we are anointed in Baptism, the priest or deacon rubs the blessed oil named chrism on the top of our head, making the Sign of the Cross.

Leader: Come forward one at a time. Let us remember that we belong to Christ.

The children come forward and the leader rubs oil on the top of each child's head, saying,
(Name), remember that you belong to Jesus Christ.
In the name of the Father,
and of the Son,
and of the Holy Spirit.

All: **Amen.**

We Remember

Draw a line to connect the word in the left column with the correct description of the word in the right column.

Confirmation	This is at the center of the Church's celebration of the liturgy and completes our initiation into the Body of Christ, the Church.
Eucharist	Through the celebration of this sacrament, we are first joined to Christ and become members of his Body, the Church.
Baptism	This sacrament strengthens the grace of Baptism.

To Help You Remember

1. The seven sacraments have been given to the Church by Christ. They make us sharers in the life of God through the power of the Holy Spirit.
2. Baptism, Confirmation, and Eucharist are the three Sacraments of Initiation.
3. By receiving all three Sacraments of Initiation we are joined to Christ and become full members of the Church.

12 With My Family

This Week . . .

In chapter 12, "Sharing in Christ's Life and Work," your child learned about the sacraments. The sacraments are the seven major celebrations of the liturgy. Given to us by Christ, they make us sharers in the life of the Holy Trinity. The three sacraments of Baptism, Confirmation, and Eucharist are the Sacraments of Initiation. These three sacraments are the foundation of the Christian life. Baptism is the first sacrament we receive. Confirmation strengthens the grace of Baptism. The Eucharist joins us more fully to Christ and the Church. By receiving all three of these sacraments we become fully united with Christ and one another and become full members of the Church, the Body of Christ.

For more on the teachings of the Catholic Church on the sacraments in general and on the Sacraments of Initiation in particular, see *Catechism of the Catholic Church* paragraph numbers 1113–1130, 1210–1274, 1285–1314, and 1322–1405.

Sharing God's Word

Read together 1 Corinthians 12:12–34. Emphasize that Baptism, Confirmation, and Eucharist are the Sacraments of Initiation and are the foundation of the Christian life.

Praying

In this chapter your child prayed, using a ritual of anointing. Read and pray together the prayer on page 111.

Making a Difference

Choose one of the following activities to do as a family or design a similar activity of your own.

- Keep a bowl of holy water in your home this week. Encourage each other to bless yourselves when you come and go and before bedtime.
- Talk about how your family continues the work of Jesus. How does your parish continue the work of Jesus? Look in the bulletin or on the web site for ideas.

For more ideas on ways your family can live your faith, visit the "Faith First for Families" page at **www.FaithFirst.com.** Click on "Games" to review the seven sacraments with your child.

Jesus Feeds the People
A Scripture Story

We Pray

LORD, feed your people forever!
BASED ON PSALM 28:9

Lord God, thank you for the gift of the Bread of Life, the Eucharist. Amen.

What is your favorite kind of bread?

Almost everyone eats bread in one form or another. Bread was an important food in the diet of the people of the Bible.

What Bible stories do you know about bread?

Jesus and the disciples thanking God for his blessings

Bible Background

Faith Focus

What is God saying to us through the Bible story of Jesus feeding the people with bread?

Faith Vocabulary

Exodus. The journey of the Israelites under the leadership of Moses from slavery in Egypt to freedom in the land promised them by God.

manna. The breadlike food the Israelites ate in the desert during the Exodus.

Manna in the Desert

There are many stories about bread in the Bible. One very important bread story in the Old Testament is part of the **Exodus** story. During the Exodus the Israelites became very tired and hungry and they began to lose trust in God. Listening to the complaining of his people, God said to Moses,

> "I will now rain down bread from heaven for you. Each day the people are to go out and gather their daily portion."
>
> Exodus 16:4

The "bread from heaven" was **manna.** Each day the Israelites gathered enough manna for the day. They baked it and ate it until they were satisfied. For Moses and the Israelites, eating the manna was a sign of love for them.

What are some signs of God's loving care for you?

Reading the Word of God

Jesus Feeds Five Thousand People

In the Gospel according to Luke in the New Testament, we read about this miracle of Jesus.

> A crowd of people followed Jesus to a deserted place. The people were hungry and tired. Jesus said to the disciples, "Give the people some food." The disciples replied, "We only have five loaves and two fish." Jesus took the five loaves and the two fish. Looking up to heaven, he said the blessing over them, broke them, and gave them to the disciples to give to the crowd. They all ate and were no longer hungry.
>
> BASED ON LUKE 9:11–13, 16–17

Jesus fed five thousand people with only five loaves of bread and two fish. There were even twelve baskets of food left over.

Pretend you are in the crowd who followed Jesus. What would you tell your family and friends about Jesus?

Understanding the Word of God

God Cares for His People

In the Old Testament story God led his people out of Egypt and fed them with manna. In the Gospel story, Jesus, the Son of God, fed the people with bread. In both stories, the people ate and were satisfied.

The story in Luke also reminds us of the food that Jesus, the Bread of Life, gave the Church at the Last Supper, his own Body and Blood. At the Last Supper, Jesus "took the bread, said the blessing, broke it, and gave it to them, saying, 'This is my body, which will be given for you; do this in memory of me' " (Luke 22:19).

God's message is the same in all three stories. We can trust that God always cares for us. God is always present with us. We call God's caring love for his people and all creation divine Providence.

What can you do to help people come to know God's love for them? Make a plan and put it into action.

Our Church Makes a Difference

Signs of God's Caring Love

The people of Saint Elizabeth Ann Seton Parish have their own bread story to tell. They learned that many of the people of another parish were out of work and were having a difficult time feeding and clothing their families. The people of Saint Elizabeth's asked, "How can we show that we care?"

That was several years ago. Today the people of both parishes have become like one family. Each month they spend time together and always ask, "How else can we help each other?"

We believe God loves us and cares for us. We, the People of God, reach out and share that caring love with others.

What are some ways your parish could care for people who are not members of your own parish family?

Our Catholic Identity

Almsgiving

Almsgiving is sharing our blessings with others, especially with people in need. The word *alms* comes from a Latin word meaning "an act of mercy or kindness." Christians treat others with mercy and kindness as God is merciful and kind to us.

What Difference Does Faith Make in My Life?

You are kind to people in many ways. When you are, you are a sign to others of God's caring love for them. Your kind words and actions help people see how much God loves them and cares for them.

Write a poem, song, or story that describes you and your friends being kind to others.

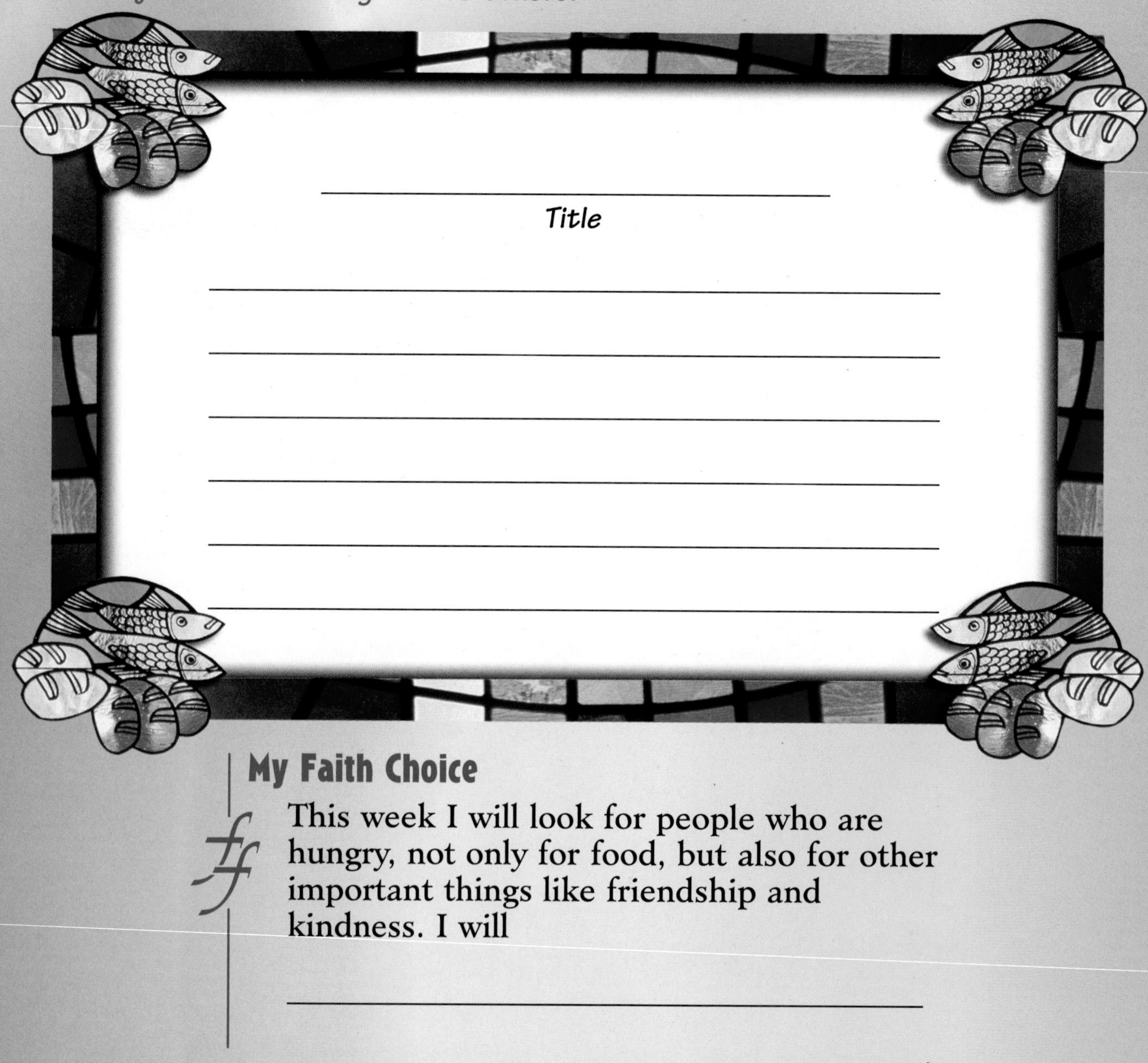

My Faith Choice

This week I will look for people who are hungry, not only for food, but also for other important things like friendship and kindness. I will

____

______________________________.

Jesus, the Bread of Life

This litany is based on part of a poem that is read at Mass on the Solemnity of the Body and Blood of Christ.

Leader: Jesus, Good Shepherd and true Bread,
All: **be merciful and kind to us.**

Leader: Jesus, source of our happiness,
All: **be merciful and kind to us.**

Leader: Jesus, you know and can do all things;
All: **be merciful and kind to us.**

Leader: Jesus, make us your guests in heaven;
All: **be merciful and kind to us.**

We Remember

Compare and contrast the story of Moses and the manna in the desert with the story of Jesus feeding the crowd. How are the two stories alike and how are they different?

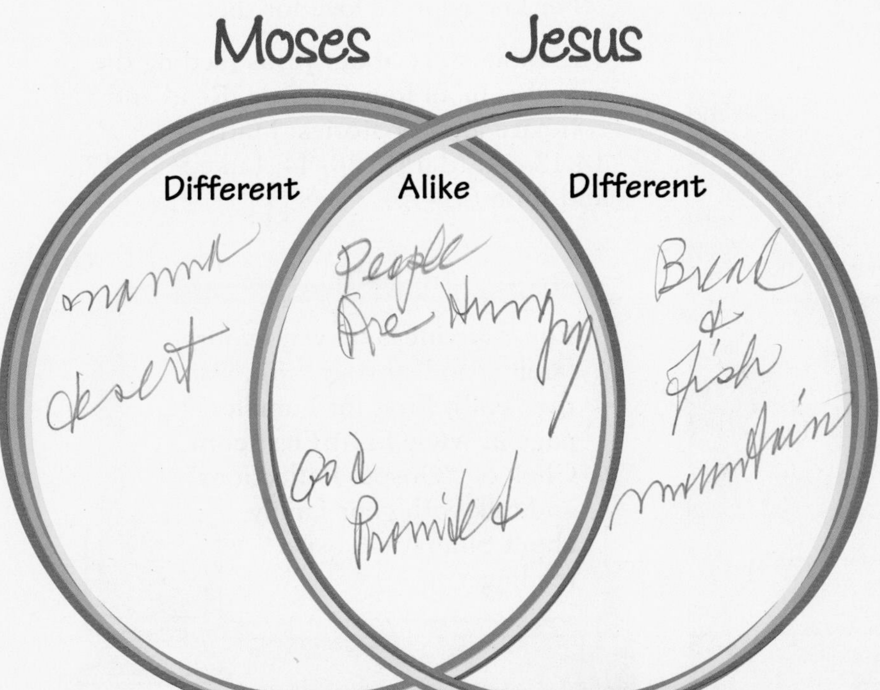

To Help You Remember

1. God fed his people, the Israelites, with manna during the Exodus.
2. Jesus fed five thousand people with five loaves of bread and two fish.
3. The bread stories in the Bible invite us to believe and trust in God's caring love for us.

13 With My Family

This Week . . .

In chapter 13, "Jesus Feeds the People: A Scripture Story," your child learned about the meaning of two bread stories in the Bible. The Israelites were fed with manna in the desert during the Exodus. Jesus fed five thousand people by multiplying five loaves of bread and two fish. In both stories the people ate until they were satisfied. In both stories God reveals his ever-present caring love for people. The Church names this caring love of God for people and for all creation divine Providence. The Gospel story of Jesus feeding the people also reminds Christians of the Eucharist, the spiritual food of the Body and Blood of Jesus.

For more on the teachings of the Catholic Church on divine Providence and the effects, or graces, of the Eucharist, see *Catechism of the Catholic Church* paragraph numbers 302–314, 1094, 1334, 1363, and 1391–1405.

Sharing God's Word

Read together the Bible story in Luke 9:10–17 about Jesus feeding the crowd or read the adaptation of the story on page 115. Emphasize that Jesus feeding the people is a sign of God's caring love.

Praying

In this chapter your child prayed a litany. Read and pray together the litany on page 119.

Making a Difference

Choose one of the following activities to do as a family or design a similar activity of your own.

- We all know that good nutrition and exercise help keep our bodies healthy. Talk about how participating in Mass helps our spiritual health.
- Jesus fed the crowd to help people understand God's love for them. How do the members of your family help each other know God's love for them?
- The Bible story about Jesus feeding the crowd is in all four Gospels. Read and compare all four stories: Matthew 14:13–21, Mark 6:30–44, Luke 9:10–17, and John 6:1–15.

For more ideas on ways your family can live your faith, visit the "Faith First for Families" page at **www.FaithFirst.com.** Click on "Gospel Reflections" and talk with your family about Sunday's Gospel reading.

Jesus' Work of Healing

We Pray

Heal me, LORD.
PSALM 6:3

**All-holy Father,
make us living signs
of your healing love
for everyone to see.
Amen.**

What kinds of healing do people need?

When we think of healing, we usually think of a cut or a broken bone. In Jesus' life on earth we see God's work of healing at work among us.

What stories do you know about Jesus healing people?

Jesus Heals and Forgives

Faith Focus

How does Jesus' work of healing continue in the world today?

Faith Vocabulary

Sacraments of Healing. The sacrament of Anointing of the Sick and the sacrament of Reconciliation, or Penance.

sin. Freely choosing to turn away from God's love and weakening or breaking one's friendship with God and the Church community.

Look at the photos on this page. Describe how the people are continuing Jesus' work of healing.

The Healing Work of Jesus

Jesus brought forgiveness and healing to the world. There are many stories in the New Testament that tell about Jesus healing people.

Once an officer in the Roman army asked Jesus to heal his paralyzed servant. The officer did not want Jesus to come to his home, so he said, "Lord, I am not worthy to have you enter under my roof; only say the word and my servant will be healed." Jesus responded by praising the man for his great faith. Then he said to the officer, "You may go; as you have believed, let it be done for you." The officer went home to find his servant healed (based on Matthew 8:8, 10, 13).

The Church continues Jesus' work of healing. It especially makes that work present among us through the two **Sacraments of Healing**—the sacrament of Reconciliation and the sacrament of Anointing of the Sick.

Reconciliation

Forgiveness is an important kind of healing. God forgives our sins because of the work of Jesus Christ. If we **sin**, we turn away from God's love and weaken or break our friendship with God and the Church community.

When we sin, the Holy Spirit invites us to ask for forgiveness and to heal the harm our sin has caused. We do this in the sacrament of Reconciliation for any sins we have committed after Baptism. This sacrament is sometimes called Confession or Penance. The celebration of this sacrament always includes:

- **Contrition, or repentance.** We are truly sorry for our sins and promise to try not to sin again.
- **Confession.** We tell our sins in private to a priest or a bishop. We must tell the priest our serious, or mortal, sins.
- **Penance, or satisfaction for our sins.** We accept the prayer or action the priest gives us as a way to heal the damage caused by our sin.
- **Absolution.** God forgives us through the words and actions of a bishop or a priest.

In this sacrament we are reconciled with God and the Church community.

What are some of the ways you can show that you forgive others?

Faith-Filled People

John Vianney

Saint John Vianney is the patron saint of parish priests. People came from all over to confess their sins to Father John Vianney. He would spend twelve to sixteen hours each day hearing confessions. So many people came that a special railroad track was built to his town. The Church celebrates the feast day of Saint John Vianney on August 4.

Anointing of the Sick

In all his healing work on earth, Jesus invited people to have faith and trust in God. Jesus continues his ministry of healing among the sick in the Church today especially through the sacrament of Anointing of the Sick. Through this sacrament we receive God's grace to help us when we are seriously ill, weak from old age, or in danger of death.

In this sacrament a priest anoints our hands and forehead with the oil of the sick. While he does this, he prays that we receive the special graces of this sacrament. These are the graces we receive in this sacrament:

Create a get-well note. Include a faith message to the person who is sick.

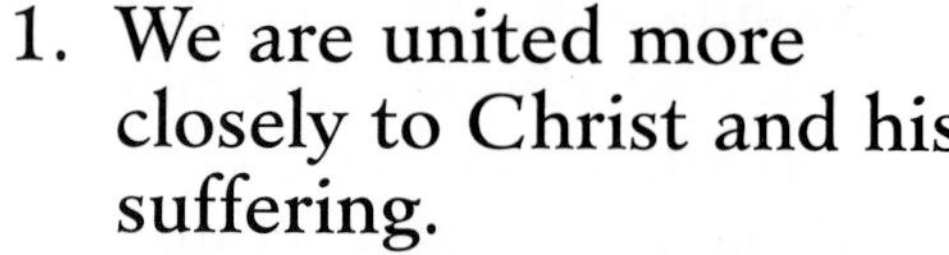

1. We are united more closely to Christ and his suffering.
2. We receive the strength, peace, and courage to deal with our suffering.
3. We receive forgiveness for our sins if we are not able to confess our sins in the sacrament of Reconciliation.
4. Our health may be restored if that would help us grow in holiness.
5. We are prepared for death and our journey to God in heaven.

In all his healing work on earth, Jesus invited people to have faith and trust in God. The Church does the same when it celebrates the Sacraments of Healing.

Our Church Makes a Difference

Parish Ministers to the Sick

At Mass on Sunday, you may see one or more extraordinary ministers of Holy Communion come forward at the end of the Communion Rite. You will hear the priest tell them to bring Holy Communion to the sick of the parish.

Parish ministers to the sick continue the healing work of Christ that began in the earliest days of the Church. These parish ministers remind the sick and the dying and their families that Jesus is present with them.

Ministers to the sick are at work not only on Sundays but all week long. They visit the sick in their homes, in hospitals, and in other places that care for the sick and elderly. They are signs to the sick that the whole Church is praying for them.

Describe how parish ministers to the sick are signs of God's love.

Our Catholic Identity

Oil of the Sick

Oil helps to heal us. The Church uses the oil of the sick in the celebration of Anointing of the Sick. The Church uses oil of the sick and the two other holy oils in the celebration of the sacraments. All the holy oils are kept in a special place in the church called an ambry.

What Difference Does Faith Make in My Life?

When you reach out and help a friend who is sick, Jesus is there with you. When you forgive someone who has hurt you, Jesus is there with you.

Think about a time when you reached out to forgive someone who hurt you. Describe what happened.

Forgiving Others

My Faith Choice

This week I will do my best to continue the healing work of Jesus. I will

____

______________________________________.

We Pray

Act of Contrition

One way to say "I'm sorry" and ask for God's forgiveness is by praying an act of contrition. Learn this or another act of contrition by heart. Pray it at bedtime each day.

My God,
I am sorry for my sins with all my heart.
In choosing to do wrong
and failing to do good,
I have sinned against you
whom I should love above all things.
I firmly intend, with your help,
to do penance,
to sin no more,
and to avoid whatever leads me to sin.
Our Savior Jesus Christ
suffered and died for us.
In his name, my God, have mercy.

We Remember

For each of the letters in the word Healing *write something about the Sacraments of Healing.*

H
E
A
L
ANOINT
N
G

To Help You Remember

1. The Church continues Jesus' work of healing and forgiveness in the Sacraments of Healing.
2. In the sacrament of Reconciliation we receive forgiveness for sins committed after we are baptized.
3. In the sacrament of Anointing of the Sick we receive the grace to become closer to Christ and join our suffering with his.

14 With My Family

This Week . . .

In chapter 14, "Jesus' Work of Healing," your child learned about the Sacraments of Healing—Reconciliation and Anointing of the Sick. Through these sacraments Jesus is present with his Church, continuing his work of healing and forgiveness in the world today. In the sacrament of Reconciliation we ask for and receive God's forgiveness for the sins we commit after we are baptized. In the sacrament of Anointing of the Sick we are united more closely to Christ and his suffering. The Holy Spirit strengthens our faith and trust in God so we can deal with our sufferings.

For more on the teachings of the Catholic Church on the Sacraments of Healing, see *Catechism of the Catholic Church* paragraph numbers 1420–1484 and 1499–1525.

Sharing God's Word

Read together the Bible story in Matthew 8:5–13 about the officer in the Roman army who asked Jesus to heal his paralyzed servant or read the adaptation of the story on page 122. Emphasize that Jesus continues his work of healing through the Church.

Praying

In this chapter your child prayed an act of contrition. Read and pray together the prayer on page 127.

Making a Difference

Choose one of the following activities to do as a family or design a similar activity of your own.

- The oil of the sick is used in the celebration of Anointing of the Sick. This holy oil is kept in the church, in the ambry. When you go to Mass this weekend, find the ambry.
- We are to forgive people as God forgives us. As a family choose a way that you can celebrate forgiveness when a family members says "I'm sorry."
- Look at two other Bible stories about Jesus healing people. Read Mark 2:1–2 and Matthew 8:14–15.

For more ideas on ways your family can live your faith, visit the "Faith First for Families" page at **www.FaithFirst.com.** Click on "Make a Difference" for ideas of how your family can share God's love with others this week.

Jesus Heals a Young Girl

A Scripture Story

We Pray

[T]he LORD hears
when I call out.

PSALM 4:4

God, our Father, show our sick brothers and sisters the power of your loving care. Amen.

What are some things that cause people to suffer?

We all know people who have been sick or have suffered in some way. The Bible has many stories about people who suffered.

What does the Bible tell us about God when we are suffering?

Jesus healing the daughter of Jairus

Bible Background

Faith Focus

What does the Gospel story about Jesus and Jairus's daughter tell us?

Faith Vocabulary

synagogue. A building in which Jewish people gather to pray and to read and study the Scriptures and the Law of God and other teachings of the Jewish religion.

Suffering in the Bible

The Bible story of creation tells us that God created everything and everyone good. God created us to be happy with him and one another here on earth and forever in heaven. God's plan of creation did not include sickness and suffering.

Suffering and illness came into the world as a result of our first parents' sin. Some people blame God for the suffering in the world. They sometimes turn away from God. Other people trust in God's great love for them when they suffer. They reach out to God in prayer. We can read many of these prayers in the Book of Psalms in the Old Testament.

Look up Psalm 4 in the Bible. Choose a verse to comfort someone who is sick or suffering in some way. Write the verse in the space.

Reading the Word of God

Jesus Heals a Young Girl

People turned to Jesus in times of suffering. One time Jairus, an official of the **synagogue**, came to Jesus. Read what happened.

One day when Jesus and his disciples were entering a town, Jairus came to Jesus. He fell on his knees and begged Jesus to come to his house because his twelve-year-old daughter was dying.

Jesus went with him and as they came toward Jairus's home, someone from his house came and said to Jairus, "Your daughter is dead; do not trouble the teacher any longer." On hearing this, Jesus said, "Do not be afraid; just have faith and your daughter will be saved."

Hearing what Jesus said, many people ridiculed him because they knew that the little girl was dead. So Jesus went over to Jairus's daughter, took her by the hand, and called to her, "Child, arise!" The girl immediately arose.

BASED ON LUKE 8:40–42, 49–50, 53–55

We believe and trust in Jesus. We turn to him when we or other people are suffering.

What did Jairus ask Jesus? What might you ask Jesus when you or a member of your family is sick?

Faith and Trust in God

Jairus's neighbors and friends did not have the same faith in Jesus as Jairus did. They tried to convince Jairus that he should leave Jesus alone.

That is exactly what Jesus does not want us to do. The Holy Spirit invites us to reach out to Jesus when we are sick or suffering in any way. We are to trust and believe in Jesus as Jairus did.

We pray for ourselves and for others who are sick or suffering. We trust that we are never left alone in our suffering.

Look at the photos of the people reaching out to people who are suffering. In the space draw or write about yourself helping someone who is suffering in some way.

Our Church Makes a Difference

Saint John of God

Christians have always shared the good news of God's caring love with people who are suffering. John of God was one of those Christians.

John was born in Portugal in 1495. He served his country as a soldier, worked as a shepherd, and, at times, sold books. In 1538, things changed for John. After listening to a sermon, he decided to dedicate his life to caring for people who were sick. Soon others joined him, and he opened a hospital. Today more than 40,000 followers of Saint John of God care for people who are sick and suffering all over the world.

The Church has named John of God a saint. He is the patron saint of hospitals, people who are sick, and nurses. His feast day is celebrated on March 8.

What does the example of Saint John of God and his followers teach us about God's love?

Our Catholic Identity

Catholic Hospitals

The word *hospital* comes from two Latin words meaning "house for guests." The first Christian hospitals cared for weary travelers and the sick. Today there are more than 2,000 Catholic hospitals in North America and South America.

Saint John of God caring for a man who is sick

What Difference Does Faith Make in My Life?

When have you helped a member of your family who was sick? When you did, you were doing the same work that Jesus did. The Holy Spirit helped you be a sign of God's caring love for that person.

List some of the things you and other young people can do to help people who are sick or are suffering in some way.

Caring for Others

My Faith Choice

This week when I hear or read about someone or some people who are suffering, I will be a sign of God's love. I will

____

____.

We Pray

Lord, Hear Our Prayer

In a prayer of intercession we pray for other people. Pray this prayer of intercession for people who are sick or suffering.

Leader: God of love,
you are always present with us.

All: **Bless** *(Name)* **with your love.**
Each child repeats the sentence with the name of a friend or family member.

Leader: Send your Holy Spirit to help him/her
believe and trust in your love
in this time of sickness.
We ask this through
Christ, our Lord. Amen.

We Remember

Retell the Gospel story about Jesus and Jairus. Include the words in the word bank.

Jesus	**Jairus**	**daughter**
faith	**sick**	**neighbors**

____

____

____

____

____

To Help You Remember

1. The Bible has many stories that describe how people deal with their sickness and suffering.
2. Jairus believed and trusted that Jesus would heal his daughter.
3. We are to reach out to Jesus in faith and trust when we are sick or suffering.

15 With My Family

This Week . . .

In chapter 15, "Jesus Heals a Young Girl: A Scripture Story," your child learned about the Gospel story of Jesus healing Jairus's daughter. This is a story of faith and trust. It is a story that reveals that God is ever present among us, in good times and in bad times. The Holy Spirit gives us comfort and courage in times of sickness and suffering. The Holy Spirit gives us the grace to trust and believe in Jesus as Jairus did. We receive the comfort and the courage to join our sufferings to those of Christ and witness God's ever-present love in our lives.

For more on the teachings of the Catholic Church on illness and suffering in the world, see *Catechism of the Catholic Church* paragraph numbers 309–314 and 1500–1510.

Sharing God's Word

Read together the Bible story in Luke 8:40–55 about Jesus healing the daughter of Jairus or read the adaptation of the story on page 131. Emphasize that we can turn to Jesus when we or other people are suffering.

Praying

In this chapter your child prayed a prayer of intercession for people who are sick or suffering in some way. Read and pray together the prayer on page 135.

Making a Difference

Choose one of the following activities to do as a family or design a similar activity of your own.

- Find out if your parish has a group that prays every day for people in the parish who are sick. If your parish does, have your family become part of that group.
- Although everything that God created is good, suffering is a part of everyone's life. Talk about what we can learn from the Bible about suffering.
- Name some ways that your family can reach out to others who are suffering. Choose one thing that you will do as a family this week.

For more ideas on ways your family can live your faith, visit the "Faith First for Families" page at **www.FaithFirst.com.** Check out "Bible Stories." Read and discuss the Bible story as a family this week.

Signs of God's Love

We Pray

[LORD God,] holy and
awesome is
your name.

PSALM 111:9

God, our Father, we are your adopted sons and daughters. Help us live as signs of your love for all people. Amen.

What do community workers do in your town or city?

People in our community work hard each day to build up our neighborhoods. The sacraments of Matrimony and Holy Orders set aside members to build up the Church.

What do bishops, priests, deacons, and married couples do to build up the Church?

Called to Holiness

Faith Focus

What do the sacraments of Holy Orders and Matrimony celebrate?

Faith Vocabulary

holiness. Life in communion with God.

Sacraments at the Service of Communion. The sacraments of Holy Orders and Matrimony.

The Sacraments at the Service of Communion

God calls each of us to live our life in communion with him. When we live our life this way, we are living a life of **holiness.** Our words and actions show that we are children of God.

Write a way that priests, deacons, and married couples serve the Church.

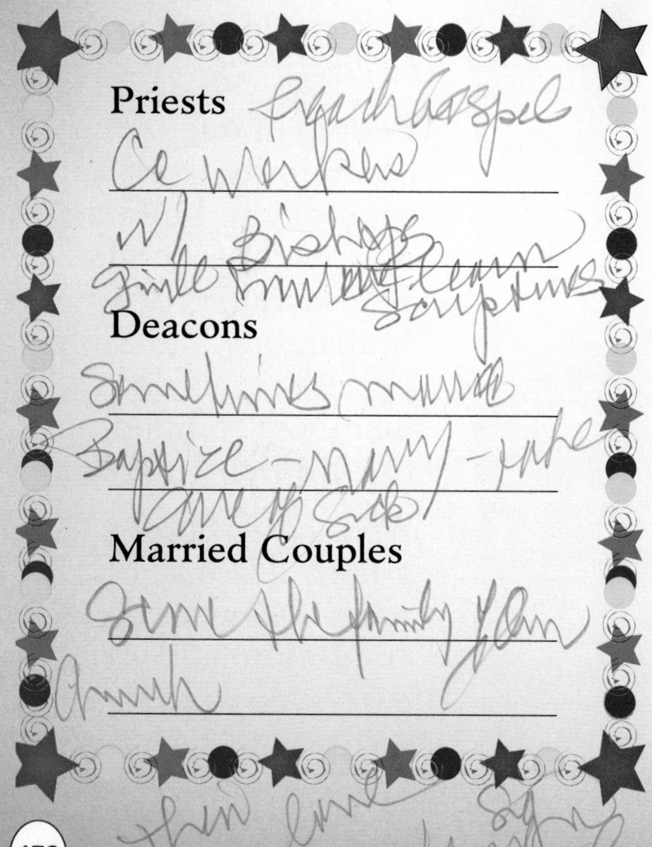

Some members of the Church are chosen to help us live our Baptism and our call to holiness in a special way. They are consecrated, or set aside, and given God's grace for this work in the **Sacraments at the Service of Communion.** These sacraments are the sacraments of Holy Orders and Matrimony.

Bishops, priests, deacons, and married couples help the whole Church live a holy life. They help the members of the Church live as children of God by keeping the commandments as Christ taught us.

Faith-Filled People

The Pope

The pope is the successor of Saint Peter the Apostle and the bishop of Rome. He is the shepherd of the whole Church and has supreme authority over the universal Church. By his life and teachings, he guides all the people of the Church to live holy lives.

Holy Orders

Since the beginning of the Church, bishops, priests, and deacons have served the whole Church. They are ordained for this service in the sacrament of Holy Orders. They serve the Church by teaching what Jesus taught, by leading the Church community in divine worship, and by governing the Church.

Jesus chose the Apostles to serve the Church in his name (Mark 3:13–14). Bishops are the successors of the Apostles. Under the authority of the pope and together with the pope, bishops are the chief teachers in the Church.

Priests are coworkers with the bishops. They preach the Gospel and lead us in the celebration of the sacraments. Priests guide us in understanding the Sacred Scripture and the teachings of the Church.

Deacons, who are sometimes married, are also ordained. They help bishops. They proclaim God's word, baptize, and marry people. They care for the sick and those in need.

Without bishops, priests, and deacons, one cannot speak of the Church. The ordained ministry is part of the Church founded by Jesus Christ.

Describe what you see happening in the photos on this page.

Matrimony

Matrimony is also a Sacrament at the Service of Communion. In this sacrament a baptized man and a baptized woman are consecrated to serve the family of our Church. They freely promise to enter into a lifelong marriage with each other. Their love becomes a sign of Jesus' love for the Church.

In Matrimony the couple promises to answer God's call to have a family. The Christian family is called the domestic church. The word *domestic* comes from the Latin word *domus,* which means "home," or "household." The members of our family are the first people to tell us about Jesus. From them we first learn about God and God's love for us. They help us learn the ways we can live the commandments by loving God and others as Jesus taught.

Write an invitation to your family. Invite them to work with you on doing something as a family.

You're Invited

____

____

____

____

____

Our Church Makes a Difference

Our Catholic Identity

Vows and Promises

The members of religious communities make sacred promises or vows to God and to the Church. This helps them live their call to holiness. They promise not to marry, to live simple and poor lives, and to obey the leaders of their community and the Church.

Religious Sisters and Brothers

Some members of the Church choose not to marry but to become members of religious communities. They share everything they have. They work together, pray together, and help one another live a holy life. They are living signs of the call of everyone to live a holy life.

Take a moment to pray that people will serve the Church as members of a religious community.

Religious sisters and religious brothers also serve the other members of the Church in many ways. They teach and care for the sick and dying. They work for peace and justice among people. They work in their own countries and they travel to other countries. Every day they pray for the Church and all people.

What Difference Does Faith Make in My Life?

You are a member of both a family and a parish. Together with the other members of your family and your parish you help one another live your call to holiness.

Create a poster that will encourage you and your friends to help one another live holy lives.

Serving Others

My Faith Choice

This week I can try to work with my family or parish to live a holy life. I will

____

____.

We Pray

Prayer for Vocations

God calls each of us to live a holy life. He calls us to do this in different ways. We call this our vocation. Pray this prayer for vocations now as a group and pray it alone each day.

Lord God,
help me understand
how you want me to live.
I will give all my heart to the work
of being a sign of your love
for all to know.
Amen.

We Remember

These three statements are false. On the line write the word or words that would make them true.

1. The two Sacraments at the Service of Communion are Holy Orders and ~~Reconciliation~~. Matrimony

   ____

2. In Holy Orders a baptized man and a baptized woman promise to be faithful to each other.

   Matrimony

3. Bishops, priests, and married couples are called in a special way through the sacrament of Holy Orders.

   and Matrimony for couples

To Help You Remember

1. The Sacraments at the Service of Communion set aside members of the Church to help all the members of the Church live holy lives.
2. Bishops, priests, and deacons are ordained to serve the whole Church in the sacrament of Holy Orders.
3. In the sacrament of Matrimony, a baptized man and a baptized woman are consecrated to serve the family of the Church.

16 With My Family

This Week . . .

In chapter 16, "Signs of God's Love," your child learned that all the baptized have the vocation of living a life of holiness. The Sacraments at the Service of Communion—Holy Orders and Matrimony—set aside some members of the Church to serve the whole Church in living that vocation. In the sacrament of Holy Orders a baptized man is ordained and consecrated to serve the whole Church as a bishop, priest, or deacon. In Matrimony a baptized man and a baptized woman are united in a lifelong bond of faithful love as a sign of Christ's love for the Church. Bishops, priests, deacons, and married couples help the whole Church live a holy life. They help the members of the Church live as children of God as Jesus taught.

For more on the teachings of the Catholic Church on the Sacraments at the Service of Communion, Holy Orders and Matrimony, see *Catechism of the Catholic Church* paragraph numbers 1533–1589 and 1601–1658.

Sharing God's Word

In the Gospel Jesus asks us to pray for vocations. Read together Luke 10:1–2. Emphasize that in the two Sacraments at the Service of Communion, Matrimony and Holy Orders, some members of the Church are consecrated to serve the whole Church.

Praying

In this chapter your child prayed for vocations. Read and pray together the prayer on page 143.

Making a Difference

Choose one of the following activities to do as a family or design a similar activity of your own.

- Talk about how your parish priest and deacons live out their vocation to serve the Church. How do they help you and other members of the parish live out your Baptism?
- Write a note to a deacon, priest, bishop, or married couple thanking them for serving the Church community.
- Families are holy. They encourage one another. They trust each other. They celebrate important days together. Talk about all the ways your family is holy.

For more ideas on ways your family can live your faith, visit the "Faith First for Families" page at **www.FaithFirst.com.** You will find it helpful to take a look at "Questions Kids Ask" this week.

Unit 2 Review

Name ______________________________

A. The Best Word

Fill in the blanks. Use the words in the word bank to complete the sentences.

Service	**liturgy**	**Initiation**
Paschal Mystery	**Healing**	**sacraments**
Exodus	**liturgical year**	

1. The ______________________________ is the Church's work of worshiping God.
2. The ______________________________ is Christ's work of salvation accomplished by his Passion, death, Resurrection, and Ascension.
3. The ______________________________ is made up of feasts and seasons that help us celebrate and share in God's great plan of saving love.
4. The Sacraments of ______________________________ are the foundation of the Christian life.
5. Through the seven ______________________________ a person shares in the saving work of Jesus Christ and the life of the Trinity.
6. The ______________________________ was the journey of the Israelites from slavery in Egypt to freedom in the land God promised them.
7. Reconciliation and Anointing of the Sick are the two Sacraments of ______________________________.
8. Holy Orders and Matrimony are the Sacraments at the ______________________________ of Communion.

B. Sacraments

1. *Put an R next to those items that relate to the sacrament of Reconciliation. Put an A next to those items that relate to the sacrament of Anointing of the Sick.*

A anointing with oil   R absolution

R penance   A prepare us for death

2. *Put an H next to those items that relate to the sacrament of Holy Orders. Put an M next to items that relate to the sacrament of Matrimony.*

H bishops, priests, and deacons   M domestic church

H ordained ministers   M a baptized man and a baptized woman

C. What I Learned

1. *Name three things you learned in this unit. Share them with the group.*

____

____

____

2. *Look at the list of words on page 96. Circle the ones you know now.*

D. From a Scripture Story

The story of Jairus's daughter invites us to believe and trust in God. Write two more ideas that you learned from this Gospel story.

____

____

____

Unit 3 • We Live

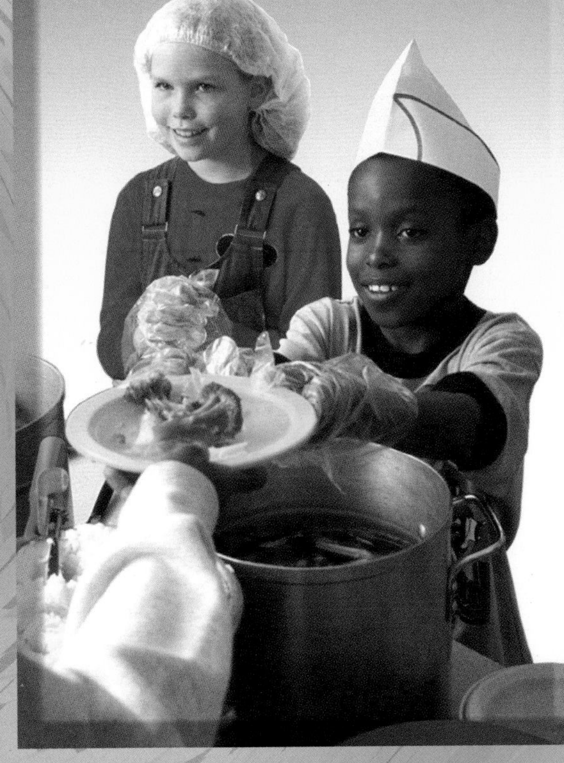

What do these pictures tell you about happiness?

Getting Ready

What I Have Learned

What is something you already know about these faith terms?

Conscience and making moral decisions

____

____

Happiness

____

____

The Lord's Day

____

____

Words to Know

Put an X next to the faith terms you know. Put a ? next to faith terms you need to know more about.

Faith Vocabulary

_____ soul
_____ deliberate actions
_____ Beatitudes
_____ conscience
_____ sin
_____ gifts of the Holy Spirit
_____ reparation
_____ mercy

Questions I Have

What questions would you like to ask about living the Beatitudes?

____

____

A Scripture Story

Moses and the Ten Commandments

Where did Moses receive the Ten Commandments from God?

Created in God's Image

We Pray

[LORD God,] your
hands made me
and fashioned me.
PSALM 119:73

Lord God, may we receive your word of life with open hearts, live it with joy, and share it with love. Amen.

What is one way you are different from other people? What is one way you are the same?

All people are in some ways different from one another. Every person is alike too. Everyone is created in God's image and likeness.

What do you think it means to be created in God's image and likeness?

Created in God's Image

Faith Focus

What powers has God given us to make choices to live a holy life?

Faith Vocabulary

intellect. The part of every person that gives us the ability to know God, ourselves, and other people.

free will. The part of every person that gives us the ability to choose to love and serve God and others.

The Real You

In the creation story, God tells us about the most important thing we can ever know about ourselves and other people. We read,

> God created man in his image;
> in the divine image he created him;
> male and female he created them.
>
> GENESIS 1:27

God creates every person with a spiritual soul. The soul is the spiritual part of every person that makes us like God and that lives forever. Our soul also gives us two wonderful powers—**intellect** and **free will**. With the power of our intellect, we can know God, ourselves, and other people. With the power of our free will, we can choose to love and serve God and others.

Jesus taught us about these wonderful powers. He said,

> " 'You shall love the Lord your God with all your heart, with all your soul, with all your mind, and with all your strength. . . . You shall love your neighbor as yourself.' "
>
> MARK 12:30–31

Give an example of a proper use of the gift of free will.

Choices! Choices! Choices!

Every day we use our intellect and free will to make choices. The choices we freely understand and make are called deliberate actions. We have the responsibility to use our intellect and free will to make good deliberate actions.

We use our intellect and free will responsibly when we choose what we know is good. When we choose something we know is against God's laws, we are not using our intellect and free will responsibly. We are always responsible for our deliberate actions. All of our choices, even the simple choices we make each day, have consequences. Consequences are the good or bad effects of our choices. We are responsible for the consequences of our actions.

It is not always easy to know what is good and to choose it. When we are not sure about what to do, we need to ask for help. We need to learn what the Church teaches about good and bad choices. We need to pray to the Holy Spirit. The Holy Spirit gives us the help to know and do and say what is good and to avoid what is against God's laws.

Write what helps you make good choices. Then write what gets in the way of making good choices.

Faith-Filled People

Peter the Apostle

Saint Peter the Apostle made some very big choices in his life. When Jesus was on trial, Peter let his feelings and emotions get in the way of making a good decision. He denied that he ever knew Jesus. After that happened, he immediately went out and wept. Peter was truly sorry for the bad choice that he made. The Church celebrates the feast of Saint Peter the Apostle on June 29.

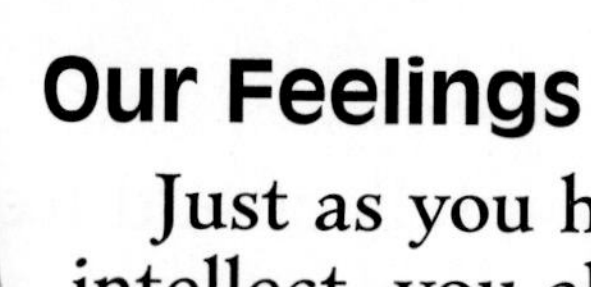

Our Feelings

Just as you have a free will and an intellect, you also have emotions. Emotions are feelings inside us that have the power to influence the choices we make. Feelings are part of what makes us human. Feelings are neither good nor bad. It is how we use them that is important.

Emotions, or feelings, are God's gifts to us. They can help us choose to do or say what is good. They can also influence us to choose to do or say what is evil.

We might feel angry when we see someone being treated unfairly. We can use the feeling of anger to work for fairness and kindness. We might feel sad when we see a friend who is sick. We can use the feeling of sadness to help people when they are sick or in trouble. Through each and every emotion, God calls us to live a good and holy life.

Read Luke 22:54–65 and answer these questions.

Feelings and Choices

How did Peter's feelings influence the choices he made?

Denid he Knw Jesus
then he was sorry

Name a feeling that helped you choose to say or do something good. Describe what happened.

Our Church Makes a Difference

Saint Augustine's Choices

Some Christians have become model decision makers. Saint Augustine's choice to follow Jesus has become famous. It has helped many people make good choices.

When Augustine was a young man, he made many bad choices that he thought would bring him happiness. His mother, Saint Monica, prayed over and over again for her son. She prayed that Augustine would learn to stop making choices that were harmful to him and others.

When he was twenty-nine years old, Augustine heard Saint Ambrose preach. Ambrose made Augustine think about his life and the choices he had been making. Augustine soon made the decision to change his ways and live as Jesus taught.

Augustine wrote a book about his life. The book is called *Confessions.* People still read it today, and it continues to help people make good choices and live a holy life.

Who helps you learn to make good decisions?

Our Catholic Identity

The Church Teaches

The Church is our teacher. One way the Church teaches is through letters. Pope John Paul II has written many letters that teach us about living the faith of the Church. One of these letters, "The Gospel of Life," teaches that every person is created in the image of God.

Saint Ambrose baptizing Saint Monica's son Augustine

What Difference Does Faith Make in My Life?

You are created in the image and likeness of God. You show that by the many choices you make each day to live a holy life. The good choices that you make have consequences that help you and others live as children of God.

Read the situation below. Fill in two consequences for a good choice you could make and two consequences for a bad choice.

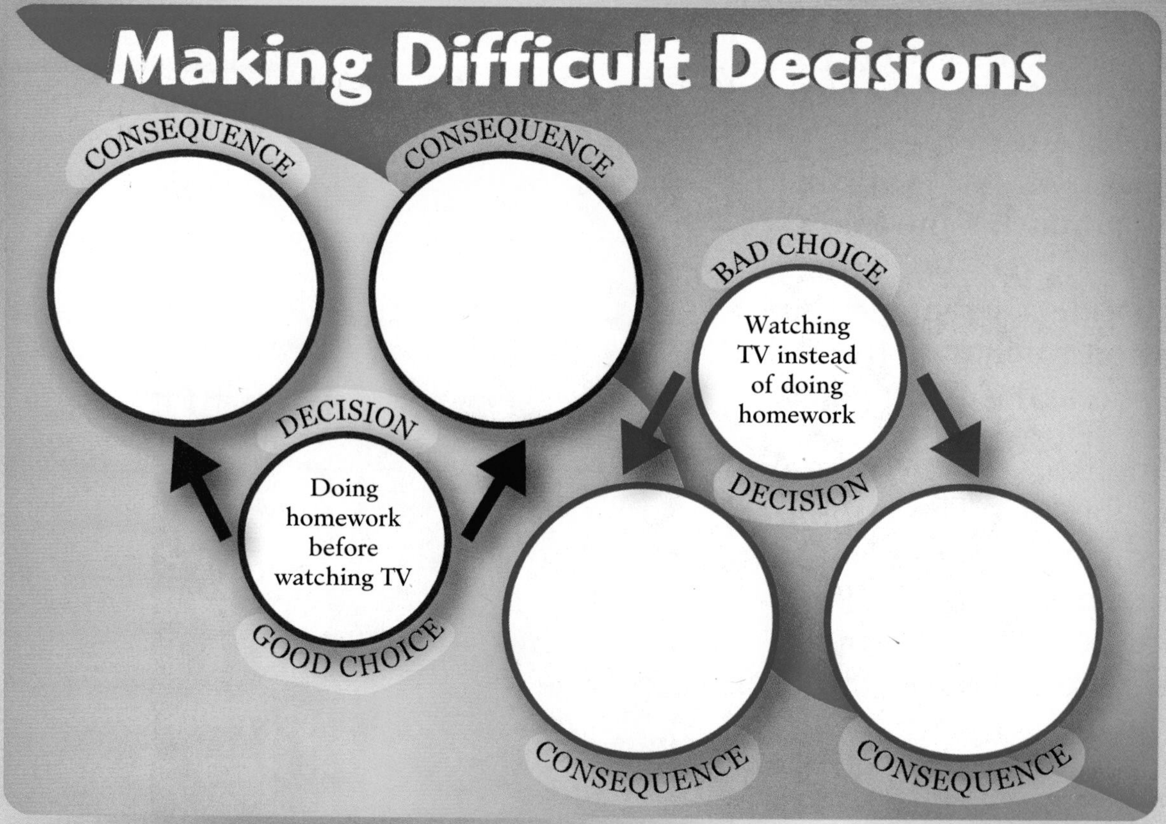

Making Difficult Decisions

CONSEQUENCE

CONSEQUENCE

DECISION
GOOD CHOICE
Doing homework before watching TV

BAD CHOICE
DECISION
Watching TV instead of doing homework

CONSEQUENCE

CONSEQUENCE

My Faith Choice

This week I will think carefully about the consequences of my decisions before I make them. As a reminder to do this, I will

____

____.

We Pray

Prayer of Saint Augustine

Pray this prayer of Saint Augustine. Ask the Holy Spirit to help you live a holy life.

Group 1: Breathe in me, O Holy Spirit,
That my thoughts may all be holy;
Group 2: Act in me, O Holy Spirit,
That my work, too, may be holy;

Group 1: Draw my heart, O Holy Spirit,
That I love but what is holy;
Group 2: Strengthen me, O Holy Spirit,
That I defend all that is holy;

All: **Guard me, then, O Holy Spirit,**
That I always may be holy. Amen.

We Remember

Unscramble the letters of the faith words. Match the words to the descriptions.

FAITH WORDS

1. G E M A I
Image

2. E R E F L W L I
Free Will

3. O N M O T I S E
Emotions

4. T E L L C T E N I
intellect

DESCRIPTIONS

__1__ **a.** Term used in the Bible that reveals that we are created in God's likeness

__3__ **b.** Feelings we experience that influence our choices

__4__ **c.** The power to know God, others, and ourselves, and to learn new things

__2__ **d.** The power to choose between good and evil

To Help You Remember

1. We are all created with a spiritual soul that makes us like God and that lives forever.
2. We are created with the gifts of an intellect and a free will to help us make good decisions to live a holy life.
3. We are created with emotions, or feelings, that influence our decisions to live a holy life.

17 With My Family

This Week . . .

In chapter 17, "Created in God's Image," your child learned that every person is created in the image and likeness of God. God creates every person with a spiritual soul. This makes us images of God. God gives us an intellect and free will. These wonderful gifts help us know, love, and serve God and others. God has also blessed us with emotions, or feelings. These gifts, which are neither good nor bad in themselves, influence the way we make choices. All our choices have consequences. We are responsible for our choices and their consequences.

For more on the teachings of the Catholic Church on the dignity of each person and our responsibility for all our choices and their consequences, see *Catechism of the Catholic Church* paragraph numbers 33–35 and 1699–1742.

Sharing God's Word

Read together the Bible passage Genesis 1:27 about God creating people or read the adaptation of the story on page 150. Emphasize that God created all people in his own image.

Praying

In this chapter your child prayed the Prayer of Saint Augustine. Read and pray together the prayer on page 155.

Making a Difference

Choose one of the following activities to do as a family or design a similar activity of your own.

- Name and talk about the many ways your family helps each other make good decisions.
- Go to the library or to the Internet to find out more about Saint Augustine of Hippo. Saint Augustine was born in 354 in North Africa. He did not become a Christian until he was thirty-three years old.
- Make a list of the steps your family can use to make good decisions. Post it where all the family members can see it and be reminded to follow the steps.

For more ideas on ways your family can live your faith, visit the "Faith First for Families" page at **www.FaithFirst.com.** Take time to read an article from "Just for Parents" this week.

The Beatitudes

We Pray

Happy the people
whose God is
the LORD.

PSALM 144:15

God, we bless you and thank you. You made us to be happy with you now and forever. Amen.

What makes you happy?

Everyone wants to be happy. Jesus taught what real happiness is all about.

What did Jesus teach about happiness?

The Way to Happiness

Faith Focus

What do the Beatitudes teach us about making good choices that bring us true happiness?

Faith Vocabulary

Beatitudes. The sayings or teachings of Jesus that describe real happiness, the happiness of people blessed by God.

The Way to Real Happiness

Many people and things here on earth make us happy. The happiness that we experience here on earth is really trying to tell us about the happiness God wants us to have. It is the happiness of being with God and all the saints forever in heaven.

Jesus taught his disciples that real happiness is being one with God. It is being a friend of God now on earth and forever in heaven.

Use the code to discover a message about real happiness.

A	B	C	D	E	F	G	H	I	J	K	L	M
1	2	3	4	5	6	7	8	9	10	11	12	13

N	O	P	Q	R	S	T	U	V	W	X	Y	Z
14	15	16	17	18	19	20	21	22	23	24	25	26

__ __ __ __ __   __ __   __ __ __
8 1 16 16 25   9 19   20 8 5

__ __ __ __ __ __   __ __ __
16 5 18 19 15 14   23 8 15

__ __ __ __ __ __   __ __   __ __ __
20 18 21 19 20 19   9 14   20 8 5

__ __ __ __ !
12 15 18 4

BASED ON PROVERBS 16:20

The Beatitudes

The **Beatitudes** are sayings and teachings of Jesus that describe real happiness. In each of the Beatitudes, Jesus describes one thing people do that leads to the happiness God wants us to have. It is the happiness of people who give their heart to God.

Read the Beatitudes to discover what Jesus teaches about the happiness that comes from being blessed by God.

> "Blessed are the poor in spirit,
> for theirs is the kingdom of heaven."
> MATTHEW 5:3

The poor in spirit have faith in God and trust in his love for them.

> "Blessed are they who mourn,
> for they will be comforted." MATTHEW 5:4

Those who mourn are sad because people suffer. They do what they can to help.

> "Blessed are the meek,
> for they will inherit
> the land." MATTHEW 5:5

The meek are kind and treat others with respect.

> "Blessed are they who hunger
> and thirst for righteousness,
> for they will be satisfied."
> MATTHEW 5:6

People who hunger for righteousness treat others fairly and work for justice.

Name someone you know who does the things that one of these four Beatitudes describes.

Faith-Filled People

Louise de Marillac

Saint Louise de Marillac grew up never knowing her mother. Then as an adult, she founded the Daughters of Charity with Saint Vincent de Paul. The Daughters of Charity work with the poor and the sick and with children whose parents left them when they were born. Saint Louise de Marillac is the patron saint of social workers. The Church celebrates the feast day of Saint Louise de Marillac on March 15.

More Beatitudes

The Beatitudes are like signposts on the road of life. They point us in the right direction. They guide us to make choices that lead to the happiness God wants every person to enjoy. Here are four more Beatitudes that Jesus taught.

> "Blessed are the merciful,
> for they will be shown mercy."
> MATTHEW 5:7

People who are merciful forgive others just as God forgives them.

> "Blessed are the clean of heart,
> for they will see God." MATTHEW 5:8

The clean of heart keep God first in their lives.

> "Blessed are the peacemakers,
> for they will be called children
> of God." MATTHEW 5:9

Peacemakers solve problems without hurting anyone.

> "Blessed are they who are persecuted
> for the sake of righteousness,
> for theirs is the kingdom
> of heaven." MATTHEW 5:10

Those persecuted for the sake of righteousness do what God wants, even when others laugh at them or threaten to harm them.

Living the Beatitudes leads to the happiness that will last forever in heaven.

Name the Beatitudes the people in the pictures are living.

Our Church Makes a Difference

The Joyful Saint

The story of our Church is filled with people who were really happy. These people were happy because they knew they were true friends of God. Saint Francis of Assisi is one of these people. Many have said that Francis was the happiest person they ever knew or ever read about.

Francis's family was wealthy. Having a lot of money did not give Francis happiness. He went about telling everyone and singing about the happiness that comes from sharing in God's friendship. People called Francis the "joyful troubadour of God." A troubadour writes and sings love songs.

Many people became followers of Saint Francis. They learned from him the secret to finding happiness.

Why do you think Saint Francis of Assisi has become the most loved of all the saints?

Our Catholic Identity

Canticles

People of faith, such as Saint Francis of Assisi, sing about the happiness that comes from sharing in the gifts of God's friendship. Saint Francis gave us "The Canticle of the Sun." A canticle is a sacred song. The "Benedictus" of Zechariah, the father of John the Baptist, and the "Magnificat" of the Blessed Virgin Mary are two important canticles from the Bible.

What Difference Does Faith Make in My Life?

You, like everyone else, want to be happy. When you think about it, the choices you make each day are ways you try to find happiness.

Write or draw how you can live one Beatitude. Describe the consequence of living that Beatitude.

The Way to True Happiness

Beatitude

Consequence

____

____

My Faith Choice

This week I will try my best to live the Beatitude I described in the activity. I will

____

____.

We Pray

The Canticle of the Sun

Join with Saint Francis and pray this part of his canticle.

Group 1: Be praised, my Lord, with all your creatures, especially Brother Sun!

All: **God be praised!**

Group 2: Be praised, my Lord, for Sister Moon and Stars! They are bright and lovely and fair.

All: **God be praised!**

Group 1: Be praised, my Lord, for our Sister Earth who feeds us, and produces fruits and colorful flowers.

All: **God be praised!**

We Remember

Write the Beatitude that would help you respond best to this situation.

No one ever seems to choose Sam to be on their team. The next day at recess you are chosen to be one of the two captains who chooses players for the kickball teams.

____

____

____

____

To Help You Remember

1. God wants everyone to be blessed and truly happy.
2. The Beatitudes guide us in making choices that lead to the happiness that comes from being blessed by God.
3. Living the Beatitudes leads to the happiness God wants us to have.

18 With My Family

This Week . . .

In chapter 18, "The Beatitudes," your child learned about the Beatitudes. The Beatitudes are the teachings from the Sermon on the Mount that describe the qualities and actions of the people blessed by God. Many things can bring us happiness, but some things do not give true and lasting happiness. Living the Beatitudes helps us discover the happiness God wants us to have.

For more on the teachings of the Catholic Church on the human calling to happiness, see *Catechism of the Catholic Church* paragraph numbers 1716–1724.

Sharing God's Word

Read together the Bible verses known as the Beatitudes. You can find these verses on pages 159–160 or in Matthew 5:3–10. Emphasize that in each Beatitude Jesus describes one thing people do that leads to the happiness that God wants us to have.

Praying

In this chapter your child prayed part of Saint Francis of Assisi's Canticle of the Sun. Read and pray together the prayer on page 163.

Making a Difference

Choose one of the following activities to do as a family or design a similar activity of your own.

- Play a game of charades using the Beatitudes as the statements to be acted out.
- Make a mural or poster to show how living the Beatitudes leads to happiness. Hang it where it will serve as a reminder to everyone to live the Beatitudes.
- Choose one of the Beatitudes and make a decision based on it this week. Explain what you will do.

For more ideas on ways your family can live your faith, visit the "Faith First for Families" page at **www.FaithFirst.com**. Learn more about this week's Gospel reading by clicking on "Gospel Reflections."

Living a Holy Life

19

We Pray

**Happy are all . . .
who walk in the
ways of God.**

Psalm 128:1

**God of love,
you are always kind
and merciful. Amen.**

What are some of the good choices that you have made this week?

We make choices every day. Living our faith includes making choices to live as children of God.

How do you know what makes a good choice that helps you live as a child of God?

Our Call to Holiness

Faith Focus

How does God help us make good choices?

Faith Vocabulary

conscience. The gift God gives to every person that helps us know and judge what is right and what is wrong.

sanctifying grace. The gift of God sharing his own life with us, the gift of holiness.

Making Good Choices

God calls everyone to make good choices and to live a holy life. Our **conscience** and the four moral, or cardinal, virtues are two of the many gifts God gives us to help us live holy lives.

Our conscience helps us know and judge what is right and wrong. We need to train our conscience to do a good job. We need to pray, read the Bible, learn the teachings of the Church, and ask people for good advice. It is important to train our conscience correctly. We have an obligation to do what it says is right and not do what it says is wrong.

The four moral virtues are habits of doing what is good. The moral virtues are prudence, justice, fortitude, and temperance. They help us use our feelings correctly and do what our conscience and our faith tell us is the right thing to do or say. We must remember that good habits come from practice.

Think about making an important decision. Tell how your conscience can guide you.

Making Bad Choices

Sometimes people and other things try to get us to choose not to live holy lives. These are called temptations. Temptations are not sins but can lead us to sin. We sin when we knowingly and freely choose to do or say something we know is against God's will. Sin always hurts our friendship with God and other people.

The Church speaks about mortal sin and venial sin. Mortal sin is a serious failure in our love for God, our neighbor, ourselves, or creation. Mortal sin causes us to lose the gift of holiness. All other sins are venial sins. Venial sins weaken our love for God and for one another.

Believe it or not, we can train ourselves to do what we know is against God's will. We can grow in bad habits, or vices. The Church teaches us about seven main vices. These vices are pride, greed, envy, anger, lust, gluttony, and laziness. When we let these bad habits grow in our lives, we train ourselves to sin. Then it is very difficult to live a holy life.

Faith-Filled People

Thomas More

Saint Thomas More was the chief lawyer for the king of England. When he was faced with choosing between the wrong that the king wanted him to do and the good he believed God wanted him to do, Thomas followed his conscience. He chose to serve God. The Church celebrates the feast day of Saint Thomas More on June 22.

Training Our Conscience

Check 4 things that help you learn to make good choices, say no to temptation, and avoid sin.

___ Read the Bible
___ Discuss my choices with my parents
___ Pray to the Holy Spirit
___ Ask my friends for help
___ Think quietly about my choices
___ Listen to my teachers
___ Talk to the priest in my parish

The Gifts of the Holy Spirit

Grace is a free gift from God. At Baptism we receive the gift of **sanctifying grace.** The word *sanctifying* means "making holy." Sanctifying grace is the gift of God's own life that he shares with us. It is given by the Holy Spirit to heal us of sin and to make us holy.

At Baptism we receive the seven gifts of the Holy Spirit. These gifts help us live our friendship with God. The Holy Spirit always gives us the grace to live a holy life and to do and say what we know is the right thing to do. If we choose to sin, the Holy Spirit helps us turn away from sin. The Holy Spirit will help us turn our hearts back toward God's love.

Name someone you know who is living one of the gifts of the Holy Spirit. Write a haiku, a three-line poem, about this person. Follow the directions under each line.

____
(Title)

____
(Five syllables)

____
(Seven syllables)

____
(Five syllables)

1 **Wisdom** helps us see the world through the eyes of faith. We are helped to see the world as God sees it.

2 **Understanding** helps us see the connection between knowing our faith and living it.

3 **Right judgment, or counsel,** helps us make good moral choices.

4 **Fortitude, or courage,** gives us the strength to make decisions to live as God wants us to live.

5 **Knowledge** helps us see the truth of all that God has made known to us.

6 **Reverence, or piety,** helps us call God Abba, or Father, with love and trust.

Wonder and awe, or fear of the Lord, help us praise, thank, and bless God.

Our Church Makes a Difference

Operation Rice Bowl

The Church is our mother and our teacher who guides us in living holy lives. During Lent the Church in the United States invites Catholics to take part in Operation Rice Bowl.

Operation Rice Bowl asks families, schools, parishes, and other faith communities to pray, fast, learn, and give to people in need. We give up something like desserts or snacks or something we really like. The money we save is put into the Operation Rice Bowl box. At the end of Lent, each family brings the money to church. It is collected and the Church uses it to help people.

Operation Rice Bowl helps us put our faith into action. Our choices show our love for God and for other people.

What things does your parish do to help you follow Jesus?

Lenten Practices

During the season of Lent the Church guides us to eat less, to pray, and to share our blessings with others, especially people in need. These Lenten practices of prayer, fasting, and almsgiving are ways the Church teaches us to live holy lives.

What Difference Does Faith Make in My Life?

Each year you are learning more and more about how to make good choices to live a holy life. Your family and the Church family guide you to make those choices. The Holy Spirit gives you the grace to know and choose the way God wants you to live.

Who helps you learn to live a holy life as a follower of Jesus Christ? How do they help you?

Becoming Closer to Jesus

People	How I Am Helped
______________	______________________________
	______________________________
	______________________________
	______________________________
______________	______________________________
	______________________________
	______________________________
	______________________________

My Faith Choice

This week I will live a holy life by following my conscience and making good choices. One good choice I will make is

____

____.

We Pray

Examination of Conscience

Examining our conscience helps us grow in living the Great Commandment to love God and our neighbor as ourselves. It helps us learn to make good choices to live holy lives.

Leader: Let us ask the Holy Spirit to help us think about the choices we have made. Holy Spirit, help us think about the ways we have chosen to show or not to show our love for God.

All: *Silently and privately reflect.*

Leader: Holy Spirit, help us think about the ways we have chosen to show or not to show our love for other people and for ourselves.

All: *Silently and privately reflect.*

Leader: God, our loving Father, you sent Jesus to teach us to live the Great Commandment. Send us the Holy Spirit to help us live holy lives as Jesus taught us to do.

All: **Amen.**

We Remember

Write T next to the true statements. Write F next to the false statements. Make the false statements true.

T 1. God calls and helps every person live a holy life.

T 2. Our conscience helps us know and judge what is right and what is wrong.

T 3. The moral virtues help us do what our conscience and faith tell us God wants us to do.

F 4. The gifts of the Holy Spirit are prudence, justice, fortitude, and temperance.

To Help You Remember

1. Our conscience and the moral virtues help us make choices to live holy lives.
2. Sin is freely choosing to do or say something we know is against God's will.
3. The gifts of the Holy Spirit help us know and choose to live as children of God and followers of Jesus.

19 With My Family

This Week . . .

In chapter 19, "Living a Holy Life," your child learned that at Baptism we receive the gift of sanctifying grace. Every person is born with a conscience that we need to form and develop correctly throughout our life. Our conscience helps us know and judge what is right and what is wrong, what is in agreement with and what is not in agreement with God's will. The moral, or cardinal, virtues of prudence, justice, fortitude, and temperance and the gifts of the Holy Spirit strengthen us to make choices that contribute to our living holy lives. However, we sometimes knowingly and freely sin. We choose not to live holy lives. When we sin, God invites us back to a life of friendship with him.

For more on the teachings of the Catholic Church on holiness, conscience, the virtues and gifts of the Holy Spirit, and sin and grace, see *Catechism of the Catholic Church* paragraph numbers 1776–1794, 1803–1832, 1846–1869, and 1996–2004.

Sharing God's Word

Read together Psalm 128:1. Emphasize that our conscience, the moral virtues, and the gifts of the Holy Spirit help us make good choices to live by God's commands.

Praying

In this chapter your child learned about and used a brief examination of conscience. Read and pray together the examination of conscience on page 171.

Making a Difference

Choose one of the following activities to do as a family or design a similar activity of your own.

- Share with each other some of the good choices you each made this past week. Talk about why you made the choices and what happened after you made the choices.
- Saint Thomas More was faced with the difficult decision to follow the king or to follow God. Go to the library or to the Internet to find out more about Saint Thomas More.
- Identify someone who is living one of the gifts of the Holy Spirit. Talk about the gift of the Holy Spirit that person is living and how it might help your family live as a Christian family.

For more ideas on ways your family can live your faith, visit the "Faith First for Families" page at **www.FaithFirst.com**. Click on "Contemporary Issues" for some interesting insights this week.

Living God's Covenant A Scripture Story

We Pray

Happy those who
observe God's
decrees . . .
with all their heart.
PSALM 119:2

**Lord God,
open our eyes
to see clearly your
teachings. Send the
Holy Spirit to teach
us your ways.
Amen.**

What are you learning about the great leaders and events of our nation?

There are so many ways the story of a nation is passed on from one generation to the next. The story of our faith has also been passed on from generation to generation.

What have you learned about God's people?

Moses holding the Ten Commandments

Bible Background

Faith Focus

What does the story of the Exodus tell us about God's people?

Faith Vocabulary

Hebrews. The name given to God's people, the Israelites, when they lived in Egypt.

Ten Commandments. The laws of the Covenant revealed to Moses on Mount Sinai that teach us to love God, others, and ourselves.

Moses and the Exodus

Moses was one of the great leaders of God's people. God chose Moses to lead the Israelites, or **Hebrews** as they were also called, out of slavery in Egypt to a new homeland. This journey from slavery to freedom is known as the Exodus.

The heart of the Exodus story is the Covenant, or solemn agreement, God made with the Israelites. God promised to be faithful and loyal to the Israelites forever. The Israelites in turn promised,

> "Everything the LORD has said, we will do."
> EXODUS 19:8

Name the abilities that Moses would need to be a good leader of God's people. Choose one and describe how it would help Moses.

Mountain in Southern Sinai in Egypt

Reading the Word of God

The Ten Commandments

The Bible tells us that Moses saw the people's faith in God growing weak as they journeyed across the desert. So Moses went up Mount Sinai. He prayed there to learn what he could do.

When Moses came down, he told the elders that God said, "I am coming to you in a dense cloud, so that when the people hear me speaking with you, they may always have faith in you also."

For three days the Israelites prepared themselves to meet God. On the morning of the third day, the LORD called Moses, and he went up to the top of Mount Sinai. God gave Moses the Ten Commandments.

BASED ON EXODUS 19:9, 14–16, 20; 20:1

When we live the **Ten Commandments**, we grow in our faith and hope in God and our love for God.

Ask the Holy Spirit to help you learn how to live the Ten Commandments.

Understanding the Word of God

The Decalogue

The Decalogue is another name for the Ten Commandments. The word *decalogue* means "ten words." The Ten Commandments are the basic laws that teach us how to love God, other people, and ourselves.

Jesus, the Son of God, came to show us how to live the Ten Commandments. The choices we make to live the Ten Commandments are signs of our faith and hope in God and of our love for God.

Design these tablets containing the Ten Commandments with words and symbols that remind you to live the Commandments.

Love God with All Your Heart

1. I am the LORD your God: you shall not have strange gods before me.
2. You shall not take the name of the LORD your God in vain.
3. Remember to keep holy the LORD'S Day.

Love Your Neighbor as Yourself

4. Honor your father and your mother.
5. You shall not kill.
6. You shall not commit adultery.
7. You shall not steal.
8. You shall not bear false witness against your neighbor.
9. You shall not covet your neighbor's wife.
10. You shall not covet your neighbor's goods.

Our Church Makes a Difference

Saint Peter Claver, "The Apostle of the Slaves"

The story of the Church is filled with leaders who lived the Ten Commandments. Peter Claver is one of those people.

Peter was the son of a farmer. He left his home in Spain and braved crossing the Atlantic Ocean. He traveled to Cartagena, which is now in Colombia in South America. Each year more than ten thousand enslaved people arrived by ship in Cartagena and were forced to work as slaves in the mines.

Boarding the ships, Peter climbed down into the hulls and cared for the slaves. He followed them into the mines and fed them, took care of their wounds, clothed them, and prayed with them. The slave owners and even some of the people of his parish church ridiculed Peter as "the slave of the slaves." Others honored Peter with the title "The Apostle of the Slaves."

The work of Peter Claver shows us what happens when we respect the dignity and life of every person as the Ten Commandments teach us to do. The Church honors Peter as a saint and celebrates his feast day on March 9.

Describe a leader you know who helped people by putting the Ten Commandments into action.

Our Catholic Identity

Social Teachings of the Catholic Church

The social teachings of the Catholic Church help us live the Ten Commandments. The Church has summarized its social teachings around seven themes, or main ideas. Two of those themes are (1) every human life is sacred and (2) we have a responsibility to care for people who are treated unjustly.

What Difference Does Faith Make in My Life?

Each day you learn about people who are working to free people who are slaves to drugs, food, money, and other things. The Holy Spirit helps you live the Ten Commandments and be free from things such as this.

In the circle write one thing people need to be freed from. In the space around the circle write what you can do to keep yourself and others free from what you have written in the circle.

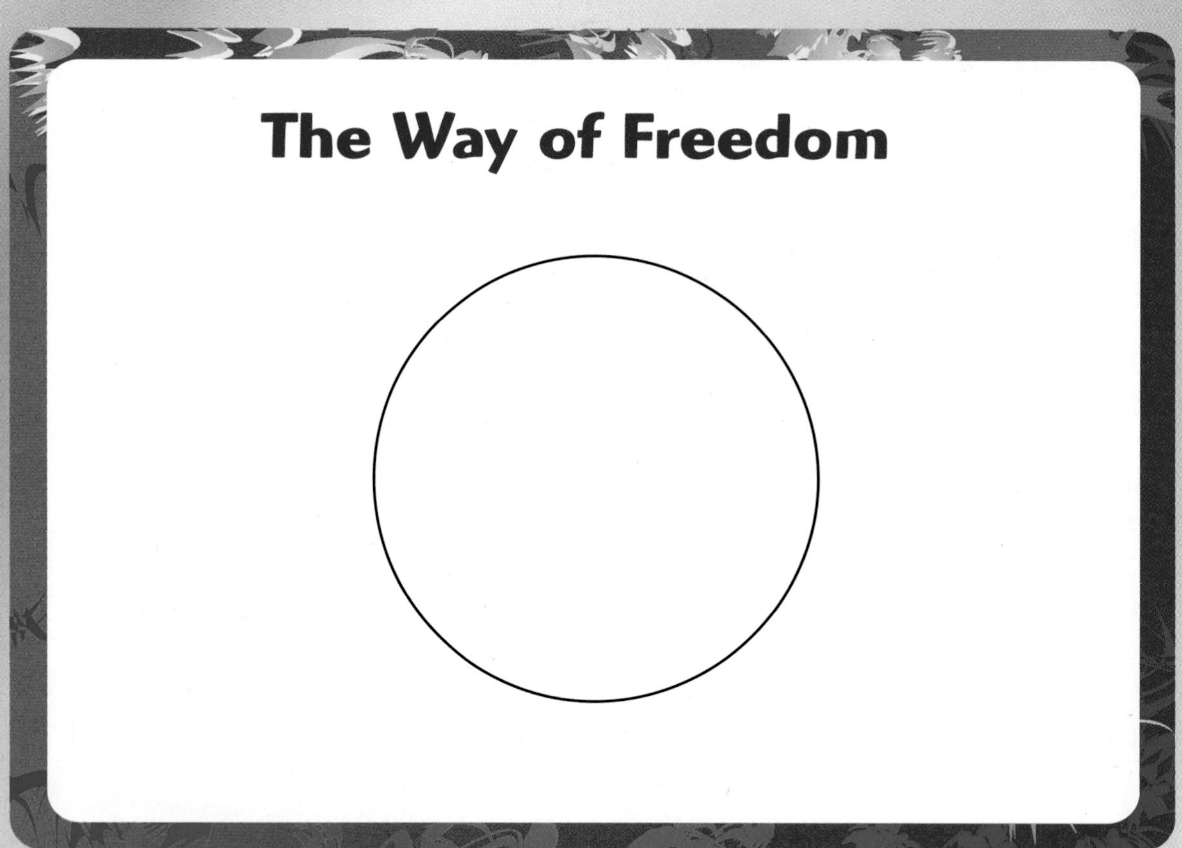

My Faith Choice

This week I will think about my actions and put the Ten Commandments into action. I will

____

______________________________________.

We Pray

A Prayer of Meditation

A meditation is a prayer in which we use our imagination. We ask the Holy Spirit to teach us to live as Jesus taught. This helps us be signs of God's love in the world.

1. Close your eyes. Remember that the Holy Spirit lives within you.
2. Recall the story of Moses leading God's people out of Egypt through the desert.
3. Imagine that you are Moses and that God is speaking to you. Read or listen as your catechist reads Exodus 19:9–20.
4. Remember that Jesus came to fulfill the Ten Commandments. Spend some quiet time in prayer and conversation with God.
5. Ask the Holy Spirit to teach you to live the Ten Commandments and be a sign of faith and hope and love for others.

We Remember

Place the letter of each word in the right column in front of the phrase in the left column that best describes it.

C	1. Another name for the Israelites	a. Decalogue
D	2. Led God's people out of slavery in Egypt	b. Covenant
E	3. Shows us how to live the Commandments	c. Hebrews
A	4. Another name for the Ten Commandments	d. Moses
B	5. The solemn agreement God made with the Hebrews	e. Jesus

To Help You Remember

1. During the Exodus, God gave Moses the Ten Commandments on Mount Sinai.
2. The Ten Commandments are the basic laws that teach us how to love God and our neighbors as ourselves.
3. Jesus came to show us how to live the Ten Commandments.

20 With My Family

This Week . . .

In chapter 20, "Living God's Covenant: A Scripture Story," your child learned that God revealed the Ten Commandments to Moses and the Israelites. The Ten Commandments are the basic laws that guide all people to love God with all their heart and to love their neighbor as themselves. Jesus affirmed the importance of the Ten Commandments when he taught that he came to fulfill and not to do away with them. He also taught that we should not lose sight of the heart of the Ten Commandments—they are guideposts to live the Great Commandment. The two parts of the Great Commandment were first revealed to the people of the Old Covenant and are stated in the Book of Deuteronomy and the Book of Numbers.

For more on the teachings of the Catholic Church on the revelation and nature of the Ten Commandments, see *Catechism of the Catholic Church* paragraph numbers 2052–2074, 2083, and 2196.

Sharing God's Word

Read together the Bible story in Exodus 19:9–20 about Moses and the Ten Commandments or read the adaptation of the story on page 175. Emphasize that by living the Ten Commandments, God's people are signs of their love for God.

Praying

In this chapter your child prayed a meditation. Pray together the meditation on page 179.

Making a Difference

Choose one of the following activities to do as a family or design a similar activity of your own.

- Moses was a good leader because he had the courage to stand up for what he believed in. Name the ways your family stands up for the Ten Commandments.
- Talk together about why rules and laws are necessary. Discuss the rules and laws that help your family live as a Christian family.
- What leaders do you know who are like Moses? Who do you know who has helped people by putting the Ten Commandments into action? Be sure that all family members share their ideas.

For more ideas on ways your family can live your faith, visit the "Faith First for Families" page at **www.FaithFirst.com**. Click on "Family Prayer." Plan to say the prayer together this week.

Love God with All Your Heart

We Pray

[LORD God], in your holy name we trust.
PSALM 33:21

**Blessed be God.
Blessed be
his holy name.
Amen.**

Who is someone you consider to be Number 1 or the best at doing something?

Everyone wants to be Number 1. Almost every day we hear the cheer and claim, "We're Number 1!" And almost every day the Number 1 team or song or movie changes. Jesus taught us that God is always and only Number 1—and that never changes!

How do you show that God is Number 1 in your life?

Christ the Redeemer,
Rio de Janiero, Brazil

God, the Center of Our Lives

Faith Focus

How do the first three Commandments help us show our love for God?

Faith Vocabulary

worship. To honor and respect above all else; to give adoration and praise to God.

Lord's Day. The name given to Sunday by Christians because Sunday is the day of the Lord's Resurrection.

With a partner come up with a list of ways fourth graders can show that God is Number 1 in their lives. Share your ideas with the whole group.

The First Commandment

The First, Second, and Third Commandments teach that we are to love God with all our heart, with our whole mind, and with our whole soul. The First Commandment is

> "I am the LORD your God: you shall not have strange gods before me."
>
> BASED ON EXODUS 20:2–3

The First Commandment teaches that God is Number 1 in our lives and this should never change. Only God is worthy of our **worship.** To worship someone or something means that the person or thing is the center of our lives, or Number 1 in our lives. We honor and love God above all else.

Jesus taught that no person or thing can ever take the place of God in our lives. We are not to allow any person or any thing to weaken or break our friendship with God.

"The LORD alone is God."

BASED ON DEUTERONOMY 6:4

The Second Commandment

One of the most important ways that we show our respect and love for someone is by the way we speak about them, or use their name. The Second Commandment is

> "You shall not take the name of the LORD your God in vain." EXODUS 20:7

The Second Commandment teaches that we use God's name with respect. Respect is a virtue that helps us honor God by everything we say or do. We especially never use God's name to make people believe that a lie is the truth.

The Second Commandment also teaches that we must use the name *Jesus,* the name *Mary,* and the names of the saints with respect. We are to treat holy things and holy places with respect. When we live this way, we do not take God's name in vain. We show our respect and love for God.

Faith-Filled People

Isaiah the Prophet

Isaiah and the other prophets preached the message, "Make God Number 1 in your life again." We use Isaiah's prayer, "Holy, holy, holy is the Lord of hosts" (Isaiah 6:3) at Mass.

Use one of the names for God in the border. Create a banner that shows you love and honor God above all else.

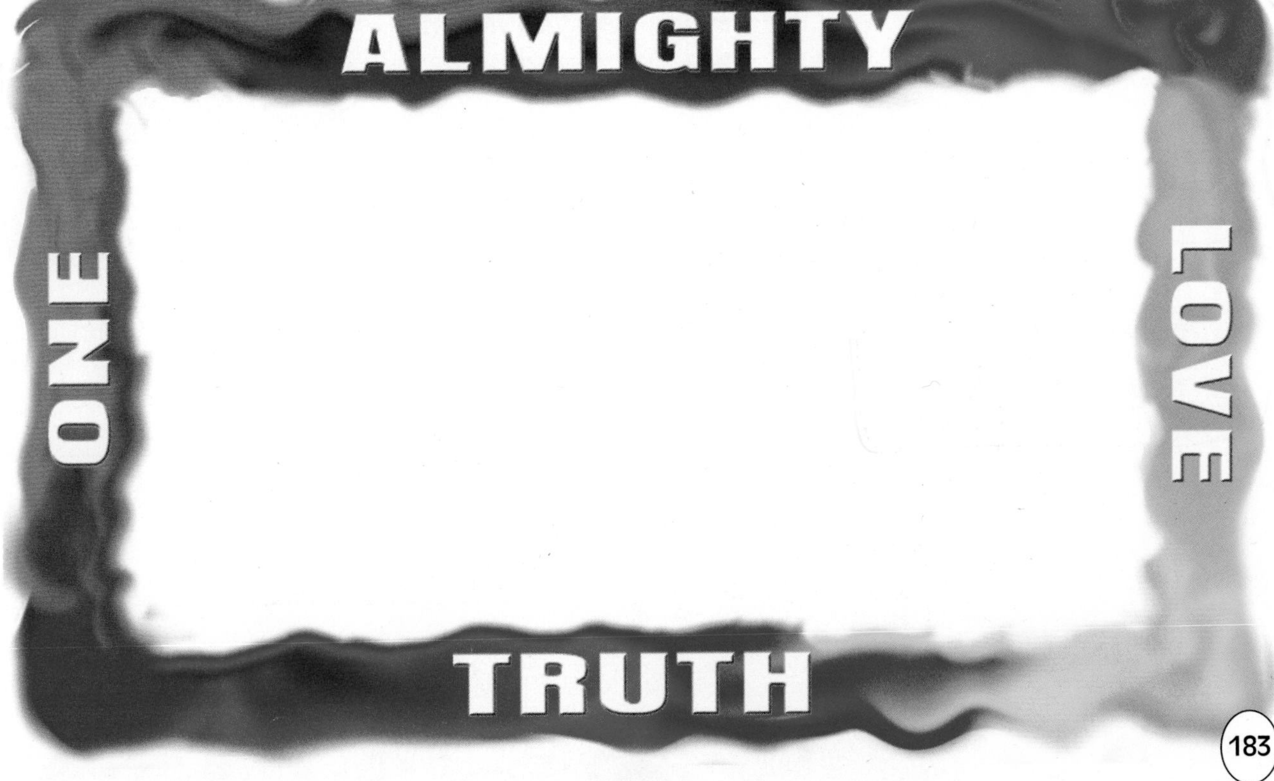

The Third Commandment

The Third Commandment teaches that we must set aside one day each week for the Lord God. For Christians, Sunday is the **Lord's Day.** It is the day of the Lord's Resurrection. The Third Commandment is

"Remember to keep holy the LORD's Day." BASED ON EXODUS 20:8

Catholics live the Third Commandment by gathering for Mass on Saturday evening or Sunday to worship God. Catholics also gather for Mass on holy days of obligation.

We also live the Third Commandment by resting from unnecessary work on Sundays. On the Lord's Day, we do things that celebrate and keep God at the center of our lives all week long.

Name one way you might live the First, Second, or Third Commandment this week.

Our Church Makes a Difference

Saint Joan of Arc

The things the saints did and said help people, families, and nations keep God at the center of their lives. Joan of Arc lived by the motto "Let God be served first."

Joan grew up in a time of war between France, the country she lived in, and England. Joan believed that God was calling her to help France. Joan became a soldier and led France in their war with England. Joan of Arc's decision changed her life and the life of the French people.

Joan became very unpopular with the leaders of France. They thought she was a witch doing the work of the devil. Joan never stopped doing the things she believed God called her to do. At the age of nineteen, she was executed.

The Church has named Joan of Arc a saint. Today she is the patron saint of France. Her feast day is May 30.

Describe how the motto "Let God Be Served First" might help the leaders make decisions.

Our Catholic Identity

Precepts of the Church

The precepts of the Church are rules the Church gives us. The precepts of the Church help us meet our responsibilities to worship God and grow in our love for God and our neighbor.

What Difference Does Faith Make in My Life?

You do many things each day that show God is Number 1 in your life. These things help others see the good things that happen when people put God first and live by his commandments.

Create a bulletin board that shows why keeping God at the center of your life makes a difference.

God Is Always Number 1!

#1

My Faith Choice

This week I will try to remember to keep God Number 1 in my life. I will

____

______________________________________.

We Pray

The Divine Praises

The Divine Praises is a prayer written to praise and honor God. Kneel and repeat each of the phrases after the leader.

Blessed be God.
Blessed be his holy name.
Blessed be Jesus Christ, true God and true man.
Blessed be the name of Jesus.
Blessed be his most sacred heart.
Blessed be his most precious blood.
Blessed be Jesus in the most holy sacrament of the altar.
Blessed be the Holy Spirit, the Paraclete.
Blessed be the great Mother of God, Mary most holy.
Blessed be her holy and immaculate conception.
Blessed be her glorious assumption.
Blessed be the name of Mary, virgin and mother.
Blessed be Saint Joseph, her most chaste spouse.
Blessed be God in his angels and in his saints.

We Remember

Match the terms in column A with the Commandments in column B. One of the Commandments can be used more than one time.

Column A	Column B
__C__ **1.** Lord's Day	**a.** First Commandment
__b__ **2.** respect	**b.** Second Commandment
__a__ **3.** worship	**c.** Third Commandment
__C__ **4.** holy days of obligation	

To Help You Remember

1. The First Commandment teaches that we are to worship only God.
2. The Second Commandment teaches that we are to show our love and respect for the name of God and all that belongs to God.
3. The Third Commandment teaches that we are to set aside one day each week as the Lord's Day. Christians set aside Sunday as the Lord's Day.

21 With My Family

This Week . . .

In chapter 21, "Love God with All Your Heart," your child learned more about the first three commandments. The First Commandment teaches that God is and should always be at the center of our lives. In all we do and say, we strive to give glory and honor to God. The Second Commandment teaches that we are to show respect for God's name and for all holy people, places, and things. The Third Commandment teaches that we must make one day each week the Lord's Day. For Christians, Sunday is the Lord's Day. On Sundays, Catholics gather to celebrate Mass. All we do and say refreshes us and helps us keep God at the center of our lives throughout the week.

For more on the teachings of the Catholic Church on the First, Second, and Third Commandments, see *Catechism of the Catholic Church* paragraph numbers 2084–2132, 2142–2159, and 2168–2188.

Sharing God's Word

Read together the first part of the Great Commandment on page 289 or in Matthew 22:37. Emphasize that the First, Second, and Third Commandments help us keep God at the center of our lives.

Praying

In this chapter your child prayed the Divine Praises. Read and pray together the prayer on page 187.

Making a Difference

Choose one of the following activities to do as a family or design a similar activity of your own.

- Look through magazines or take a walk through a shopping mall as a family. Talk about how the displays might tempt people not to keep God as Number 1 in their lives.
- Talk about the poor language used in many prime-time television shows. Write a family letter to the head of programming of a major network stating your thoughts and feelings on that topic.
- Talk about the ways your family keeps Sunday holy. Choose one thing you will do this week to keep Sunday holy.

For more ideas on ways your family can live your faith, visit the "Faith First for Families" page at **www.FaithFirst.com**. Visit the "Games" site. Ask your child to show you the game they most like.

Love Your Neighbor as Yourself

We Pray

Trust in the LORD
and do good.

PSALM 37:3

**Lord God,
loving Father, send
us the Holy Spirit
to guide us to live
as Jesus, your Son,
taught. Amen.**

How did you treat each person you met today?

We see people treated in many ways. The Fourth through the Tenth Commandments teach us that we are to honor and respect other people.

What are some ways you show respect for yourself and for other people?

Honor and Respect One Another

Faith Focus

How do the Fourth, Fifth, Sixth, and Ninth Commandments help us live as Jesus taught?

Faith Vocabulary

honor. To have special respect for someone, to hold someone in high regard.

respect. To give someone or something the honor they deserve.

The Fourth Commandment

The Fourth Commandment teaches about being good family members, neighbors, and citizens. The Fourth Commandment is

"Honor your father and your mother."

EXODUS 20:12

We are to **honor** and **respect** our parents. We are to care about them and think of them with love. We are to obey them and show our thanks to them for all that they do to help us grow.

Parents share their faith with us. They help us come to know Jesus and they teach us ways to live as his followers. In our families we first come to know and trust in the love that God the Father, Son, and Holy Spirit has for us. That is what we mean when we say that the family is a sign of the Holy Trinity.

The Fourth Commandment also teaches that we are to respect other family members and other people who have the responsibility to care for us. We are to respect our teachers and all legitimate authority in our community. We are to be good and responsible citizens.

Draw or write one way that you show you are living the Fourth Commandment.

Living the Fourth Commandment

The Fifth Commandment

God creates every person in the image and likeness of God. All life belongs to God and is a gift from God. That means that the life of every person is sacred, or holy. The Fifth Commandment teaches that we must treat all life as sacred. The Fifth Commandment is

> "You shall not kill." EXODUS 20:12

We live the Fifth Commandment when we:

- care for and respect all human life.
- respect our own life and body and the lives and bodies of the other people.
- care for our own health and the health of others.
- use food and medicine wisely.
- act safely.

The Fifth Commandment also tells us that we must not deliberately hurt or kill innocent people or misuse alcohol, drugs, or food. We are not to bully others, commit acts of terrorism, or harm or end our own lives by suicide.

Jesus taught his followers how to live this Commandment. We are to make peace with those who hurt us. We are not to take revenge, or get even with people who hurt us. We are to be careful not to let our feelings of anger turn into hatred. We are to love our enemies.

Faith-Filled People

Sister Helen Prejean

Sister Helen Prejean lives as a follower of Jesus by visiting and caring for prisoners, prisoners' families, and the families of victims of violent crimes.

SCHOOL SPONSORS ANTI-DRUG PROGRAM

Local Church Helps Earthquake Victims

PEOPLE DONATE MONEY FOR HOMELESS SHELTERS

Mothers Against Drunk Driving (MADD) Speak at Local Community Center

Talk about how each of these headlines shows people living according to the Fifth Commandment.

The Sixth and Ninth Commandments

Friendship is a gift from God. Marriage is a special kind of friendship between a man and a woman. At their wedding a man and a woman promise to love and honor each other their whole lives. The Sixth and Ninth Commandments teach us about what a husband and wife and others must do to honor the love between a husband and a wife. The Sixth Commandment is

> "You shall not commit adultery."
>
> EXODUS 20:14

This Commandment teaches that a husband and a wife must honor and not betray the love they promised to share only with each other.

The Ninth Commandment is

> "You shall not covet your neighbor's wife."
>
> EXODUS 20:17

Create a collage of words using qualities of a good and true friend.

The word *covet* means "to want or desire wrongfully what belongs to someone else." This Commandment teaches that family, friends, and neighbors are to help a husband and a wife grow in their love. No one should ever break up, or even want to break up, the love a husband and a wife share.

We prepare to live this kind of married love when we are young. We respect our body and the bodies of others. We demand that others treat our bodies with respect. We keep the promises we make. We work at being loyal friends.

Our Church Makes a Difference

L'Arche Communities

L'Arche communities are communities of faith. The word *l'Arche* means "the ark" or "the covenant." L'Arche communities live the Covenant we have with God and with one another.

L'Arche communities believe in the dignity and value of every person. They bring together Catholics and other Christians to form a family with people who have severe disabilities. All the members of a L'Arche community live and work together. Everyone shares whatever blessings God has given them with everyone else.

Every day all throughout the world, L'Arche communities show that all human life is sacred. Everyone is loved and valued as a child of God.

What do the members of your parish do to show that they respect human life as sacred?

Our Catholic Identity

Respect Life Sunday

Each year on the first Sunday of October, Catholics in the United States celebrate Respect Life Sunday. We celebrate that every human life is sacred. We make decisions to work for programs that respect the dignity of every person, born and unborn.

Members of a L'Arche community

What Difference Does Faith Make in My Life?

Every day you show that you honor and respect people. When you do, you build a caring school, family, and community. You build a world that respects the dignity of every person. You are living the Ten Commandments as Jesus taught.

Describe a covenant on which you and your friends build your friendship. Tell what each of you promises to do to keep your friendship strong.

A Friendship Covenant

This week I will look for opportunities to show my respect for people as Jesus taught. I will

____

______________________________________.

We Pray

A Prayer for All People

Leader: God, Creator and Father, all life is your gift to us.
Hear our prayers as we pray *(pause)* for all people
that they value the gift of life as a sacred gift from you,

All: **God of life, hear our prayer.**

Leader: For all children who suffer from abuse,
from lack of food and a place to call their home,

All: **God of life, hear our prayer.**

Leader: For all unborn children that they are taken
care of so that they are born healthy,

All: **God of life, hear our prayer.**

Leader: For all people who suffer from acts
of injustice, terror, and violence,

All: **God of life, hear our prayer.**

Leader: Let us pray together as Jesus taught us.

All: **Our Father . . .**

We Remember

Read each story. On the lines write the number of the Commandment each of these people is living.

1. Jane has a decision to make. Should she eat another candy bar or should she eat some fruit? She decides on the fruit. 5
2. Tom has a habit of teasing his friends. One of his friends tells him to stop and reminds him that they need to respect each other. 5/6
3. The teacher asks John to stop talking and bothering the class. He immediately stops and apologizes. 4

To Help You Remember

1. The Fourth Commandment teaches about our responsibilities as family members, neighbors, and citizens.
2. The Fifth Commandment teaches that we are to respect and honor all human life, born and unborn, as sacred and as a gift from God.
3. The Sixth and Ninth Commandments teach that we must express and share our friendship and love in appropriate ways.

22 With My Family

This Week . . .

In chapter 22, "Love Your Neighbor as Yourself," your child learned more about the Ten Commandments. The Fourth through Tenth Commandments teach us to live the second part of the Great Commandment, "You shall love your neighbor as yourself" (Matthew 22:37). The Fourth Commandment teaches that we honor and respect our parents and live as good family members, neighbors, and citizens. The Fifth Commandment teaches that all human life is sacred and a gift from God. We are to respect and care for all life to the best of our ability. The Sixth and Ninth Commandments teach that we respect and honor marriage as a faithful lifelong commitment between a man and a woman.

For more on the teachings of the Catholic Church on the Fourth, Fifth, Sixth, and Ninth Commandments, see *Catechism of the Catholic Church* paragraph numbers 2196–2246, 2258–2317, 2331–2391, and 2514–2527.

Sharing God's Word

Read together the second part of the Great Commandment in Matthew 22:37 or on page 291. Emphasize that the Sixth through Tenth Commandments teach us to respect and love our neighbors as ourselves.

Praying

In this chapter your child prayed a prayer of intercession. Read and pray together the prayer on page 195.

Making a Difference

Choose one of the following activities to do as a family or design a similar activity of your own.

- Ask family members to share an experience when they felt they were treated disrespectfully. Discuss how important it is for you to treat all people with respect.
- Ask each person to share two situations in the past week when they followed the Ten Commandments in making a choice.
- What does your parish do to show respect for all people, all human life? Look in your parish bulletin or on your parish web site for ideas.

For more ideas on ways your family can live your faith, visit the "Faith First for Families" page at **www.FaithFirst.com**. Check out this week's "Just for Parents" article.

Love One Another as I Have Loved You

We Pray

LORD, . . .
I fulfill your
commands.
PSALM 119:166

**Lord God,
may the Helper,
the Holy Spirit
who comes from
you, lead us to all
truth. Amen.**

What is one way you show you love others?

People show their love for their family and friends in many ways. The Ten Commandments teach us to love others as God wants us to show our love for them.

What do you know about the Seventh, Eighth, and Tenth Commandments and what they teach us about showing that we love others?

Faith Focus

How do the Seventh, Eighth, and Tenth Commandments help us live as Jesus taught?

Faith Vocabulary

reparation. The work of repairing or making up for harm we have wrongfully caused.

perjury. Lying under oath.

The Seventh Commandment

The Seventh, Eighth, and Tenth Commandments help us show our love for people. They guide us in using the things we have and respecting the belongings of others. The Seventh Commandment is

"You shall not steal." Exodus 20:15

This Commandment teaches that we are to respect the gifts God gives to others. We must use the things with which God has blessed us justly.

We must not steal, cheat, or damage what belongs to someone else. When we borrow things, we are to use them carefully and return them in good condition.

If we steal something or we damage or lose something that someone has let us use, we must make **reparation.** We have the responsibility to give back what we have stolen or repair what we have damaged or replace what we have lost.

Describe how the children in this photo are living or not living the Seventh Commandment.

The Eighth Commandment

Jesus said, "I am the truth" (John 14:6). Disciples of Jesus are to be honest and truthful. The Eighth Commandment helps us live this way. The Eighth Commandment is

> "You shall not bear false witness against your neighbor."
> EXODUS 20:16

This Commandment teaches that we must

- speak the truth.
- take responsibility for all our words and actions.

We must not lie about ourselves or damage the good name or reputation of others by lying about them. We are not to gossip and put other people down, or to blame others for the wrong we have done.

We are not honest or truthful when we bear false witness, or tell lies, about others. Lying under oath, or committing **perjury**, is especially serious.

We must make reparation for all of these things. We need to tell the truth and repair the damage we have wrongfully caused.

Faith-Filled People

Stephen the Deacon

Saint Stephen was one of the first followers of Jesus. He was a deacon who helped widows and orphans and other Christians in need. When an angry crowd asked Stephen about Jesus, he was honest and told the truth about Jesus. The crowd put Stephen to death. The Church celebrates the feast day of Saint Stephen on December 26.

Read this situation. Write your own ending.

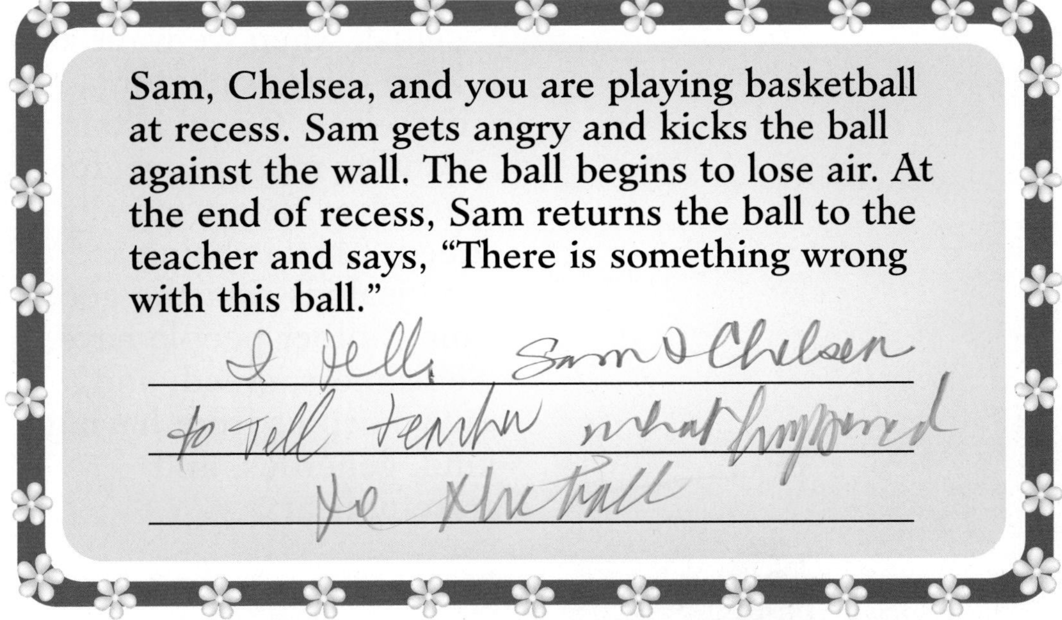

Sam, Chelsea, and you are playing basketball at recess. Sam gets angry and kicks the ball against the wall. The ball begins to lose air. At the end of recess, Sam returns the ball to the teacher and says, "There is something wrong with this ball."

The Tenth Commandment

Jesus taught about our desire to want things. He taught,

> "Your father wants you to live in the kingdom of God. Do not want things too much. They can get in the way of your getting to heaven. For your heart will always be where your treasure is."
>
> BASED ON LUKE 12:32–34

The Tenth Commandment talks about our heart and what it wants. The Tenth Commandment is

> You shall not covet your neighbor's goods.
>
> BASED ON EXODUS 20:17

This Commandment teaches that we are to have a generous, kind, and grateful heart. We must try to be as generous and kind to other people as God is to us. We are to thank God for all the blessings he gives to us and others.

The Tenth Commandment warns against selfishness, greed, and envy. We are selfish when we want and keep things only for ourselves. Greed is our wanting more things for ourselves than we really need. Envy is being sad and jealous over the good things other people have. Selfishness, greed, and envy keep us from having a kind, generous, and grateful heart.

Draw or write about one of your favorite possessions. Tell how you can share it with someone else.

Our Church Makes a Difference

The Potato Project: Love by the Truckload

Each year Christians and people of other religions join together for the Society of St. Andrew's Potato Project. They collect about twenty million pounds of potatoes that businesses are going to throw away. Businesses do not want the potatoes because they are the wrong size or shape or have marks on their skins.

The Potato Project volunteers save food from being thrown away and wasted. They make sure that the good food that God has blessed our farms with is shared by all. The volunteers bring the potatoes to food pantries, churches, and other places where people who are hungry come to get food. Many who are hungry are fed.

How do you see people unselfishly sharing their blessings with others?

Our Catholic Identity

The Collection at Mass

In the first days of the Church, when Christians gathered for Eucharist, they brought food to church. The food was collected and given to people in need. Today some of the money we give in the collection at Mass is used to help people in need.

What Difference Does Faith Make in My Life?

Each day you make choices to live the Ten Commandments. You are honest and truthful. You are kind and generous. Through your actions, you continue the work of Jesus.

Describe one person or group who is kind and generous to you.

Being Kind and Generous

Name Mom

What They Share ______________________

____

What Difference This Makes in My Life ______________________

____

My Faith Choice

When I am honest and truthful and kind and generous, I am following the way of Jesus. This week I will be especially kind and generous. I will

____

______________________.

We Pray

Signs of Mercy

Learn to sign this prayer. Teach it to your friends and your family. Pray it often each day.

God, **you** **always**

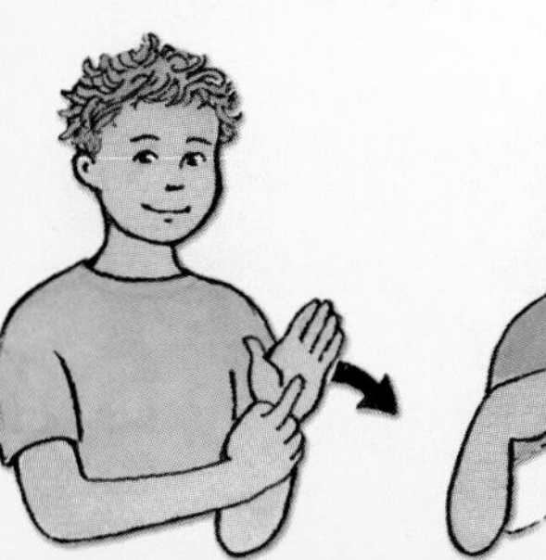

show **us** **mercy.**

We Remember

Match the virtues in the left column with the Commandments in the right column.

VIRTUES	COMMANDMENTS
b a 1. honesty	a. Seventh Commandment
C 2. generosity	b. Eighth Commandment
C 3. kindness	c. Tenth Commandment
b 4. truthfulness	

To Help You Remember

1. The Seventh Commandment teaches that we are to respect the property of others.
2. The Eighth Commandment teaches that we are to be honest and truthful.
3. The Tenth Commandment teaches that we are to be grateful and generous.

23 With My Family

This Week . . .

In chapter 23, " 'Love One Another as I Have Loved You,' " your child learned more about the Ten Commandments. God has given the world and all the good in it to all people. We are to respect the world, use it wisely, and generously share our blessings with a grateful heart. The Seventh Commandment teaches that we are to respect the gifts of others. The Eighth Commandment teaches us to be honest and truthful. We are to respect the good name of other people. The Tenth Commandment teaches us to have a kind, generous, and grateful heart. Living all of the Ten Commandments helps us love God and one another as Jesus taught.

For more on the teachings of the Catholic Church on the Seventh, Eighth, and Tenth Commandments, see *Catechism of the Catholic Church* paragraph numbers 2401–2449, 2464–2503, and 2534–2550.

Sharing God's Word

Read the teaching of Jesus in Luke 12:32–34 about gathering possessions or read the adaptation of the story on page 200. Emphasize the importance of being honest and truthful, kind and generous, and just.

Praying

In this chapter your child learned to sign a prayer of mercy. Read, sign, and pray together the prayer on page 203.

Making a Difference

Choose one of the following activities to do as a family or design a similar activity of your own.

- Talk about the people you know who unselfishly share their blessings with others. Then choose one thing you can do this week to share your blessings with others.
- Look up the Corporal Works of Mercy and the Spiritual Works of Mercy on page 286. Talk about the ways that the works of mercy help you to be generous and kind.
- How does your parish live like the early Christians and share its blessings with others? Look in the bulletin or on the web site.

For more ideas on ways your family can live your faith, visit the "Faith First for Families" page at **www.FaithFirst.com**. Click on "Make a Difference" this week to learn how your family can share God's love with others.

Unit 3 Review

Name ______________________

A. The Best Word

Fill in the blanks to complete each of the sentences.
Use the words from the word bank.

Hebrews	**happiness**	**Decalogue**
intellect	**worship**	**deliberate actions**
honor	**conscience**	

1. Our ______________ gives us the power to know God.

2. The choices we freely understand and make are called ______________________________.

3. The Beatitudes are sayings and teachings of Jesus that describe the true ______________________ of people blessed by God.

4. Our ______________ helps us judge right from wrong.

5. Moses led the Israelites, or ______________, on a journey from slavery in Egypt to freedom in the land God promised them.

6. The ______________________ is another name for the Ten Commandments.

7. The First Commandment says that only God is worthy of ______________________________.

8. The Fourth Commandment calls us to ______________ and obey our parents.

B. Words and Phrases

Match the items in column A with those in column B.

Column A

a 1. Person or thing that leads us to choose to do what we know is against God's will

b 2. A choice we make that causes us to lose the gift of holiness

d 3. A moral virtue that gives us courage to make good choices

c 4. "You shall not kill."

e 5. "You shall not commit adultery."

Column B

a. temptation

b. mortal sin

c. Fifth Commandment

d. fortitude

e. Sixth Commandment

C. What I Learned

1. *Name three things you learned in this unit. Share them with the group.*

___

___

___

2. *Look at the faith terms on page 148. Circle the ones you know now.*

D. From a Scripture Story

In each blank write ways Jesus fulfilled the Law and the Prophets by his actions and his words.

Words	Actions
___	___
___	___
___	___
___	___

Unit 4 • We Pray

Talk about different ways that Catholics pray.

Getting Ready

What I Have Learned

What is something you already know about these three things about prayer?

The different kinds of prayer

____

____

The Our Father

____

____

Prayer partners

____

____

Words to Know

Put an X next to the faith terms you know. Put a ? next to faith terms you need to know more about.

Faith Vocabulary

______ vocal prayer
______ meditation
______ contemplation
______ prayers of thanksgiving
______ prayers of praise
______ prayers of blessing and adoration
______ prayers of petition
______ prayers of intercession

Questions I Have

What questions would you like to ask about prayer?

____

____

____

A Scripture Story

Jesus praying with his disciples

What is one thing we ask of God when we pray the Our Father?

People of Prayer

We Pray

O God, hear my prayer. PSALM 54:4

Father, we join with all creation, on earth and in heaven. We lift up our hearts to praise you. Amen.

How do you like to spend time with your friends?

Spending time together and sharing thoughts and feelings with a friend helps a friendship grow. The same is true for our friendship with God.

What is your favorite time or place to spend time with God?

God Is Always with Us

Faith Focus

In what ways does the Church pray?

Faith Vocabulary

pray. Raising our minds and hearts to God, who is Father, Son, and Holy Spirit; talking and listening to God.

Liturgy of the Hours. The daily, public, communal prayer of the Church.

Spending Time with God

The Holy Spirit invites us and teaches us to **pray.** When we pray, we share with God what is on our minds and in our hearts. We pray to God the Father, to Jesus, and to the Holy Spirit. Whether we pray alone or with others, we believe that God is always with us. Whether we pray quietly in our hearts or aloud, God is always there listening to us.

Praying strengthens our friendship with God. It celebrates our love for God. It expresses our faith and trust in God the Father, the Son, and the Holy Spirit. It is a sign of our love for God.

Share your favorite prayer with a partner.

The Church Prays

The Church is a people of prayer. From the very beginning of the Church, the followers of Jesus Christ have always gathered for prayer. Praying is something the Church does every day, all year long, year after year.

Celebrating the liturgy is the main form of prayer of the Church. The liturgy of the Church centers around the Eucharist and the other sacraments. All the other prayers we pray arise out of the liturgy.

Every day the Church prays the **Liturgy of the Hours.** In the morning, at midday, in the evening, and at night, the Church offers prayerful thanks to God for his great love for us. We ask God to help us live as his children and as followers of Christ.

Benedict and Scholastica

Saint Benedict and Saint Scholastica were twins. Benedict wrote about living the Gospel. Everything he wrote can be summed up in the words "Pray and work." Scholastica followed the advice of her brother. Many other men and women did too, and still do today. They are called Benedictines. We celebrate the feast day of Saint Benedict on March 21 and the feast day of Saint Scholastica on February 10.

Make a chart that shows the places and times you might pray each day.

Professing Our Faith in God

Praying is a sign of our faith in God. Faith is one of God's gifts to us. Faith gives us the ability to listen to God, to come to know God, and to believe in him. Faith helps us make our friendship with God the most important thing in our lives.

From its earliest days the Church has professed its faith in God in creeds. The creeds of the Church are brief summaries of what the Church believes. We profess our faith in God and in all God has made known to us and done for us.

The two main creeds of the Church are the Apostles' Creed and the Nicene Creed. We pray the Nicene Creed at Mass at the end of the Liturgy of the Word.

Look up the Apostles' Creed and the Nicene Creed on page 284. Write on the lines two things we believe about God the Father, God the Son, and God the Holy Spirit.

Father	Son	Holy Spirit
________	________	________
________	________	________

Our Church Makes a Difference

Our Catholic Identity

Medals and Statues

Medals and statues are sacramentals. They are objects given to us by the Church that help us pray. They remind us of God's love for us.

Prayer Partners

In many parishes older children are prayer partners with younger children. When they gather to pray, the older children sit next to the younger children and pray with them. This helps the younger children learn to sing and pray out loud the words they do not know how to read.

When they gather for Mass, the younger children also learn when to sit and stand and kneel. All this helps the younger children take part in Mass and grow as people of prayer.

Who helps you pray? Who do you pray with?

What Difference Does Faith Make in My Life?

You are a person of prayer. The Holy Spirit invites you to pray anytime, anywhere. You can pray at home, in church, on your way to school, or while you are taking a walk.

God is inviting you to pray right now. Listen. Share with God what is in your heart and on your mind.

A Time to Pray

____

____

____

____

____

____

____

____

My Faith Choice

This week I will spend some time each day with God in prayer. I will

____

___________________________________.

We Pray

Holy Mary, Pray for Us

The Hail Mary honors Mary as the Mother of God and our mother. Pray the Hail Mary with your group, your family, and alone.

Leader: Lord God, Mary, the mother of your Son, Jesus, is our model of prayer. We honor her today as we remember the day that she said yes to your call to be the mother of Jesus.

Group 1: Hail Mary, full of grace,
the Lord is with you!

Group 2: Blessed are you among women,
and blessed is the fruit of your
womb, Jesus.

All: **Holy Mary, Mother of God,
pray for us sinners,
now and at the hour
of our death. Amen.**

We Remember

Write T next to the true statements. Write F next to the false statements. Make the false statements true.

_____ **1.** We pray to God the Father, Jesus, and the Holy Spirit.

_____ **2.** Praying strengthens our friendship with God.

_____ **3.** Praying before and after meals is the main form of prayer in the Church.

_____ **4.** We pray the Nicene Creed at the end of Mass.

To Help You Remember

1. Prayer is raising our minds and hearts to God.
2. The liturgy of the Church centers around the Eucharist and the other sacraments.
3. The creeds of the Church are short summaries of the faith of the Church that we use to profess our faith in God and all he has done for us.

24 With My Family

This Week . . .

In chapter 24, "People of Prayer," your child learned more about prayer. Prayer is not only talking but also listening to God. Prayer is lifting our minds and hearts to God and sharing our thoughts and feelings with God. The liturgy is the main form of prayer of the Church. The liturgy centers around the Eucharist and the other sacraments. The Church prays every day year-round. The Liturgy of the Hours is the daily public prayer of the Church. The creeds of the Church are prayers of the Church that are brief summaries of what the Church believes.

For more on the teachings of the Catholic Church on Christian prayer, see *Catechism of the Catholic Church* paragraph numbers 2558–2567 and 2650–2679.

Sharing God's Word

Read together Psalm 54:4. Emphasize that prayer is both talking and listening to God.

Praying

In this chapter your child prayed the Hail Mary. Read and pray together the prayer on page 215.

Making a Difference

Choose one of the following activities to do as a family or design a similar activity of your own.

- God invites us to pray. Invite family members to share their favorite times and places to pray.
- This is a good time to review the Nicene Creed. Use this creed all week for family prayer. Hopefully, by the end of the week, all family members will know the Nicene Creed by heart.
- Sacramentals, such as medals or statues, remind us of God's love for us and help us pray. Find all the sacramentals in your home. If they are not displayed, choose a few to display around your home.

For more ideas on ways your family can live your faith, visit the "Faith First for Families" page at **www.FaithFirst.com**. Click on "Family Prayer" and pray the prayer together this week.

We Pray in Many Ways

We Pray

**It is good to give
thanks to the LORD.**
PSALM 92:2

We give you thanks for all your blessings, almighty God, living and reigning, now and forever. Amen.
THANKSGIVING AFTER MEALS

What have you asked or told your family today?

We turn to our family and friends for many different reasons throughout the day. We also turn to God in prayer.

What are some of the ways you pray?

We Lift Our Hearts Up to God

Faith Focus

In what ways do we express our prayers to God?

Faith Vocabulary

meditation. A form of prayer using our imagination that helps us come to know God and how he wants us to live.

contemplation. A form of praying that does not use words that strengthens our love and friendship with God.

Let Us Pray

God is the center of our lives. After being with Jesus, seeing what he did, and listening to what he said, Jesus' followers came more and more to see the importance of spending time with God in prayer. One way we keep God at the center of our lives is by praying.

When we pray, we can share everything about our lives with God. Every kind of prayer is an expression of faith in God, hope in God, and love of God. Faith, hope, and love are the theological virtues. They help us keep God at the center of our lives.

Describe what you can do to remember to pray each day.

Different Kinds of Prayer

When we pray, we talk with God in many ways. The Church names five main kinds of prayer.

Prayers of Praise. We tell God that we believe he alone is God. There is only one God. We love him above everyone and everything else. He has done good things for us that no one else could ever do.

Prayers of Blessing and Adoration. We acknowledge God to be the Creator. God gives us the gift of life and shares his life and love with us.

Prayers of Thanksgiving. We thank God for the gift of creation, for our salvation in Jesus Christ, for the gift of holiness, and for every blessing.

Prayers of Petition. We ask God for forgiveness and for help in all our needs.

Prayers of Intercession. We ask God to help others. We pray that all people may know God's love for them.

Teresa of Avila

Saint Teresa of Avila was one of ten children. Her mother died when Teresa was fifteen years old. When she was twenty, Teresa entered the Carmelite monastery to become a religious sister. Teresa wrote many books that teach about the importance of prayer in our life. We celebrate the feast day of Saint Teresa of Avila on October 15.

Choose one of the five kinds of prayer. Write your own two-line prayer.

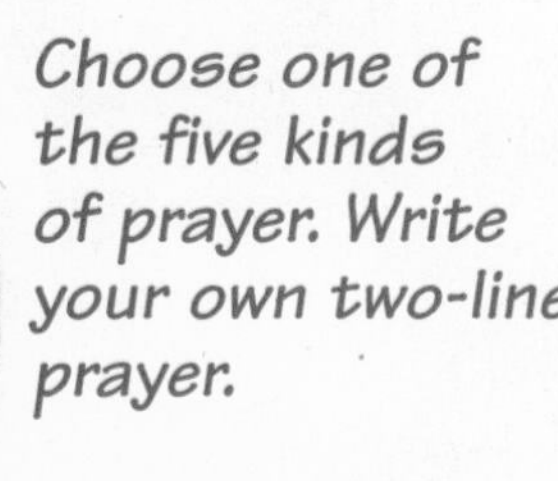

We Pray Aloud and Silently

The Church expresses its prayers in many ways. When we pray, we use our whole being. We pray aloud and silently. We pray alone and with others. We use words and our imagination. When we pray, we use our body and spirit.

Vocal Prayer. This form of prayer uses words. In vocal prayer we speak or sing our prayers. We pray our words aloud or silently in our hearts.

Meditation. This form of prayer uses our imagination. The prayer of **meditation** can start with a Bible reading. We put ourselves in that story. We listen to Jesus speaking or watch as he cures a sick person or forgives someone. We then ask, "Lord, what do you want me to do?" We ask the Holy Spirit to teach us how to live as followers of Jesus Christ.

On each line write the kind of prayer you think these young people are praying.

Contemplation. In this type of prayer, we quietly sit in God's presence and then focus on his loving closeness to us. The prayer of **contemplation** is a close sharing between friends.

Our Church Makes a Difference

A Prayer Journey

From the earliest days of the Church, Christians have made pilgrimages. A pilgrimage is a prayer journey.

Each year Christians make pilgrimages to the Holy Land. The Holy Land is the name we give to the places where Jesus lived, died, and was raised from the dead. Christians from every country in the world journey to Bethlehem, Jerusalem, Nazareth, and all the places you read about in the Gospels. They come to give praise and thanks to God. They come to pray for themselves and for other people.

Pilgrimages to the Holy Land and to other holy places invite all people to believe in, hope in, and love God. They help us know God's love at work in the world. Prayer journeys invite all people to keep God at the center of their lives.

Where would you like to visit on a prayer journey? Why would you choose that place?

Our Catholic Identity

The Holy Land

For over 800 years, the Franciscan friars have cared for the many churches and shrines in the Holy Land. The Franciscans do more than care for the many places where Jesus lived, died, and was raised from the dead. They work for peace and friendship with everyone in the Holy Land.

Views of the city of Jerusalem, Israel, today

What Difference Does Faith Make in My Life?

Think about the many ways you pray. Every time you pray, you grow closer to God.

Look at this map of the Holy Land in Jesus' time. Circle one of the places on the map and imagine that you are with Jesus in that place. Then quietly answer these questions:

- *What would you say to Jesus?*
- *What might he say to you?*

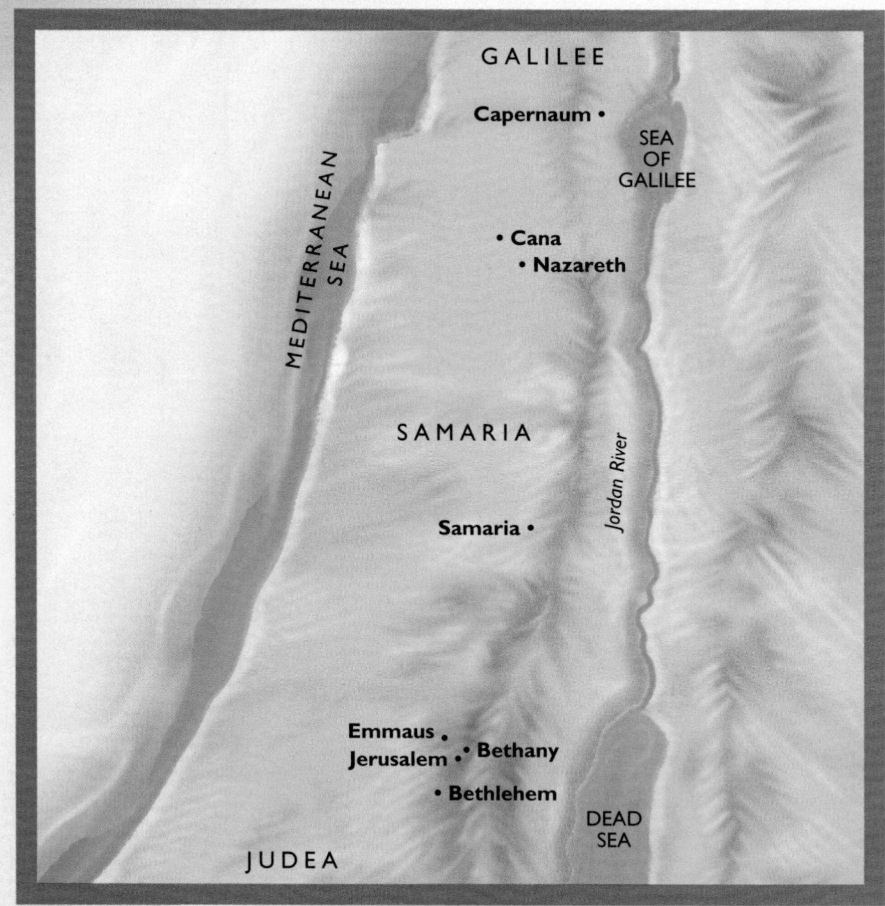

My Faith Choice

This week I will use some of the ways I have learned to pray in this chapter. I will

____

____.

We Pray

In a prayer of meditation we use our imagination and put ourselves into a Bible story. We listen to Jesus and ask the Holy Spirit to teach us to live as a follower of Jesus.

1. Sit quietly. Close your eyes. Breathe in and out very slowly.
2. Imagine you are with Jesus as he is teaching about God's love. See yourself among the people listening to Jesus.
3. You want to ask Jesus a question about what he is saying. What is the question you want to ask? Ask it. What is Jesus' reply?
4. Spend a few quiet moments thinking about the answer Jesus gives.
5. How can you put the response Jesus gave to your question into action? Make a decision to do it.

We Remember

Use the words in the box to complete the sentences.

petition vocal praise contemplation

1. We participate in __vocal__ prayer when we pray aloud.
2. In prayers of __Praise__ we tell God that he alone is God.
3. In prayers of __petition__ we ask for God's forgiveness and for help in all our own needs.
4. The prayer of __contemplation__ is a close sharing between friends.

To Help You Remember

1. The Church has named five types of prayer. They are prayers of praise, of adoration and blessing, of thanksgiving, of intercession, and of petition.
2. Every kind of prayer we pray is a sign that we believe in God, hope in God, and love God.
3. We use our body and spirit when we pray.

25 With My Family

This Week . . .

In chapter 25, "We Pray in Many Ways," your child learned about the many different ways that we pray. The Church prays prayers of praise, blessing and adoration, thanksgiving, petition, and intercession. We express these prayers, using our whole being, using our body and spirit. We use words and pray without using words. We use our religious imaginations. We pray prayers of meditation and contemplation. All our prayers are expressions of faith, hope, and love—the theological virtues that help us keep God at the center of our lives.

For more on the teachings of the Catholic Church on prayer, see *Catechism of the Catholic Church* paragraph numbers 2623–2643, 2650–2660, and 2697–2719.

Sharing God's Word

Read together Matthew 6:5–8. Praying is one way we keep God at the center of our lives.

Praying

In this chapter your child prayed a prayer of meditation. Read and pray together a prayer of meditation, using the steps on page 223.

Making a Difference

Choose one of the following activities to do as a family or design a similar activity of your own.

- List all the blessings that your family has to be thankful for. Then write a prayer of thanksgiving and pray it each day this week.
- We can learn about prayer from the saints. Go to the library or look on the Internet to find out more about Saint Teresa of Avila and what she taught about the importance of prayer.
- Talk about how your family can encourage each other to pray. Then do one thing this week that will help you remember to pray. For example, you might leave yourself a note on your pillow or on the inside of the door to your home.

For more ideas on ways your family can live your faith, visit the "Faith First for Families" page at **www.FaithFirst.com**. Read this week's "Bible Story." Talk about the Bible story with your child.

Lord, Teach Us to Pray
A Scripture Story

We Pray

To you I pray, O LORD.
PSALM 5:3

Lord God, Creator, Savior, and Sanctifier, the kingdom, the power, and the glory are yours, now and for ever. Amen.

How do you learn?

Our parents and teachers help us learn in many ways. Jesus taught us best about God and how we are to live as children of God. Jesus taught us to pray.

What stories in the Gospel do you know that tell about Jesus teaching his disciples to pray?

Bible Background

Faith Focus

What does Jesus teach us in the Our Father?

Faith Vocabulary

Rabbi. A Hebrew word meaning "Teacher," a title of honor and respect in the Bible given to someone whom people trusted to help them understand and live the Law of God.

Lord's Prayer. A name for the Our Father; the prayer Jesus, our Lord, taught his disciples to pray.

Jesus the Teacher

In Jesus' time some people were honored with the title of **Rabbi,** or Teacher. People gathered around such a teacher to understand and live God's Law. These people were disciples of that teacher. A disciple is a person who learns from and follows the teachings of another person.

Jesus was honored with the title of Rabbi, or Teacher. The disciples of Jesus traveled with him. They went to the Temple and synagogue with him. All the time they listened and watched. They asked question after question, looking for advice. They trusted him to help them understand and live faithfully the laws and customs of their religion.

The disciples of Jesus came to believe that Jesus was the One sent by God to be the Messiah. He was the One who fulfilled the Law and everything God had promised to his people.

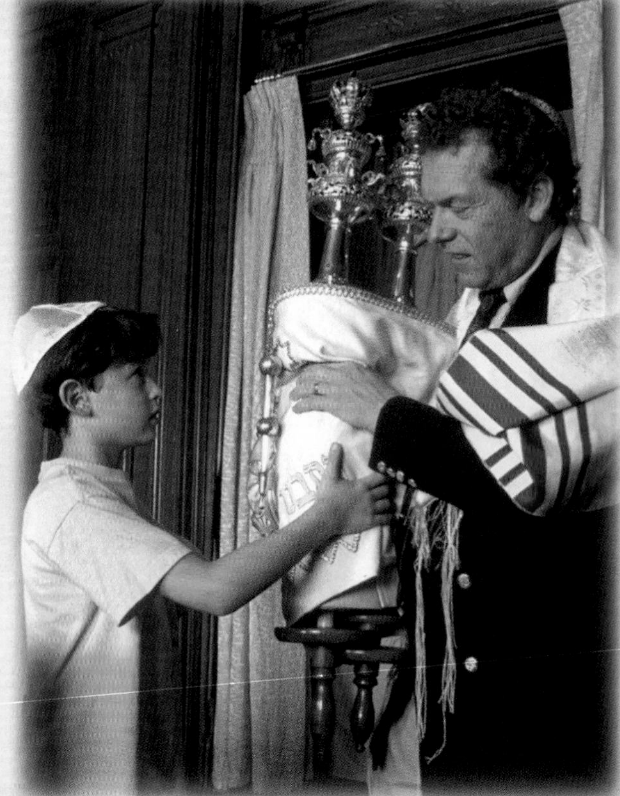

A rabbi and Jewish boy holding the Torah

Name two things you have learned about God from Jesus.

God is ______________________

____

______________________________.

God is ______________________

____

______________________________.

Reading the Word of God

Lord, Teach Us to Pray

One day the disciples were with Jesus while he was praying. When Jesus finished praying, one of the disciples asked Jesus to teach them to pray. Jesus replied,

"When you pray, say:
Father, hallowed be your name,
your kingdom come.
Give us each day our daily bread
and forgive us our sins
for we ourselves forgive everyone
in debt to us,
and do not subject us to the
final test." LUKE 11:2–4

When the disciples and the first Christians gathered, they prayed as Jesus taught them. This prayer became known as the **Lord's Prayer** or the Our Father.

Underline the words in the Scripture that are similar to the words we pray in the Our Father.

Understanding the Word of God

The Our Father

When we pray the Our Father, we tell God he is the center of our lives. We place our trust in him above everyone and everything else. Each time we pray the Our Father,

- we worship God by honoring and respecting his name as holy.
- we ask God to continue to build his kingdom. We promise God that we want to live as Jesus taught us.
- we ask God for our "daily bread." We ask for all we and others need to live as children of God.
- we ask God to forgive our sins and to help us forgive others as he forgives us. We remember that Jesus' dying and being raised from the dead was the greatest sign of God's forgiving love for us.
- we ask God to help us do good and to avoid sin. We ask God to help us follow Jesus' way of serving others.

The Our Father is the prayer of all Christians. Its words teach us both how to pray and how to live as disciples of Jesus. That is why it is called the perfect prayer for Christians.

How are the people in the pictures living the words of the Our Father?

Our Church Makes a Difference

The Gift of Hope

The children of Blessed Sacrament Parish learned that over one billion people go to bed hungry every night. They wondered what they could do. After talking with their teacher, they worked with their parents and decided to take part in the Heifer Project.

A child in Kenya with his goat provided by the Heifer Project

People who take part in the Heifer Project buy animals that are given to families around the world. These families raise the animals and give the offspring to other families in need.

The children of Blessed Sacrament Parish decided to earn enough money to buy two flocks of chicks for a family. They were living their prayer, "Give us this day our daily bread." They were giving a family the gift of food and the gift of hope.

The children of Blessed Sacrament Parish were teaching everyone that God is at work in the world. He is at work building the kingdom that Jesus taught will one day come about. Then everyone will really know that God is the Father of all people.

Describe some of the people or organizations you know who share the gift of hope with others.

Our Catholic Identity

The Doxology

We pray the Our Father at every Mass. At Mass we conclude the Our Father by singing or saying aloud, "For the kingdom, the power, and the glory are yours, now and for ever." These words are called a doxology. A doxology is a prayer of praise. The Church has prayed this doxology from the early days of the Church.

A child in the Dominican Republic with her chicken provided by the Heifer Project

What Difference Does Faith Make in My Life?

The Holy Spirit helps you understand, pray, and live the Our Father.

Choose one of the lines of the Our Father. Describe how it helps you live as a follower of Jesus.

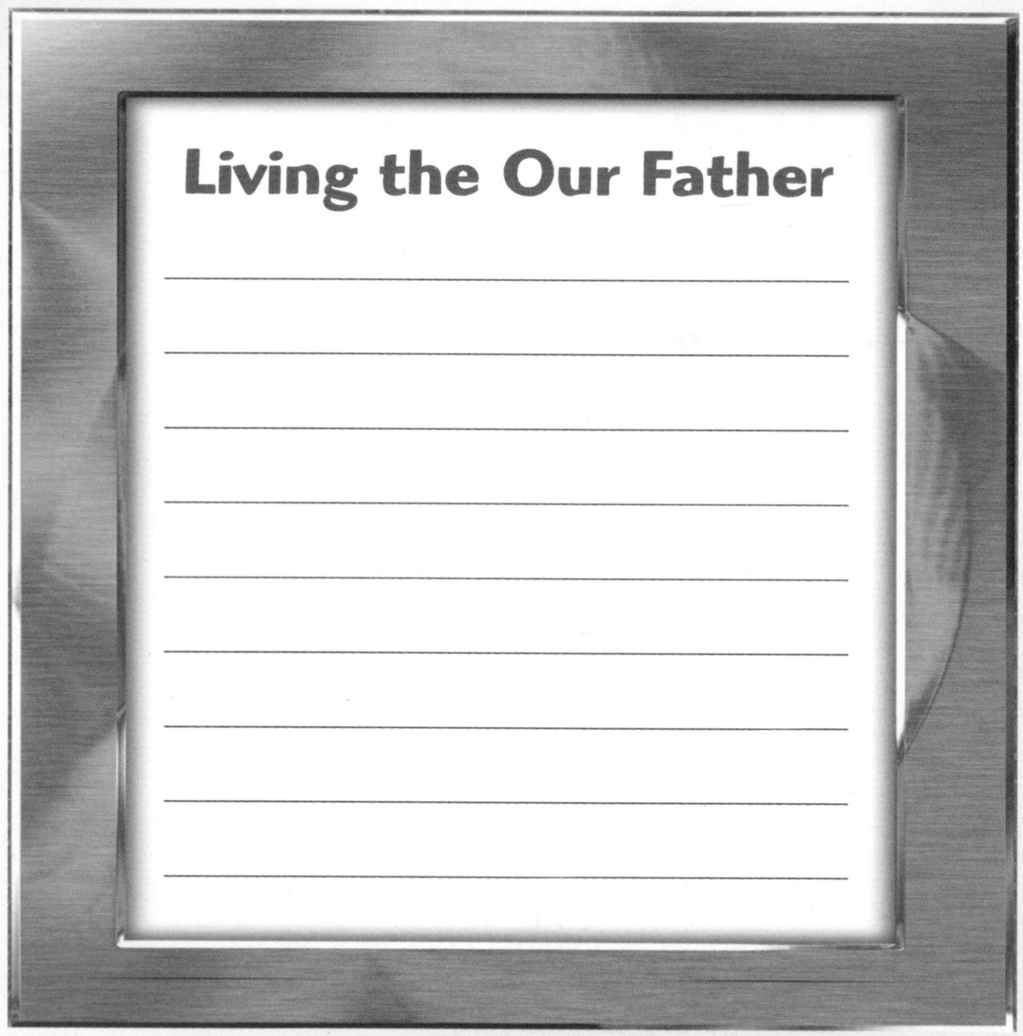

My Faith Choice

This week I will pray the Our Father every day. When I do, I will

____

______________________________________.

We Pray

The Our Father

The Church prays the Our Father every day. Join together as members of the Church. Pray as Jesus taught us.

Leader: O God, by the grace of the Holy Spirit we call you Father and live as your children. We pray as Jesus taught us.

All: **Our Father . . .**

Leader: Let us conclude by praising God.

All: **For the kingdom, the power, and the glory are yours, now and for ever. Amen.**

We Remember

Match the words from the Our Father in column A with their meanings in column B.

Column A

b 1. Hallowed be thy name.

a 2. Thy kingdom come.

c 3. Give us this day our daily bread.

e 4. Forgive us our trespasses.

d 5. Deliver us from evil.

Column B

a. The Holy Spirit works with us to prepare for the coming of the kingdom Jesus began.

b. We give glory to God who is All-holy.

c. We trust that God will give us all we need to live as his children.

d. We ask God to help us do good and avoid doing wrong. We ask him to help us follow Jesus' way of serving others.

e. We trust that God will forgive our sins.

To Help You Remember

1. Jesus is our Teacher, who helps us best understand and live as children of God.
2. Jesus taught us to call God our Father in prayer.
3. When we pray the Our Father, we tell God he is the center of our lives.

26 With My Family

This Week . . .

In chapter 26, "Lord, Teach Us to Pray: A Scripture Story," your child learned more about the Our Father. Saint Matthew's Gospel and Saint Luke's Gospel both give us accounts of Jesus teaching the disciples the Our Father. From the earliest days of the Church, Christians prayed the Our Father, or Lord's Prayer, when they gathered for prayer. When we pray the Our Father, we acknowledge that God is the center of our lives. The Our Father is the summary of the Gospel. The Our Father not only teaches us how to pray but also shows us how to live as the children of God, who is the Father of all people.

For more on the teachings of the Catholic Church on the Our Father, see *Catechism of the Catholic Church* paragraph numbers 2759–2856.

Sharing God's Word

Read together the Bible story in Luke 11:2–4 about Jesus teaching his disciples to pray or read the adaptation of the story on page 227. Emphasize that Jesus gave us the Our Father to pray.

Praying

In this chapter your child prayed the Our Father. Read and pray together the prayer on page 231.

Making a Difference

Choose one of the following activities to do as a family or design a similar activity of your own.

- The first Christian communities prayed the Our Father three times a day. Follow the example of the first Christians and do the same this week.
- Invite all family members to share the names of people they know who live the Our Father. Thank God for these generous people, for all they do, and the example they are to others.
- The Our Father is the prayer of all Christians. Learn the words of the Our Father in a language other than the language you usually use to pray.

For more ideas on ways your family can live your faith, visit the "Faith First for Families" page at **www.FaithFirst.com**. "Gospel Reflections" will continue to change each week over the summer. Don't forget to check it out.

Unit 4 Review

Name ______________________

A. The Best Word or Phrase

Fill in the blanks to complete the sentences.
Use the words from the word bank.

Meditation	**Our Father**	**Liturgy of the Hours**
Contemplation	**prayer**	**Nicene Creed**

1. The Holy Spirit invites us to raise hearts and minds up to God in ______________________.

2. ______________________ is a form of prayer that uses our imagination. It helps us come to know God and how he wants us to live.

3. In the ______________________ the Church offers prayerful thanks in the morning, at midday, in the evening, and at night.

4. We pray the ______________________ at Mass at the end of the Liturgy of the Word.

5. ______________________ is a form of prayer that does not use words and strengthens our love and friendship with God.

6. Every time we pray the ______________________, or Lord's Prayer, we place our trust in God above all else.

B. Words and Phrases

Match the types of prayers in column A with their clues in column B.

Column A

c 1. Prayers of praise

d 2. Prayers of blessing and adoration

b 3. Prayers of thanksgiving

a 4. Prayers of intercession

e 5. Prayers of petition

Column B

a. Ask God to help others.

b. Thank God for every blessing and gift.

c. Acknowledge God as the Creator of all.

d. Tell God we love him above all else.

e. Ask God for forgiveness and help with all your needs.

C. What I Learned

1. *Name three things you learned in this unit. Share them with the group.*

____

____

____

2. *Look at the faith terms on page 208. Circle the ones you know now.*

D. From a Scripture Story

Read the psalm prayers and name the kind of prayer each one is.

Enter, let us bow down in worship;
 Let us kneel before the LORD who made us. PSALM 95:6

Prayer of Blessing & Adoration

It is good to give thanks to the LORD,
 to sing praise to your name, Most High. PSALM 92:2

Prayer of Praise & Thanksgiving

We Celebrate

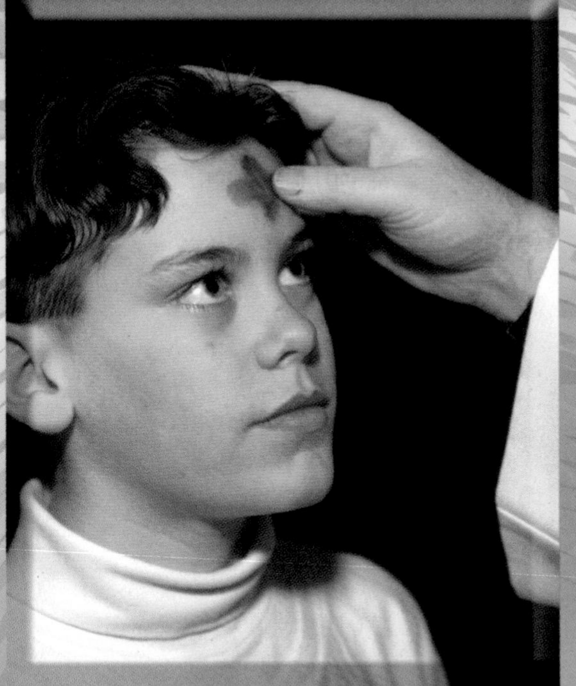

Why are celebrations during the Church's year important?

The Liturgical Year

We call the Church's celebration of the liturgy the liturgical year. The seasons of the liturgical year are Advent, Christmas, Lent, Easter, and Ordinary Time.

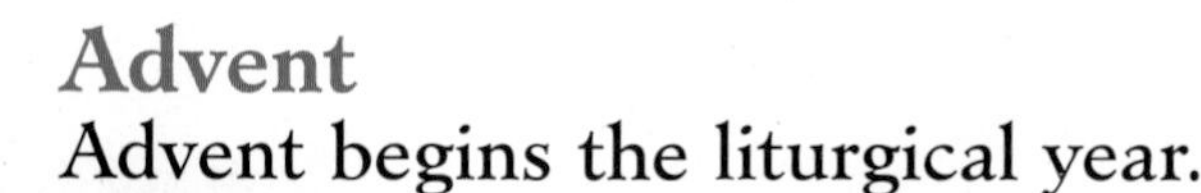

Advent
Advent begins the liturgical year.

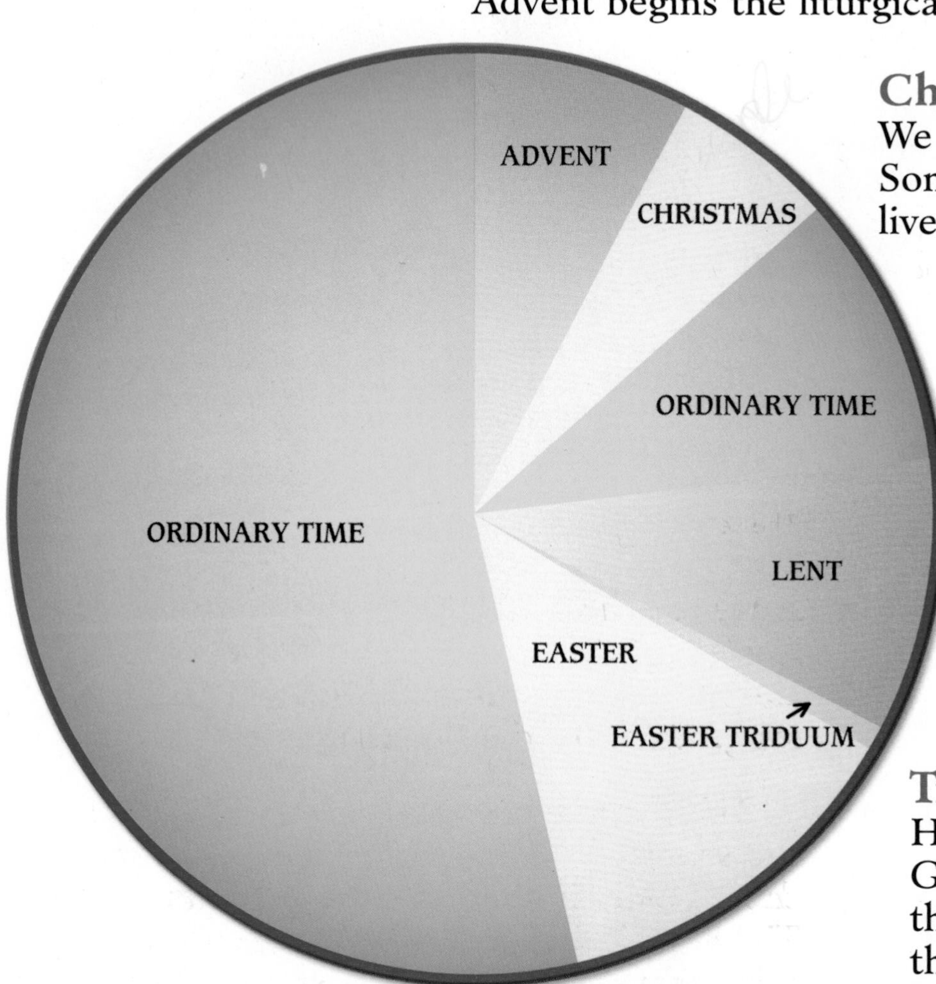

Christmas
We celebrate that the Son of God came and lived among us.

Lent
Lent is a time of penance and preparation for Easter.

Triduum
Holy Thursday, Good Friday, and the celebration of the Easter Vigil/Easter Sunday are the most important days of the liturgical year.

Easter
We celebrate the Resurrection of Jesus from death to new life and his Ascension to the Father.

Ordinary Time
We remember Jesus' life and work on earth.

Ordinary Time

Faith Focus

How do we celebrate the Church's year?

The Word of the Lord

These are the Gospel readings for the Third Sunday in Ordinary Time. Choose this year's reading and look it up in the Bible. Read and discuss the reading with your family.

Year A:
Matthew 4:12–23 or
Matthew 4:12–17

Year B:
Mark 1:14–20

Year C:
Luke 1:1–4 or
Luke 4:14–21

The seasons of the year

The Church's Year

All during the year we gather to celebrate the liturgy. We join with Jesus and the Holy Spirit to bless and give thanks to God the Father.

We call the Church's year the liturgical year. The Church's liturgical year has seasons too. They are Advent, Christmas, Lent, the Triduum, and Easter. All the other weeks of the year are called Ordinary Time. Ordinary Time is the longest part of the Church's year.

The Church uses colors to help us identify the seasons of the liturgical year. You see these colors in the priest's vestments at Mass. The liturgical year's colors are also used in other ways to decorate the church during each season.

The color purple, or violet, is used during the seasons of Advent and Lent. During Christmas and Easter the Church uses white or gold. Green is used during Ordinary Time. On Palm Sunday of the Lord's Passion, Good Friday, Pentecost, and several other feasts, the Church uses the color red.

Liturgical Colors

In each section of the circle write the name of the liturgical season. Color each season. Use the colors the Church uses for each season.

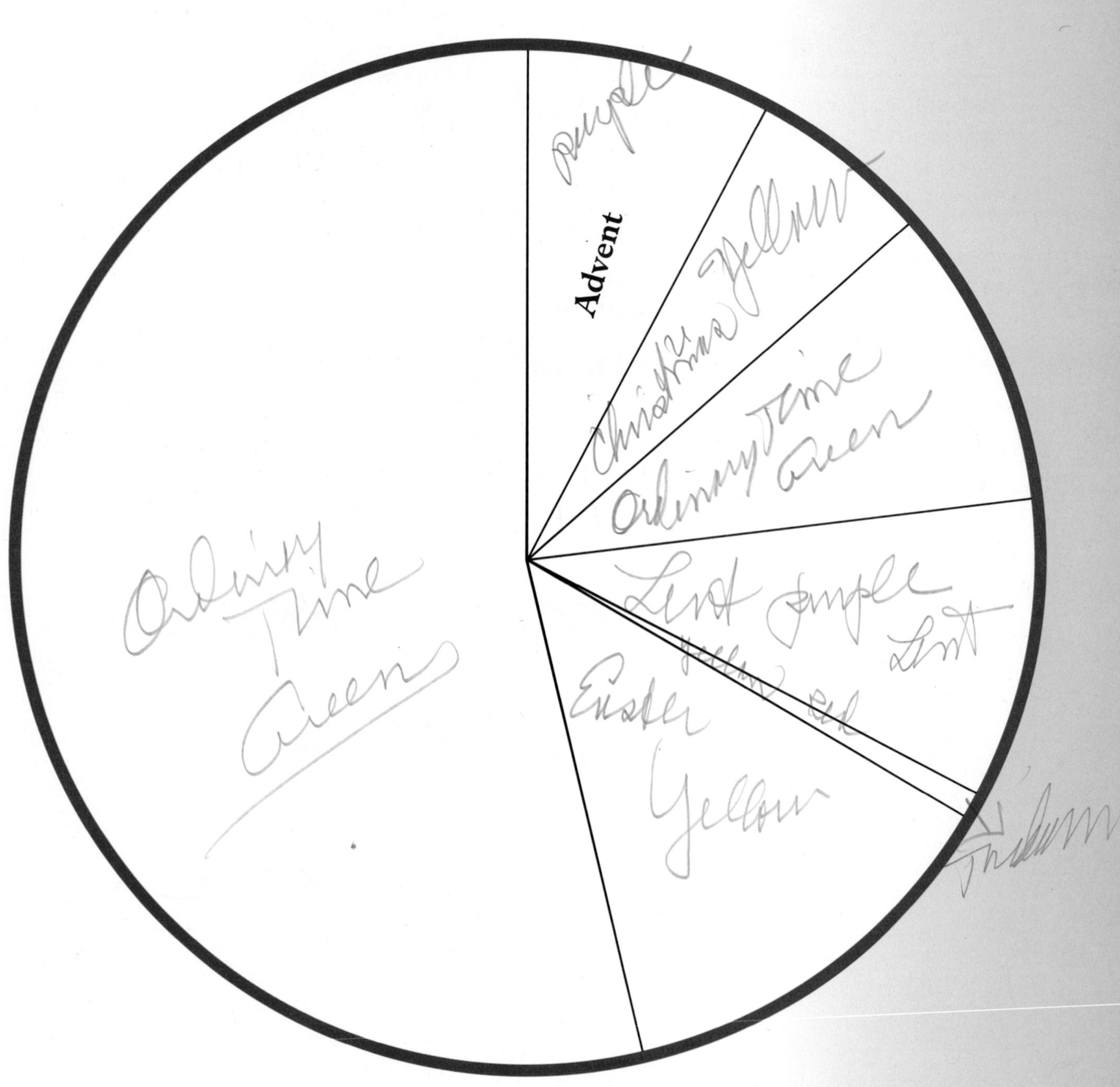

The First Week of Advent

Faith Focus

What do we prepare for during Advent?

The Word of the Lord

These are the Gospel readings for the First Sunday of Advent. Choose this year's reading and look it up in the Bible. Read and discuss the reading with your family.

Year A:
Matthew 24:37–44

Year B:
Mark 13:33–37

Year C:
Luke 21:25–28, 34–36

What You See

The tradition of the Advent wreath began in Germany. It is made of a circle of evergreens and four candles. Each week in churches and homes throughout the world, a candle is lighted and a prayer is said.

Light of the World

During the month of December, we make or buy gifts and wrap them. We decorate a tree. Families get ready for Christmas, and so does the Church.

Advent is the time we remember God's promise to send the Messiah. During the Masses of Advent we listen to stories from the Old Testament about this promise.

On each of the four Sundays of Advent, we light a candle on our Advent wreath. The candles help us count the weeks until Christmas. They also remind us that Jesus lights our world as the sun lights the earth.

We prepare for Christmas by being a light for others. We find ways to help others. We offer gifts of service. We may delight in finding ways to be secret givers. Our gifts light up the lives of others.

Be a Light in the World!

Read each situation. In each flame write one way you can be a light for others.

1. **Mom needs help at home after school.**
2. **Your parish needs five new members for the children's choir.**
3. **Your puppy needs to be walked. It is a cold day.**
4. **Alfie is having trouble with his math homework.**

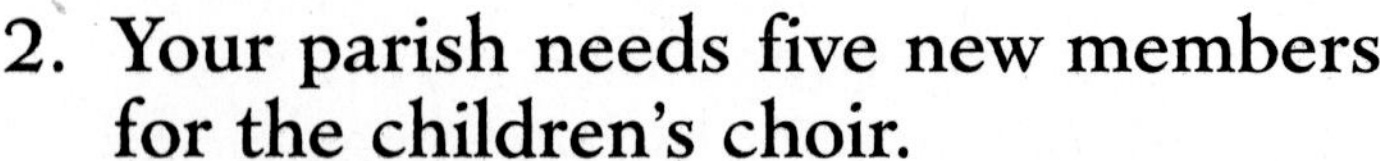

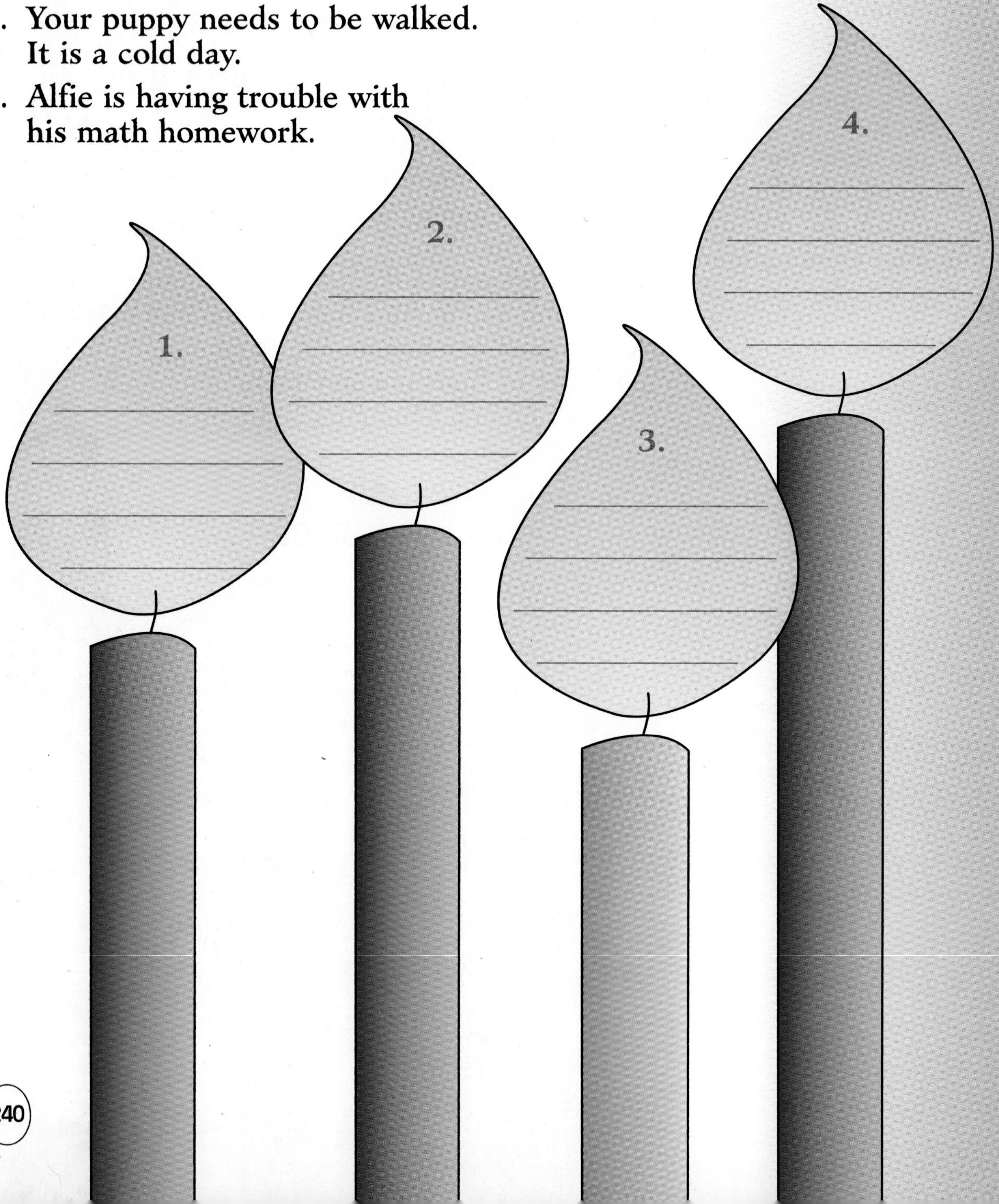

1\.

2\.

3\.

4\.

The Second Week of Advent

Faith Focus

How did John the Baptist help the people prepare for the coming of Jesus?

The Word of the Lord

These are the Gospel readings for the Second Sunday of Advent. Choose this year's reading and find it in the Bible. Read and discuss the reading with your family.

Year A:
Matthew 3:1–12

Year B:
Mark 1:1–8

Year C:
Luke 3:1–6

Saint John the Baptist preaching

God's Messenger

Telephone! E-mail! Beepers! We get messages today in many different ways.

John the Baptist was God's messenger. His message was that the Lord, God's Promised One, was coming.

John's good news came with a warning. The people were to repent and change. Then they would be ready to welcome the Lord when he came.

We listen to the stories of John the Baptist preaching on two Sundays in Advent. His message of preparation is important for us too. It reminds us to get ready for the coming of Jesus the Lord, God's Promised One.

Sending an Advent Message

Write an Advent round for your class to sing. Use the melody from "Are You Sleeping," or "Frère Jacques." Give your round a title.

The Third Week of Advent

Faith Focus

How does the Church help us prepare for Christmas?

The Word of the Lord

These are the Gospel readings for the Third Sunday of Advent. Choose this year's reading and find it in the Bible. Read and discuss the reading with your family.

Year A:
Matthew 11:2–11

Year B:
John 1:6–8, 19–28

Year C:
Luke 3:10–18

Be Ready

Change can be good for us. Sometimes we change to make our lives better. To become a better student, we may spend more time studying instead of playing.

John the Baptist asked people to change. He spoke loud and clear, "Prepare the way of the Lord, / make straight his paths" (Mark 1:3). The people listened. They asked John how they could make a clear path to the Lord. They wanted nothing to keep them from God.

John said they should repent. Then he baptized them with water. This was a sign that they were willing to give up their old ways and live as children of God.

We too want nothing to keep us away from God. During Advent the Church helps us do this. We prepare ourselves to welcome Jesus at Christmas. The Church reminds us of the message of John the Baptist: "Prepare the way of the Lord" (Mark 1:3).

Present-day mountain area outside Jerusalem

On Your Way

Place a ✔ in the box next to the things that show how you can follow John the Baptist's words "Prepare the way of the Lord."

- ❐ I will help at home after school.
- ❐ I will light the Advent candle tonight with my family.
- ❐ I will tell others about the low grade my friend got on the test.
- ❐ I will read the Bible with my family at bedtime tonight.
- ❐ I will ask for lots of presents for Christmas.
- ❐ I will play with my friends and be late for dinner.

Other things I can do that show I am listening to John the Baptist's message:

____

____

____

Faith Focus

What does the name Jesus mean?

The Word of the Lord

These are the Gospel readings for the Fourth Sunday of Advent. Choose this year's reading and find it in a Bible. Read and discuss the reading with your family.

Year A:
Matthew 1:18–24

Year B:
Luke 1:26–38

Year C:
Luke 1:39–45

God Saves

Your name has a special meaning. Perhaps your parents named you after a saint or a grandparent. God gave his Promised One a special name too.

The angel Gabriel came to Mary and asked her to be the mother of the Son of God. Gabriel told her to name him Jesus. This name means "God saves."

Mary said yes to God's request. She said, "Behold, I am the handmaid of the Lord. May it be done to me according to your word" (Luke 1:38). Mary is truly the Mother of God because she is the mother of Jesus, the eternal Son of God made man, who is God himself.

An angel also came to Joseph to tell him that the child Mary was expecting was to be named Jesus. The angel repeated the message he told to Mary.

During Advent we remember that Jesus is our Savior. We prepare to welcome him into our hearts just as Mary and Joseph did.

Mosaic of Mary and the angel Gabriel

The Name of Jesus

The name *Jesus* in Hebrew is similar to the name *Joshua.* This is how it is written.

Jesús is the Spanish spelling for Jesus. *Jésus* is the French spelling for Jesus. Each is pronounced differently.

Hearing-impaired people say and read the name *Jesus* by signing it. This is how to sign the name *Jesus.*

People who cannot see use Braille as a way to read. The surface of flat paper is dappled with a code of dots. People who cannot see can "read" Braille by feeling the raised dots.

The name *Jesus* in Braille looks like this:

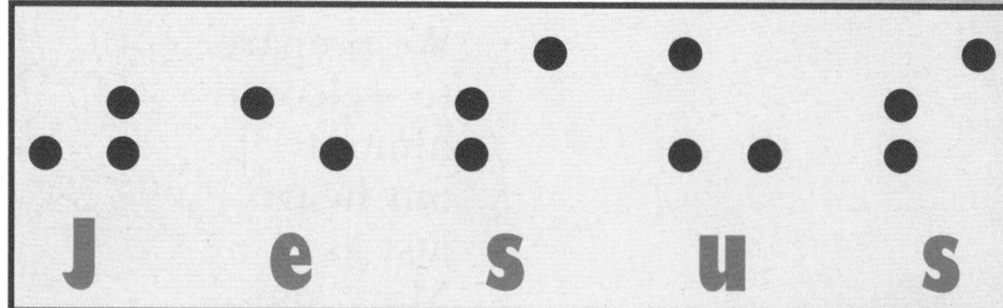

Trace this pattern of dots on a white sheet of paper. To make a raised dot, use the tip of a ball-point pen and puncture a hole through the dot from the bottom side of the paper. Then close your eyes and run your fingertip over your homemade Braille and read the name Jesus.

Faith Focus

What did the shepherds do when they heard the angels' message about Jesus?

The Word of the Lord

These are the Gospel readings for Mass on Christmas Day. Choose one reading and find it in the Bible. Read and discuss the reading with your family.

Years A, B, and C:
John 1:1–18 or
John 1:1–5, 9–14

The Birth of Jesus

When you were born, your whole family rejoiced! Many rejoiced when Jesus was born too.

The Gospel tells us that the glory of the Lord shone in the dark night over the place where shepherds were watching their sheep. The shepherds were afraid but the angels brought this good news: "[T]oday in the city of David a savior has been born for you who is Messiah and Lord" (Luke 2:11).

Jesus was born in Bethlehem, which is called the "city of David." Many years before, Israel's greatest king, David, had been born in Bethlehem.

The angels did not announce the birth of Jesus, the Savior, to great kings. The angels announced his birth to shepherds who then left their sheep and went to see the Child born in Bethlehem. Then the shepherds went about "glorifying and praising God for all they had heard and seen, just as it had been told to them" (Luke 2:20).

Present-day countryside near Bethlehem

God's Promise

Design a Christmas message that praises God for the birth of Jesus.

Faith Focus

Who is the Savior of the world?

The Word of the Lord

This is the second reading for the feast of the Epiphany. Find it in the Bible and read and discuss it with your family.

Years A, B, and C:
Ephesians 3:2–3, 5–6

Savior of the World

Name a leader for whom you have great respect. Why do you respect this leader? How do you show your respect for this person?

At the time Jesus was born, some wise men, called Magi, studied the stars to find signs of the birth of a great and holy leader. One night the Magi saw a great star in the sky. They believed the star would lead them to this great leader.

The Magi set out on a long journey and followed the star. It led them to Bethlehem. There they found Jesus, Mary, and Joseph. They offered gifts of gold, frankincense, and myrrh to Jesus to honor him as a king and show their great respect for him.

God's salvation is for all people—the poor shepherds, the royal Magi, us, and everyone.

From the painting *The Wise Men Journey to Bethlehem* by Vladimir Mazuranic, 1910

Finding Jesus

The Magi followed the star to find Jesus. Help the Magi find their way to Bethlehem.

The Magi followed the star and found Jesus and his mother Mary.

BASED ON LUKE 2:9–10

The First Week of Lent

Faith Focus

Why does the Church celebrate Lent?

The Word of the Lord

These are the Gospel readings for the First Week of Lent. Choose this year's reading and look it up in a Bible. Read and discuss the reading with your family.

Year A:
Matthew 4:1–11

Year B:
Mark 1:12–15

Year C:
Luke 4:1–13

What You Hear

The word *alleluia* is not used during Lent. Before the reading of the Gospel, only a psalm verse is read.

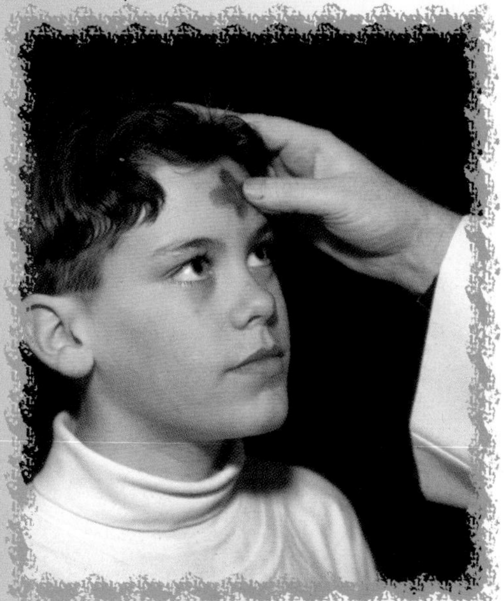

The blessing of ashes on Ash Wednesday

The Church's Sacred Springtime

When spring comes, we put on lighter and more comfortable clothing. We often do spring cleaning around our home. Spring is a time to enjoy a fresh, new colorful season of the year.

Lent is the Church's springtime. It is the time of the Church's year that we spend preparing for our Easter celebration of Jesus' Resurrection to new life.

Lent begins on Ash Wednesday. On Ash Wednesday, as a cross is traced on our forehead with ashes, we hear the words, "Turn away from sin and be faithful to the Gospel."

Lent is a time to remember the new life of Christ given to us through Baptism. We renew our efforts to live the Gospel by loving God and one another.

Treasure Search

Unscramble the words in each jewel to discover a virtue that helps you live the Gospel. Clue: Read Colossians 3:12–15 in your Bible.

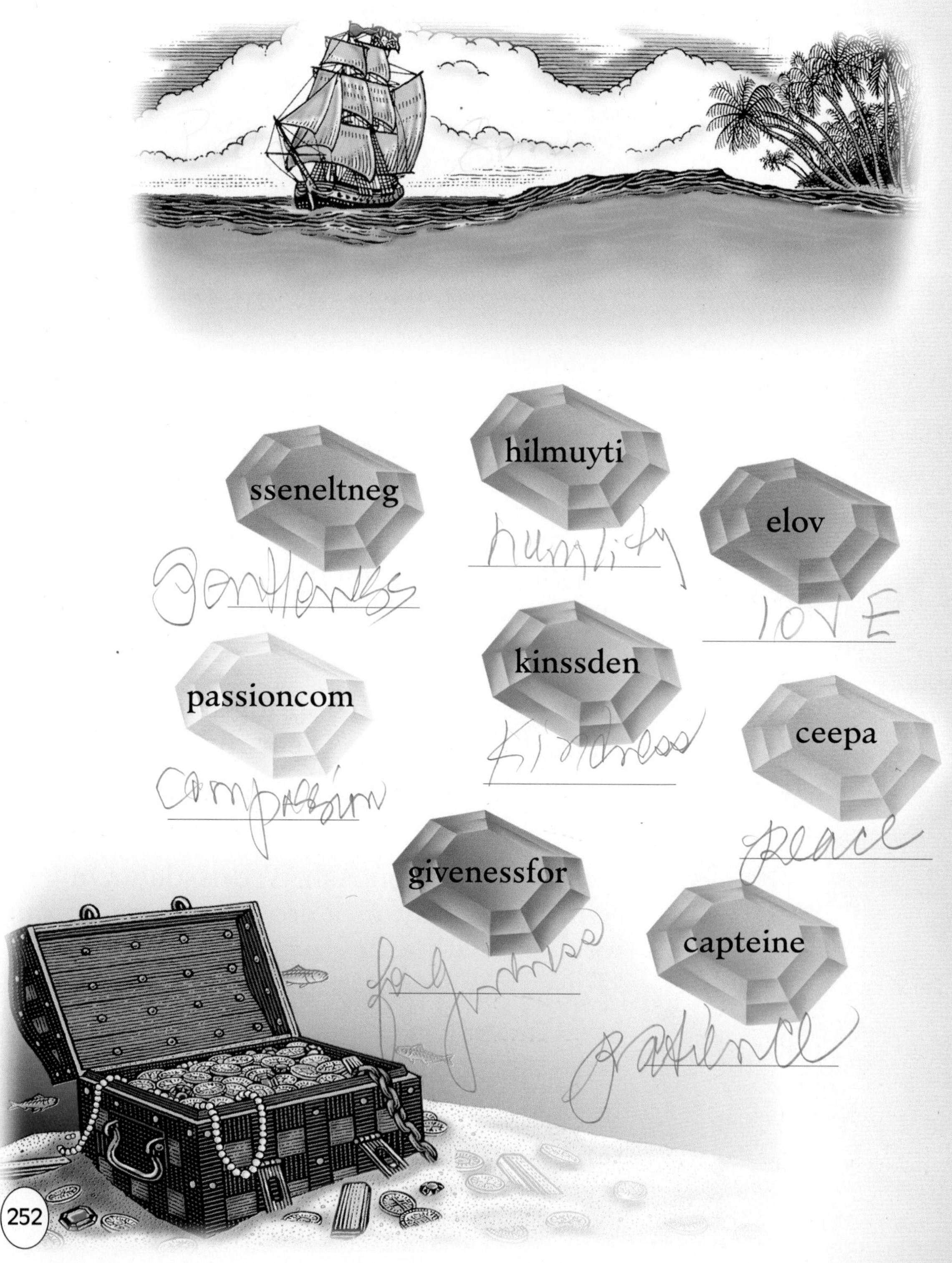

The Second Week of Lent

Faith Focus

How does celebrating Lent help us become forgiving people?

The Word of the Lord

These are the Gospel readings for the Second Sunday of Lent. Choose this year's reading and find it in a Bible. Read and discuss the reading with your family.

Year A:
Matthew 17:1–9

Year B:
Mark 9:2–10

Year C:
Luke 9:28–36

Celebrate Forgiveness

Have you ever started out for someplace and suddenly realized you were going in the wrong direction? What did you do?

When we sin, we are going in the wrong direction. We need to stop doing those things that lead us away from God.

Lent is the season of the Church's year that reminds us about forgiveness. It is a time of the year to check on the direction we are going. At Mass we pray the words, "Forgive us our trespasses as we forgive those who trespass against us, and lead us not into temptation, but deliver us from evil." We ask God to help us live as he wants us to live.

During Lent we are also invited to participate in the celebration of the sacrament of Reconciliation. We confess our sins and ask God to forgive us and help us live the Gospel better.

Celebrate Forgiveness

Doing this activity will help you prepare to celebrate the sacrament of Reconciliation. Write your responses on the lines.

Greeting

The priest greets us with joy. He shares God's words of forgiveness from the Bible. My favorite Bible story of forgiveness is

Prodigal Son

____.

Confession and Prayer of Sorrow

We tell our sins to the priest. The priest gives us a penance. We say a prayer that tells God we are sorry for our sins.

Write a short prayer of sorrow.

____

____

____

Absolution

The priest says a prayer of forgiveness. Our sins are forgiven by God. We are reconciled with God and the Church.

Praise and Dismissal

Our celebration ends with a prayer of praise. We are sent forth to be forgiving people.

Write your own short prayer of praise.

____

____

____

Faith Focus

What does it mean to say Christians are a people of prayer?

The Word of the Lord

These are the Gospel readings for the Third Sunday of Lent. Choose this year's reading and find it in a Bible. Read and discuss the reading with your family.

Year A:
John 4:5–42 or
John 4:5–15, 19–26, 39, 40–44

Year B:
John 2:13–25

Year C:
Luke 13:1–9

Pray Always

No matter when you pray or why you pray, prayer is important. Why is that? Prayer is taking the time to tell God about your life and your needs.

Jesus taught his followers to be people of prayer. The early Christians listened to Jesus. The Acts of the Apostles tells us that they went to the Temple and joined with other Jewish people in the early morning and in the evening. Christians also gathered in their homes at certain times during the day to pray.

Today the Church continues to pray all during the day. This daily prayer of the Church is called the Liturgy of the Hours. Light and hope fill the Church's Morning Prayer. Quiet and peace mark the Church's Evening Prayer.

Lent is a special time for us to remember that we are a people of prayer. We try to remember to pray throughout our day.

Jesus praying

Morning Prayer

Pray this prayer with your family in the morning.

ALL: **Lord, open my lips. And my mouth shall proclaim your praise.**

LEADER: Come, let us worship the Lord, our God.

ALL: **Glory be to the Father, and to the Son, and to the Holy Spirit; as it was in the beginning, is now, and will be for ever. Amen.**

READER 1: Let us pray for peace in the world.

ALL: **Lord, hear our prayer.**

READER 2: Let us pray for all who are fasting and praying during Lent.

ALL: **Lord, hear our prayer.**

READER 3: Let us pray that our own prayers and good works during Lent will prepare us for Easter.

ALL: **Lord, hear our prayer.**

LEADER: Hear our prayer. Strengthen us in faith and hope. Enliven us with love. We ask this in Jesus' name.

ALL: **Amen.**

Faith Focus

What did Jesus say about sharing our blessings with others?

The Word of the Lord

These are the Gospel readings for the Fourth Sunday of Lent. Choose this year's reading and find it in a Bible. Read and discuss the reading with your family.

Year A:
John 9:1–41 or
John 9:1, 6–9, 13–17, 34–38

Year B:
John 3:14–21

Year C:
Luke 15:1–3, 11–32

A Cheerful Giver

We like people to praise us. We like compliments too. Sometimes when we do something nice, we like people to notice our good deed.

During Lent we may fast, or "give things up." This special deed, or good work, helps us remember that all our blessings are gifts from God. Jesus told us not to show off when we fast. He said that God sees the good we do. No one else needs to know about it.

During Lent the Church invites us to share our blessings with others. We especially share them with people who are in need. By sharing our blessings with others, we follow the example of Jesus.

Jesus said to look bright and happy, not gloomy and sad, when we do these things. The Apostle Paul explained this teaching of Jesus. Paul wrote, "God loves a cheerful giver" (2 Corinthians 9:7).

Jesus taught that we are to share our blessings with others quietly. We should not look for praise from people who see us doing these good deeds.

Cheer Up!

Read Matthew 6:1–4, 16–18. Illustrate the meaning of one of the verses. Write the verse below your drawing.

The Fifth Week of Lent

Faith Focus

What gift did Jesus give his followers?

The Word of the Lord

These are the Gospel readings for the Fifth Sunday of Lent. Choose this year's reading and find it in a Bible. Read and discuss the reading with your family.

Year A:
John 11:1–45 or
John 11:3–7, 17, 20–27, 33–45

Year B:
John 12:20–33

Year C:
John 8:1–11

The Gift of Peace

When Jesus began his public ministry, he told his followers, "Blessed are the peacemakers, / for they will be called children of God" (Matthew 5:9).

On the night before he died, Jesus offered his followers a gift. He said, "Peace I leave with you; my peace I give to you" (John 14:27). On the first Easter evening when the Risen Jesus appeared to his Apostles, he also said, "Peace be with you" (John 20:19).

All of Jesus' followers must share this gift of peace. Pope Paul VI reminded us that when we treat others justly and fairly, peace follows. He said, "If you want peace, work for justice." Justice means being fair and treating others as our equals.

Lent is a special time to live as peacemakers. We share Jesus' gift of peace with others by treating people justly and fairly.

Peace and Justice

Read these situations. Choose one and describe how you can work peacefully with others to solve it.

Problems:

1. Older students keep teasing younger students in the hallway.
2. The playground equipment at school has been broken. Recess has been cancelled.

Palm Sunday of the Lord's Passion

Faith Focus

What does the Church remember and celebrate on the Sunday that begins Holy Week?

The Word of the Lord

These are the Gospel readings for Palm Sunday of the Lord's Passion. Choose this year's reading and find it in a Bible. Read and discuss the reading with your family.

Year A:
Matthew 26:14–27:66 or
Matthew 27:11–54

Year B:
Mark 14:1–15:47 or
Mark 15:1–39

Year C:
Luke 22:14–23:56 or
Luke 23:1–49

Hosanna!

When you have a birthday party, you need to prepare for it in many ways. You have to decide on a time to have the party, and who to invite. Will a cake be baked or ordered?

Once when it was time to celebrate Passover, Jesus sent his disciples to Jerusalem to prepare for the celebration. They went to Jerusalem ahead of Jesus and made all the preparations.

Today on Palm Sunday of the Lord's Passion, we gather near the entrance of the church to prepare for our celebration. We are given palm branches to use in the celebration.

The priest wearing red vestments and the other ministers join us. The palm branches are blessed. Holding them in our hands we walk in procession into the church while singing, "Hosanna to the Son of David; / blessed is he who comes in the name of the Lord" (Matthew 21:9).

Palm Sunday is the beginning of Holy Week. It is the day on which the Church celebrates Jesus' entry into Jerusalem to celebrate Passover. Our celebration of Palm Sunday prepares us for our celebration of the Easter Triduum, the last three days of Holy Week.

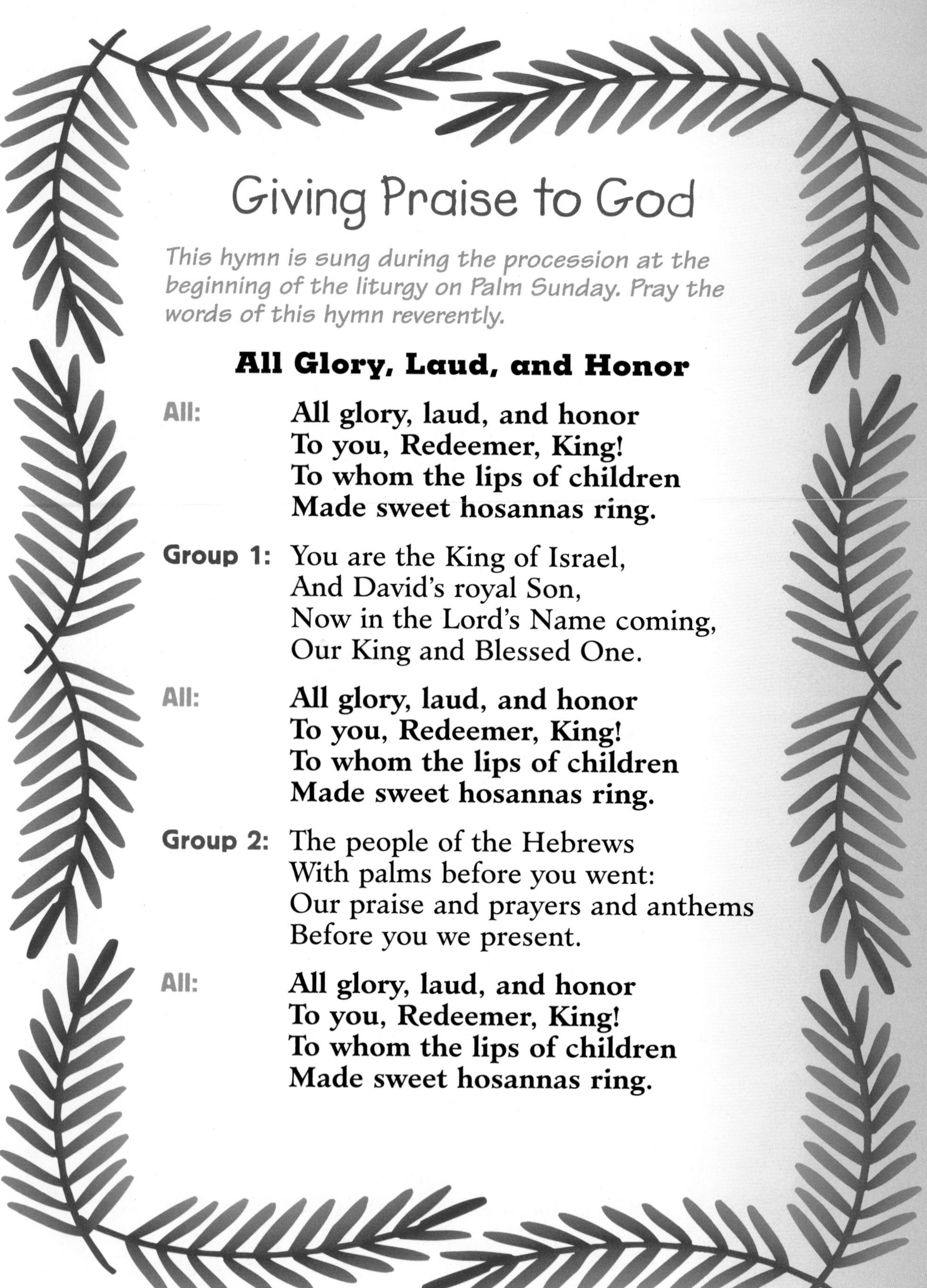

Giving Praise to God

This hymn is sung during the procession at the beginning of the liturgy on Palm Sunday. Pray the words of this hymn reverently.

All Glory, Laud, and Honor

All: **All glory, laud, and honor**
To you, Redeemer, King!
To whom the lips of children
Made sweet hosannas ring.

Group 1: You are the King of Israel,
And David's royal Son,
Now in the Lord's Name coming,
Our King and Blessed One.

All: **All glory, laud, and honor**
To you, Redeemer, King!
To whom the lips of children
Made sweet hosannas ring.

Group 2: The people of the Hebrews
With palms before you went:
Our praise and prayers and anthems
Before you we present.

All: **All glory, laud, and honor**
To you, Redeemer, King!
To whom the lips of children
Made sweet hosannas ring.

Faith Focus

What do we remember on Holy Thursday?

The Word of the Lord

These are the three Scripture readings for Mass on Holy Thursday evening. Choose one of the readings and find it in a Bible. Read and discuss the reading with your family.

First Reading:
Exodus 12:1–8, 11–14

Second Reading:
1 Corinthians 11:23–26

Gospel: John 13:1–15

What You See

Members representing the assembly come forth. The priest pours water over their feet and dries them. This reminds us that Jesus washed the disciples' feet at the Last Supper. By doing this, Jesus taught us to serve one another.

Holy Thursday

We all have favorite memories of events and celebrations. *Triduum* is a word the Church uses for the last three days of Holy Week. The three celebrations of the Triduum are Holy Thursday, Good Friday, and Easter.

The Last Supper

On Holy Thursday we remember the last time Jesus shared a meal with his disciples. Together they celebrated Passover.

During the Passover meal bread and wine were shared. When Jesus shared the bread and wine at the Last Supper, he gave it a new meaning. He took bread, said the blessing prayer, and broke the bread, and said, "This is my body, which will be given for you" (Luke 22:19). After the meal he shared the cup of wine and said, "This cup is the new covenant in my blood, which will be shed for you" (Luke 22:20).

Jesus commanded the Apostles to share this meal with one another. He said, "[D]o this in memory of me" (Luke 22:19). The Church follows Jesus' command each time we celebrate the Eucharist.

Holy Thursday

The words in the word bank are hidden in the puzzle. Circle them. Then use some of the words to write a sentence about Holy Thursday.

Triduum	**Holy Thursday**	**Good Friday**
Easter	**Passover**	**Lord's Supper**

H	X	T	U	E	L	Q	R	D	L	Y	G
Q	O	V	K	E	A	S	T	E	R	X	O
B	C	L	D	R	P	G	H	Q	S	V	O
Q	D	V	Y	S	R	D	M	T	S	S	D
L	V	Y	E	T	R	I	D	U	U	M	F
P	Z	C	X	M	H	Y	A	O	O	T	R
R	O	S	D	L	D	U	W	Y	R	V	I
P	A	S	S	O	V	E	R	L	E	O	D
B	L	K	I	B	O	S	X	S	A	I	A
A	M	V	A	E	X	R	L	H	D	B	Y
V	X	Q	P	V	Y	T	T	L	X	A	V
L	O	R	D	S	S	U	P	P	E	R	Y

____

____

Triduum/Good Friday

Faith Focus

What does the Church remember and celebrate on Good Friday?

The Word of the Lord

These are the three Scripture readings for Good Friday. Choose one of the readings and find it in the Bible. Read and discuss the reading with your family.

First Reading:
Isaiah 52:13–53:12

Second Reading:
Hebrews 4:14–16, 5:7–9

Gospel:
John 18:1–19:42

Celebrating the Lord's Passion

On Good Friday we celebrate the Passion and death of Jesus. No Mass is celebrated anywhere. Our celebration on Good Friday is made up of three parts: the Liturgy of the Word, the Veneration of the Cross, and Holy Communion.

The priest begins with a prayer asking God to watch over us and make us holy. Next we listen to the readings from the Old Testament and the New Testament. Then the Passion of Jesus is read from the Gospel according to John.

Next we join the priest in praying for the Church and its leaders, the people who are preparing for Baptism, and for all people who need our prayers.

After the Liturgy of the Word, the deacon or priest enters the church holding the cross up high. Three times he sings out loud, "This is the wood of the cross." We answer, "Come, let us worship." Then we are invited to walk up to the cross and show our reverence for it.

Now the altar is prepared and we are invited to receive Holy Communion. When our celebration ends we leave the church in silence. We thank God for his great love for us.

Venerating the cross during the Good Friday liturgy

We Celebrate Good Friday

On the line under each sentence write the part of the Good Friday liturgy it describes.

Liturgy of the Word **Holy Communion**
Veneration of the Cross

1. We listen to the Passion of Jesus read from the Gospel according to John.

   ____

2. The deacon or priest sings, "This is the wood of the cross."

   ____

3. We pray for all people who need our prayers.

   ____

4. We show our reverence for the cross.

   ____

5. We receive the Body and Blood of Jesus.

   ____

Faith Focus

What do we remember and celebrate at the Easter Vigil and on Easter Sunday?

The Word of the Lord

These are the Gospel readings for Mass on Easter Sunday. Choose this year's reading and find it in a Bible. Read and discuss the reading with your family.

Years A, B, and C:
John 20:1–9 or
Matthew 28:1–10 or
Luke 24:13–35

The Resurrection

Celebrating Easter

Easter is a special day for Christians. Some families decorate their homes with flowers. Christians around the world celebrate Easter in a special way! It is the most important season of the Church's year.

The Church invites us to celebrate joyfully the seven Sundays of the Easter season. The Church celebrates Easter for fifty days. Each of its seven Sundays recalls the new life Jesus won for us.

Throughout the Easter season, we sing and proclaim out loud for all to hear over and over *Alleluia*. *Alleluia* means "Praise the Lord!" We also remember Easter Sunday as a special day. To celebrate our joy, we sing, "This is the day the Lord has made; let us rejoice and be glad."

He Is Risen!

Pray this hymn that we sing at Mass on Easter Sunday. Decorate the border with Easter colors.

All: **Christians, to the Paschal Victim**
offer your thankful praise!

Group 1: A Lamb the sheep redeems:
Christ who only is sinless,
Reconciles sinners
to the Father. . . .

All: **Christians, to the Paschal Victim**
offer your thankful praise!

Group 2: Speak, Mary, declaring
What you saw, wayfaring.
"The tomb of Christ, who is living,
The glory of Jesus'
resurrection. . . ."

All: **Christians, to the Paschal Victim**
offer your thankful praise!

Group 3: Christ indeed from death is risen,
our new life obtaining;
Have mercy, victor King,
ever reigning!

All: **Amen. Alleluia.**

Faith Focus

How does celebrating Easter strengthen us to live as peacemakers?

The Word of the Lord

This is the Gospel reading for the Second Sunday of Easter. Find it in a Bible and read and discuss it with your family.

Years A, B, and C:
John 20:19–31

What You See

White, a symbol of joy, is worn by the priest during the Easter season.

Rejoice, the Lord Is Risen

On the first Easter day, Jesus appeared to his disciples. He came to them with a message of peace. He greeted them, saying, "Peace be with you" (Luke 24:36). Jesus gave us the gift of peace. We rejoice in his gift.

The great Easter Proclamation we sing at the Easter Vigil is called the Exultet. This Latin word means "rejoice." At the end of this great song of rejoicing, we say, "Christ . . . came back from the dead to shed his peaceful light on all mankind." We pray that Christ will shed a peaceful light over our world today.

The Church shares Jesus' gift and message of peace with all people. Each time we celebrate the Eucharist, the priest says, "The peace of the Lord be with you always." We respond, "And also with you." Then we are invited to offer one another a sign of the peace of Christ. As followers of Jesus, we commit ourselves to live as peacemakers.

Modern fishing boat on the Sea of Galilee

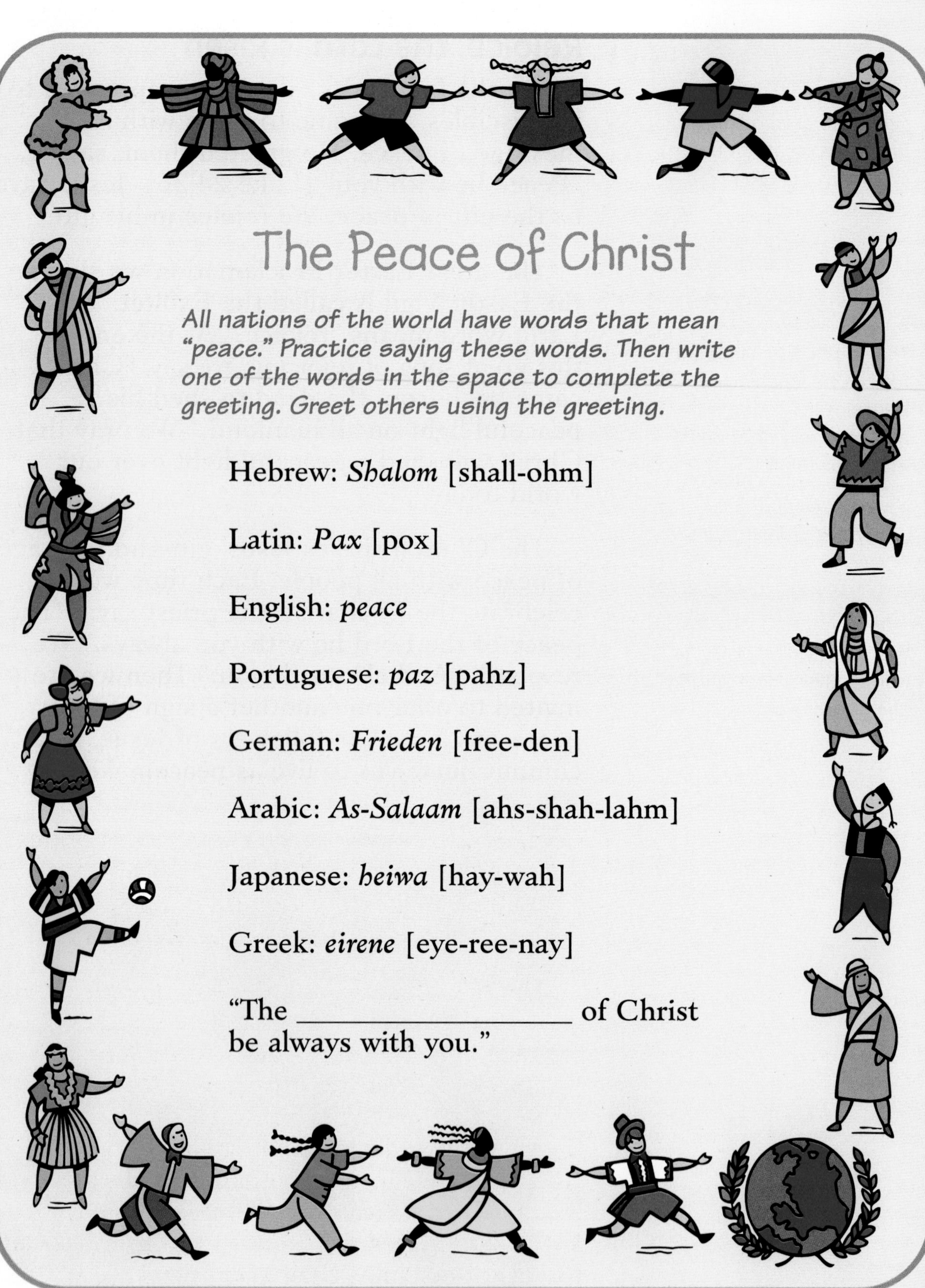

The Peace of Christ

All nations of the world have words that mean "peace." Practice saying these words. Then write one of the words in the space to complete the greeting. Greet others using the greeting.

Hebrew: *Shalom* [shall-ohm]

Latin: *Pax* [pox]

English: *peace*

Portuguese: *paz* [pahz]

German: *Frieden* [free-den]

Arabic: *As-Salaam* [ahs-shah-lahm]

Japanese: *heiwa* [hay-wah]

Greek: *eirene* [eye-ree-nay]

"The ____________________ of Christ be always with you."

The Third Week of Easter

Faith Focus

When did the disciples recognize the Risen Jesus?

The Word of the Lord

These are the Gospel readings for the Third Sunday of Easter. Choose this year's reading and find it in a Bible. Read and discuss the reading with your family.

Year A:
Luke 24:13–35

Year B:
Luke 24:35–48

Year C:
John 21:1–19 or 21:1–14

The Road to Emmaus

We can recognize our mom or dad or best friend from a distance. But once Jesus' friends did not recognize Jesus after he was raised from the dead.

On the day of the Resurrection, as two of Jesus' disciples were walking from Jerusalem to Emmaus, they did not recognize the Risen Jesus when he joined them. As they walked, they shared with this traveler the stories other disciples of Jesus had told them about Jesus' death and Resurrection. The Risen Jesus then began explaining the Scriptures to them. They were amazed at all he knew.

The two disciples and the Risen Jesus finally arrived at Emmaus, and they invited Jesus to stay with them. There they shared a meal. When Jesus took the bread, said the blessing prayer, and broke the bread to share it with them, the two disciples immediately realized it was the Risen Jesus who had joined them on the road. Then Jesus suddenly disappeared and the disciples ran back to Jerusalem to tell the other disciples their good news.

Helping Others Recognize Jesus

The disciples traveling to Emmaus recognized the Risen Jesus when he broke the bread and shared it with them. In what other ways can we help people know that the Risen Jesus is with us? Clue: Read Matthew 25:35–40.

Faith Focus

Why did Jesus' disciples proclaim the good news of Jesus' death and Resurrection?

The Word of the Lord

These are the Gospel readings for the Fourth Sunday of Easter. Choose this year's reading and find it in a Bible. Read and discuss the reading with your family.

Year A:
John 10:1–10

Year B:
John 10:11–18

Year C:
John 10:27–30

Proclaim the Good News

When we have good news, we cannot wait to pass it on. Jesus' followers could not wait to pass on the good news of Jesus' death and Resurrection.

After his Resurrection the Risen Jesus appeared to his disciples and told them to invite others to become his disciples. He commanded them to baptize people in the name of the Father, and of the Son, and of the Holy Spirit.

The Apostles did as the Risen Jesus commanded. They boldly proclaimed the good news of Jesus' death and Resurrection. They invited others to change their ways and follow the way of Jesus.

The first followers of Jesus were called people of "the Way" (Acts 24:14). Day by day the number of followers grew. Soon they were given the name *Christian.* This means "a follower of Christ."

Many people came to believe and follow Jesus because they saw the faith, hope, and love of the early Christians.

Proclaiming the Good News

Think about some of the people you know or have read about who have helped you come to know Jesus better. Tell their story here.

The Fifth Week of Easter

Faith Focus

How should we show our love for one another?

The Word of the Lord

These are the Gospel readings for the Fifth Sunday of Easter. Choose this year's reading and find it in a Bible. Read and discuss the reading with your family.

Year A:
John 14:1–12

Year B:
John 15:1–8

Year C:
John 13:31–35

Love One Another

Family members show their love for each other by words and actions. We say, "I love you," "I forgive you," "I'm proud of you." We pray together and help each other.

Throughout his life on earth, Jesus often emphasized how important it is that we love one another. On the night before he died, Jesus told his disciples, "[L]ove one another. As I have loved you, so you also should love one another" (John 13:34). We call this the New Commandment.

The early Christians took the New Commandment very seriously. This is one of the reasons the early Church grew.

We show our love to one another as the early Christians did. We forgive one another. We take care of those who are in need. We pray for one another. We bring the healing presence of Christ to those who are sick and troubled. As the early Christians did, we love one another not just by talking about Jesus but by living as he taught us to do.

An Act of Love

Leader: Jesus taught that we are to live as his disciples and not merely talk about what it means to be a Christian. Let us listen to what John the Apostle teaches.

Reader: A reading from the First Letter of John.
Read 1 John 3:18–24.
The word of the Lord.

All: **Thanks be to God.**

Leader: Let us think about the reading.

All: *Think about ways to live the message of the reading.*

Leader: Let us conclude by praying an act of love.

All: **O my God,**
I love you above all things
with my whole heart and soul,
because you are all-good
and worthy of all my love.
I love my neighbor as myself
for the love of you.
I forgive all who have injured me
and ask pardon of all whom
I have injured. Amen.

The Sixth Week of Easter

Faith Focus

How can we show others we are followers of Christ?

The Word of the Lord

These are the Gospel readings for the Sixth Sunday of Easter. Choose this year's reading and find it in a Bible. Read and discuss the reading with your family.

Year A:
John 14:15–21

Year B:
John 15:9–17

Year C:
John 14:23–29

Faith in Action

When have you been an eyewitness to an important event? What was it like?

The Apostles were eyewitnesses to the events of Jesus' life on earth. The Risen Jesus appeared to Peter and to the other Apostles and then to as many as 500 others. This so changed their lives that after Jesus' return to his Father, they spent their whole life telling others that Jesus died for our sins and was raised to new life on the third day.

The Letter of James in the New Testament reminds us that we can witness to the new life of Jesus by our good works. We show our faith by what we do. We cannot just say, "Go in peace, keep warm, and eat well" (James 2:16). We must help people who are in need of food or clothing.

We are to be witnesses to our Risen Lord. On the Sixth Sunday of Easter the Church reminds us that the Holy Spirit, the Advocate, is with us. The Holy Spirit helps us witness to our faith in Jesus.

Putting Our Faith into Action

For each letter in the word WITNESS, write a word from the lesson or another word of your own. Use the word you write to show how you can put your faith in Jesus into action.

The Seventh Week of Easter

Faith Focus

How does the Church honor Mary during the Easter season?

The Word of the Lord

These are the Gospel readings for the Seventh Sunday of Easter. Choose this year's reading and find it in a Bible. Read and discuss the reading with your family.

Year A:
John 17:1–11

Year B:
John 17:11–19

Year C:
John 17:20–26

Mary, Queen of Heaven and Earth

Rejoice, Mary!

Your parents share their lives with you. Imagine how Mary felt when she learned that Jesus had been raised from the dead. All during the Easter season we share in the great joy that Mary must have felt.

Mary showed her love for God in many ways. We remember that Mary said yes to God at the Annunciation. Mary was with Jesus when he changed water into wine. Later, Jesus said that Mary was blessed because she heard and kept God's word. When Jesus died on the cross, Mary was there. Mary now shares in the joy of life everlasting with her son in heaven.

All during the Easter season, we share in the great joy that filled Mary's heart when she saw her Risen Son, Jesus. We rejoice with Mary and pray:

Rejoice and be glad, O Virgin Mary,
alleluia!
For the Lord has truly risen, alleluia.

Mother of Jesus, Mother of God

Look up and read in a Bible one of these stories: Luke 1:26–38, Luke 2:1–7, 15–20, John 2:1–12, John 19:23–27, Acts of the Apostles 1:13–14. In the space draw or write about the story you chose. Retell the story to a friend or member of your family.

Faith Focus

What do Christians remember and celebrate on Pentecost?

The Word of the Lord

These are the Gospel readings for Pentecost. Choose this year's reading and find it in a Bible. Read and discuss the reading with your family.

Year A:
John 7:37–39
John 20:19–23

Year B:
John 7:37–39 or
John 15:26–27, 16:12–15

Year C:
John 7:37–39 or
John 14:15–16, 23–26

Dove, one of the symbols the Church uses for the Holy Spirit

The Gift of the Holy Spirit

Sometimes we hear a person speak a language we do not know. We wish we could understand.

On Pentecost, fifty days after Jesus' Resurrection, people from many places and who spoke many languages were in Jerusalem. On that day, Mary and the disciples were praying together in an upstairs room in the city of Jerusalem. Suddenly, a great wind roared through the room. Tongues of fire rested over their heads. They were filled with the Holy Spirit.

Then Peter, filled with courage, went out and addressed the crowds in the streets. He proclaimed the good news of Jesus' death and Resurrection. Everyone heard Peter in their own language and understood his message! When they asked Peter what they should do, Peter told them to change their ways and be baptized.

On Pentecost Sunday we remember that we too are filled with the Holy Spirit. We proclaim the good news of Jesus' death and Resurrection. We do this by our good, helpful, loving acts toward others.

The Work of the Holy Spirit

Solve the code to tell what happened on Pentecost.

A	B	C	D	E	F	G	H	I	J	K	L	M
1	2	3	4	5	6	7	8	9	10	11	12	13

N	O	P	Q	R	S	T	U	V	W	X	Y	Z
14	15	16	17	18	19	20	21	22	23	24	25	26

On the day of Pentecost, the

___ ___ ___ ___ ___ ___ ___ ___ were filled with
1 16 15 19 20 12 5 19

the ___ ___ ___ ___ ___ ___ ___ ___ ___ ___.
8 15 12 25 19 16 9 18 9 20

___ ___ ___ ___ ___ ___ people from many countries
10 5 23 9 19 8

heard the ___ ___ ___ ___ of the ___ ___ ___ ___
23 15 18 4 12 15 18 4

in their own native language. Thousands were

___ ___ ___ ___ ___ ___ ___ ___. They became
2 1 16 20 9 26 5 4

followers of ___ ___ ___ ___ ___ that day.
10 5 19 21 19

BASED ON ACTS OF THE APOSTLES 2:1, 4–6, 41

Catholic Prayers and Practices

Sign of the Cross

In the name of the Father,
and of the Son,
and of the Holy Spirit. Amen.

Glory Prayer

Glory to the Father,
and to the Son,
and to the Holy Spirit:
as it was in the beginning, is now,
and will be for ever. Amen.

Lord's Prayer

Our Father, who art in heaven,
hallowed be thy name;
thy kingdom come;
thy will be done on earth
as it is in heaven.
Give us this day our daily bread;
and forgive us our trespasses
as we forgive those who trespass
against us;
and lead us not into temptation,
but deliver us from evil.
Amen.

Prayer to the Holy Spirit

Come, Holy Spirit, fill the hearts
of your faithful.
And kindle in them the
fire of your love.
Send forth your Spirit and
they shall be created.
And you will renew the
face of the earth.

Hail Mary

Hail Mary, full of grace,
the Lord is with you!
Blessed are you among women,
and blessed is the fruit
of your womb, Jesus.
Holy Mary, Mother of God,
pray for us sinners,
now and at the hour of our death.
Amen.

Act of Contrition

My God,
I am sorry for my sins
with all my heart.
In choosing to do wrong
and failing to do good,
I have sinned against you
whom I should love above all things.
I firmly intend, with your help,
to do penance,
to sin no more,
and to avoid whatever leads me to sin.
Our Savior Jesus Christ
suffered and died for us.
In his name, my God, have mercy.

Apostles' Creed

I believe in God,
the Father almighty,
creator of heaven and earth.

I believe in Jesus Christ,
his only Son, our Lord.
He was conceived by the power
of the Holy Spirit
and born of the Virgin Mary.
He suffered under Pontius Pilate,
was crucified, died, and was buried.
He descended to the dead.
On the third day he rose again.
He ascended into heaven,
and is seated at the right hand
of the Father.
He will come again to judge
the living and the dead.

I believe in the Holy Spirit,
the holy catholic Church,
the communion of saints,
the forgiveness of sins,
the resurrection of the body,
and the life everlasting. Amen.

Nicene Creed

We believe in one God,
the Father, the Almighty,
maker of heaven and earth,
of all that is, seen and unseen.

We believe in one Lord, Jesus Christ,
the only Son of God,
eternally begotten of the Father,
God from God, Light from Light,
true God from true God,
begotten, not made, one in Being
with the Father.
Through him all things were made.
For us men and for our salvation
he came down from heaven:

by the power of the Holy Spirit
he was born of the Virgin Mary, and
became man.

For our sake he was crucified under
Pontius Pilate;
he suffered, died, and was buried.
On the third day he rose again
in fulfillment of the Scriptures;
he ascended into heaven
and is seated at the right hand
of the Father.
He will come again in glory to judge
the living and the dead,
and his kingdom will have no end.

We believe in the Holy Spirit, the Lord,
the giver of life,
who proceeds from the Father
and the Son.
With the Father and the Son he is
worshiped and glorified.
He has spoken through the Prophets.
We believe in one holy catholic and
apostolic Church.
We acknowledge one baptism for
the forgiveness of sins.
We look for the resurrection
of the dead,
and the life of the world to come.
Amen.

Morning Prayer

Dear God,
as I begin this day,
keep me in your love and care.
Help me to live as your child today.
Bless me, my family, and my friends
in all we do.
Keep us all close to you. Amen.

Grace Before Meals

Bless us, O Lord,
and these your gifts
which we are about to receive
from your goodness.
Through Christ our Lord.
Amen.

Grace After Meals

We give you thanks for all your gifts,
almighty God,
living and reigning now and for ever.
Amen.

Evening Prayer

Dear God,
I thank you for today.
Keep me safe throughout the night.
Thank you for all the good I did today.
I am sorry for what I have chosen
to do wrong.
Bless my family and friends. Amen.

A Vocation Prayer

God, I know you will call me
for special work in my life.
Help me follow Jesus each day
and be ready to answer your call.

The Angelus

Leader: The angel spoke God's message to Mary,
Response: and she conceived of the Holy Spirit.
All: Hail, Mary . . .

Leader: "I am the lowly servant of the Lord:
Response: let it be done to me according to your word."
All: Hail, Mary . . .

Leader: And the Word became flesh
Response: and lived among us.
All: Hail, Mary . . .

Leader: Pray for us, holy Mother of God,
Response: that we may become worthy of the promises of Christ.

Leader: Let us pray. Lord, fill our hearts with your grace: once, through the message of an angel you revealed to us the incarnation of your Son; now, through his suffering and death lead us to the glory of his resurrection. We ask this through Christ our Lord.
All: Amen.

The Beatitudes

"Blessed are the poor in spirit,
for theirs is the kingdom of heaven.
Blessed are they who mourn,
for they will be comforted.
Blessed are the meek,
for they will inherit the land.
Blessed are they who hunger
and thirst for righteousness,
for they will be satisfied.
Blessed are the merciful,
for they will be shown mercy.
Blessed are the clean of heart,
for they will see God.
Blessed are the peacemakers,
for they will be called children of God.
Blessed are they who are
persecuted for the
sake of righteousness,
for theirs is the kingdom of heaven.

"Blessed are you when they insult you and persecute you and utter every kind of evil against you [falsely] because of me. Rejoice and be glad, for your reward will be great in heaven."

MATTHEW 5:3–12

Corporal Works of Mercy

Feed people who are hungry.
Give drink to people who are thirsty.
Clothe people who need clothes.
Visit prisoners.
Shelter people who are homeless.
Visit people who are sick.
Bury people who have died.

Spiritual Works of Mercy

Help people who sin.
Teach people who are ignorant.
Give advice to people
who have doubts.
Comfort people who suffer.
Be patient with other people.
Forgive people who hurt you.
Pray for people who are alive and for
those who have died.

The Ten Commandments

1. I am the LORD your God: you shall not have strange gods before me.
2. You shall not take the name of the LORD your God in vain.
3. Remember to keep holy the LORD's Day.
4. Honor your father and your mother.
5. You shall not kill.
6. You shall not commit adultery.
7. You shall not steal.
8. You shall not bear false witness against your neighbor.
9. You shall not covet your neighbor's wife.
10. You shall not covet your neighbor's goods.

BASED ON EXODUS 20:3, 7–17

Precepts of the Church

1. Participate in Mass on Sundays and holy days of obligation and rest from unnecessary work.
2. Confess sins at least once a year.
3. Receive Holy Communion at least during the Easter season.
4. Observe the prescribed days of fasting and abstinence.
5. Provide for the material needs of the Church, according to one's abilities.

The Great Commandment

"You shall love the Lord,
your God, with all your
heart, with all your soul,
and with all your mind. . . .
You shall love your neighbor as yourself."

MATTHEW 22:37, 39

Rosary

Catholics pray the rosary to honor Mary and remember the important events in the life of Jesus and Mary. There are twenty mysteries of the rosary. Follow the steps from 1 to 5.

1. Make the Sign of the Cross and pray the Apostles' Creed.
2. Pray an Our Father, 3 Hail Marys, and the Glory Prayer.
3. Think of the first mystery. Pray an Our Father, 10 Hail Marys, and the Glory Prayer.
4. Repeat step 3 for each of the next 4 mysteries.
5. Pray the Hail, Holy Queen prayer. Make the Sign of the Cross.

Joyful Mysteries

1. The Annunciation
2. The Visitation
3. The Nativity
4. The Presentation
5. The Finding of Jesus in the Temple

Mysteries of Light

1. The Baptism of Jesus in the Jordan River
2. The Miracle at the Wedding at Cana
3. The Proclamation of the Kingdom of God
4. The Transfiguration of Jesus
5. The Institution of the Eucharist

Sorrowful Mysteries

1. The Agony in the Garden
2. The Scourging at the Pillar
3. The Crowning with Thorns
4. The Carrying of the Cross
5. The Crucifixion

Glorious Mysteries

1. The Resurrection
2. The Ascension
3. The Coming of the Holy Spirit
4. The Assumption of Mary
5. The Coronation of Mary

Hail, Holy Queen

Hail, holy Queen, mother of mercy,
hail, our life, our sweetness,
and our hope.
To you we cry, the children of Eve;
to you we send up our sighs,
mourning and weeping
in this land of exile.
Turn, then, most gracious advocate,
your eyes of mercy toward us;
lead us home at last
and show us the blessed fruit
of your womb, Jesus:
O clement, O loving, O sweet
Virgin Mary.

Stations of the Cross

1. Jesus is condemned to death.

2. Jesus accepts his cross.

3. Jesus falls the first time.

4. Jesus meets his mother.

5. Simon helps Jesus carry the cross.

6. Veronica wipes the face of Jesus.

7. Jesus falls the second time.

8. Jesus meets the women.

9. Jesus falls the third time.

10. Jesus is stripped of his clothes.

11. Jesus is nailed to the cross.

12. Jesus dies on the cross.

13. Jesus is taken down from the cross.

14. Jesus is buried in the tomb.

Some parishes conclude the Stations by reflecting on the Resurrection of Jesus.

The Seven Sacraments

Jesus gave the Church the seven sacraments. The sacraments are the main liturgical signs of the Church. They make the Paschal Mystery of Jesus, who is always the main celebrant of each sacrament, present to us. They make us sharers in the saving work of Christ and in the life of the Holy Trinity.

Sacraments of Initiation

Baptism

Through Baptism we are joined to Christ and become members of the Body of Christ, the Church. We are reborn as adopted children of God and receive the gift of the Holy Spirit. Original sin and all personal sins are forgiven.

Confirmation

Confirmation completes Baptism. In this sacrament the gift of the Holy Spirit strengthens us to live our Baptism.

Eucharist

Sharing in the Eucharist joins us most fully to Christ and to the Church. We share in the one sacrifice of Christ. The bread and wine become the Body and Blood of Christ through the power of the Holy Spirit and the words of the priest. We receive the Body and Blood of Christ.

Sacraments of Healing

Reconciliation

Through the ministry of the priest we receive forgiveness of sins committed after our Baptism. We need to confess all mortal sins.

Anointing of the Sick

Anointing of the Sick strengthens our faith and trust in God when we are seriously ill, dying, or weak because of old age.

Sacraments at the Service of Communion

Holy Orders

Through Holy Orders a baptized man is consecrated to serve the whole Church as a bishop, priest, or deacon in the name of Christ. Bishops, who are the successors of the Apostles, receive this sacrament most fully. They are consecrated to teach the Gospel, to lead the Church in the worship of God, and to guide the Church to live holy lives. Bishops are helped by priests, their coworkers, and by deacons in their work.

Matrimony

Matrimony unites a baptized man and a baptized woman in a lifelong bond of faithful love to always honor each other and to accept the gift of children from God. In this sacrament the married couple is consecrated to be a sign of God's love for the Church.

We Celebrate the Mass

The Introductory Rites

We remember that we are the community of the Church. We prepare to listen to the word of God and to celebrate the Eucharist.

The Entrance

We stand as the priest, deacon, and other ministers enter the assembly. We sing a gathering song. The priest and deacon kiss the altar. The priest then goes to the chair where he presides over the celebration.

Greeting of the Altar and of the People Gathered

The priest leads us in praying the Sign of the Cross. The priest greets us, and we say,

And also with you.

The Act of Penitence

We admit our wrongdoings. We bless God for his mercy.

The Gloria

We praise God for all the good he has done for us.

The Collect

The priest leads us in praying the Collect, or the opening prayer. We respond, "**Amen.**"

The Liturgy of the Word

God speaks to us today.
We listen and respond to God's word.

The First Reading from the Bible

We sit and listen as the reader reads from the Old Testament or from the Acts of the Apostles. The reader concludes, "The word of the Lord." We respond,

Thanks be to God.

The Responsorial Psalm

The song leader leads us in singing a psalm.

The Second Reading from the Bible

The reader reads from the New Testament, but not from the four Gospels. The reader concludes, "The word of the Lord." We respond,

Thanks be to God.

Acclamation

We stand to honor Christ present with us in the Gospel. The song leader leads us in singing **"Alleluia, Alleluia, Alleluia"** or another chant during Lent.

The Gospel

The deacon or priest proclaims, "A reading from the holy gospel according to (name of Gospel writer)." We respond,

Glory to you, O Lord.

He proclaims the Gospel. At the end, he says, "The gospel of the Lord." We respond,

Praise to you, Lord Jesus Christ.

The Homily

We sit. The priest or deacon preaches the homily. He helps the whole community understand the word of God spoken to us in the readings.

The Profession of Faith

We stand and profess our faith. We pray the Nicene Creed together.

The Prayer of the Faithful

The priest leads us in praying for our Church and its leaders, for our country and its leaders, for ourselves and others, for the sick and those who have died. We can respond to each prayer in several ways. One way we respond is,

Lord, hear our prayer.

The Liturgy of the Eucharist

We join with Jesus and the Holy Spirit to give thanks and praise to God the Father.

The Preparation of the Gifts

We sit as the altar table is prepared and the collection is taken up. We share our blessings with the community of the Church and especially with those in need. The song leader may lead us in singing a song. The gifts of bread and wine are brought to the altar.

The priest lifts up the bread and blesses God for all our gifts. He prays, "Blessed are you, Lord, God of all creation . . ."
We respond,
Blessed be God for ever.

The priest lifts up the cup of wine and prays, "Blessed are you, Lord, God of all creation . . ."
We respond,
Blessed be God for ever.

The priest invites us,
Pray, my brothers and sisters, that our sacrifice may be acceptable to God, the almighty Father.

We stand and respond,
May the Lord accept the sacrifice at your hands for the praise and glory of his name, for our good, and the good of all his Church.

The Prayer over the Offerings

The priest leads us in praying the Prayer over the Offerings. We respond, "**Amen.**"

Preface

The priest invites us to join in praying the Church's great prayer of praise and thanksgiving to God the Father.

Priest:	The Lord be with you.
Assembly:	**And also with you.**
Priest:	Lift up your hearts.
Assembly:	**We lift them up to the Lord.**
Priest:	Let us give thanks to the Lord our God.
Assembly:	**It is right to give him thanks and praise.**

After the priest sings or prays aloud the preface, we join in acclaiming,

Holy, holy, holy Lord, God of
power and might.
Heaven and earth are full of
your glory.
Hosanna in the highest.
Blessed is he who comes in
the name of the Lord.
Hosanna in the highest.

The Eucharistic Prayer

The priest leads the assembly in praying the Eucharistic Prayer. We call upon the Holy Spirit to make our gifts of bread and wine holy and that they become the Body and Blood of Jesus. We recall what happened at the Last Supper. The bread and wine become the Body and Blood of the Lord. Jesus is truly and really present under the appearances of bread and wine.

The priest sings or says aloud, "Let us proclaim the mystery of faith." We respond using this or another acclamation used by the Church,

Christ has died, Christ is risen,
Christ will come again.

The priest then prays for the Church. He prays for the living and the dead.

Doxology

The priest concludes the praying of the Eucharistic Prayer. He sings or prays aloud,

Through him, with him, in him, in the unity of the Holy Spirit, all glory and honor is yours, almighty Father, for ever and ever.

We stand and respond, "**Amen.**"

THE COMMUNION RITE

The Lord's Prayer

We pray the Lord's Prayer together.

The Rite of Peace

The priest invites us to share a sign of peace, saying, "The peace of the Lord be with you always." We respond,

And also with you.

We share a sign of peace.

The Fraction, or the Breaking of the Bread

The priest breaks the host, the consecrated bread. We sing or pray aloud,

Lamb of God, you take away
the sins of the world:
have mercy on us.
Lamb of God, you take away
the sins of the world:
have mercy on us.
Lamb of God, you take away
the sins of the world:
grant us peace.

Communion

The priest raises the host and says aloud,

This is the Lamb of God who takes away the sins of the world.
Happy are those who are called to his supper.

We join with him and say,

Lord, I am not worthy to receive you, but only say the word and I shall be healed.

The priest receives Communion. Next, the deacon and the extraordinary ministers of Holy Communion and the members of the assembly receive Communion.

The priest, deacon, or extraordinary minister of Holy Communion holds up the host. We bow and the priest, deacon, or extraordinary minister of Holy Communion says, "The body of Christ." We respond, **"Amen."** We then receive the consecrated host in our hand or on our tongue.

If we are to receive the Blood of Christ, the priest, deacon, or extraordinary minister of Holy Communion holds up the cup containing the consecrated wine. We bow and the priest, deacon, or extraordinary minister of Holy Communion says, "The blood of Christ." We respond, **"Amen."** We take the cup in our hands and drink from it.

The Prayer after Communion

We stand as the priest invites us to pray, saying, "Let us pray." He prays the Prayer after Communion. We respond, **"Amen."**

The Concluding Rites

We are sent forth to do good works, praising and blessing the Lord.

Greeting

We stand. The priest greets us as we prepare to leave. He says, "The Lord be with you." We respond,
And also with you.

Blessing

The priest or deacon may invite us, "Bow your heads and pray for God's blessing."
The priest blesses us, saying,
May almighty God bless you,
the Father, and the Son, and
the Holy Spirit.
We respond, "**Amen.**"

Dismissal of the People

The priest or deacon sends us forth, using these or similar words,
The Mass is ended, go in peace.
We respond,
Thanks be to God.

We sing a hymn. The priest and the deacon kiss the altar. The priest, deacon, and other ministers bow to the altar and leave in procession.

The Sacrament of Reconciliation

Individual Rite

Greeting

Scripture Reading

Confession of Sins and Acceptance of Penance

Act of Contrition

Absolution

Closing Prayer

Communal Rite

Greeting

Scripture Reading

Homily

Examination of Conscience with a litany of contrition and the Lord's Prayer

Individual Confession and Absolution

Closing Prayer

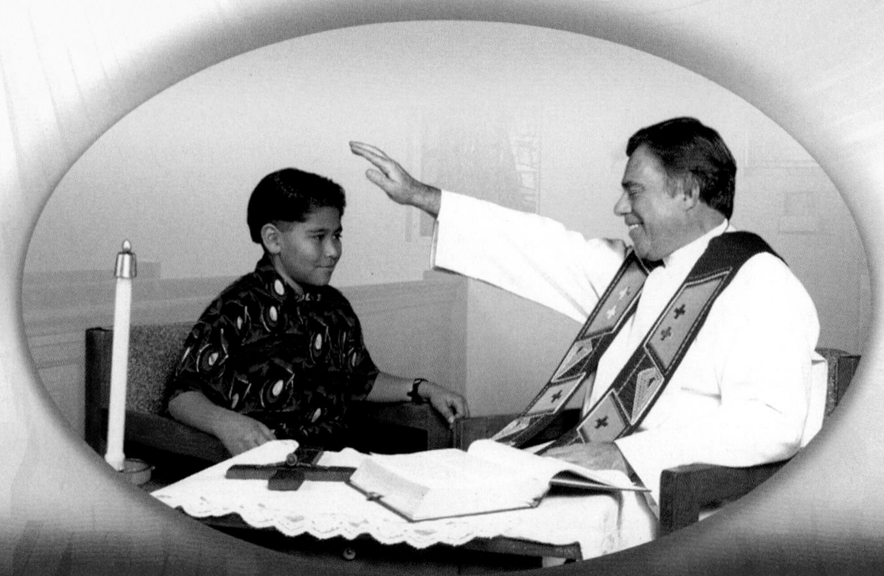

Glossary

A-B

Abba [page 39]
A word meaning "Father," which expresses the love and trust of a child for a parent.

Advocate [page 70]
A word meaning "one who speaks up for someone else," title or name Jesus used for the Holy Spirit.

Almighty [page 38]
God's power to do everything and anything good.

almsgiving [page 117]
Sharing our blessings with others, especially with people in need.

angels [page 40]
Spiritual beings, who do not have a body like humans do, and who give glory to God without stopping.

Anointing of the Sick [page 124]
The Sacrament of Healing through which we receive the grace that strengthens our faith and trust in God when we are seriously ill, weakened by old age, or dying.

Apostles [page 87]
The first shepherds of the Church, the disciples Jesus gave the responsibility and authority to baptize and to teach in his name.

Apostles' Creed [page 17]
One of the earliest creeds of the Church that names the main beliefs the Church has professed from the time of the Apostles.

Ark of the Covenant [page 30]
The decorated chest in which the Israelites kept the stone tablets on which the Ten Commandments were written.

Ascension [page 64]
The return of the Risen Jesus in glory to his Father in heaven after Jesus' work on earth had been finished forty days after the Resurrection.

Baptism [page 107]
The Sacrament of Initiation through which we are joined to Jesus Christ, become members of the Church, are reborn as adopted children of God, receive the gift of the Holy Spirit, and original sin and our personal sins are forgiven.

The words in boldface type are Faith Vocabulary words in the text.

bear false witness [page 199]
To intentionally tell a lie about someone.

Beatitudes [page 158]
The sayings or teachings of Jesus that describe real happiness, or the happiness of people blessed by God.

Bible [page 22]
The book in which the Church has collected the seventy-three holy writings, or books, inspired by God.

bishops [pages 87 and 139]
The successors of the Apostles, who under the authority of the pope and together with the pope are the chief teachers of the Church, lead us in the celebration of the sacraments, and guide us in living holy lives.

Body of Christ [page 86]
A New Testament image for the Church that teaches that the members of the Church are made one in Christ, the Head of the Church.

Body and Blood of Christ [page 108]
The Eucharist, the consecrated bread and consecrated wine that has become Jesus really and truly present by the power of the Holy Spirit and the words of the priest at Mass.

C-D

Christ [page 48]
A word meaning "Anointed One"; title for Jesus, the Anointed One of God, the Messiah.

Church [page 86]
The community of believers joined to Christ in Baptism who God has called to be the new People of God.

Communion of Saints [page 89]
All the baptized living on earth and all the faithful who have died, including the souls in purgatory and the saints in heaven.

confession [page 123]
The telling of our sins in private to a bishop or priest in the sacrament of Reconciliation.

Confession [page 123]
Another name for the sacrament of Reconciliation, or Penance.

Confirmation [page 107]
The Sacrament of Initiation that strengthens the grace of Baptism and in which we receive the gift of the Holy Spirit in a fuller way to share the good news of all that God has done for us in Jesus Christ.

conscience [page 166]
The gift God gives to every person that helps us know and judge what is right and what is wrong.

consequences [page 151]
The good and bad effects of our choices.

contemplation [page 218]
A form of prayer that does not use words and strengthens our love and friendship with God.

Corporal Works of Mercy [page 78]
Seven ways we live Jesus' command to love by helping people care for their bodily, or corporal, needs.

covenant [page 15]
A solemn agreement between human beings, or between God and human beings.

covet [page 192]
To want or desire wrongfully what belongs to someone else.

Creator [page 38]
God, who created everything and everyone, seen and unseen, out of love and without any help.

creeds [pages 17 and 212]
Symbols of faith, professions of faith, brief summaries of what the Church believes.

Crucifixion [page 63]
The putting to death of Jesus on a cross.

decalogue [page 176]
A word that means "ten words"; another name for the Ten Commandments.

deliberate actions [page 151]
Choices that we knowingly and freely make.

divine Providence [page 39]
God's caring love for us.

divine Revelation [page 14]
God making known both himself and his plan of creation and salvation for the world and all people.

domestic church [page 140]
The Christian family.

doxology [page 229]
A prayer of praise.

E-F-G-H

emotions [page 152]
Feelings inside us that have the power to influence the choices we make.

envy [page 200]
Being sad and jealous over the good things other people have.

Eucharist [page 108]
The Sacrament of Initiation in which we give praise and thanksgiving to God the Father through the power of the Holy Spirit and in which we share in the Body and Blood of Christ, who is truly and really present under the appearances of bread and wine.

Evangelists [page 24]
The writers of the four Gospels: Matthew, Mark, Luke, and John.

Exodus [page 114]
The journey of the Israelites under the leadership of Moses from slavery in Egypt to freedom in the land promised them by God.

faith [page 14]
The gift from God that helps us know him and believe in him and all that he has revealed.

free will [page 150]
The part of every person that gives us the ability to choose to love and serve God and others.

gifts of the Holy Spirit [pages 109 and 168]
Wisdom, understanding, right judgment (counsel), courage (fortitude), knowledge, reverence (piety), and wonder and awe (fear of the Lord).

gospel [page 24]
A word meaning "good news."

Gospels [page 24]
The first four books of the New Testament named after the Evangelists Matthew, Mark, Luke, and John that pass on the Good News of Jesus Christ.

greed [page 200]
Wanting more things for ourselves than we really need.

heaven [page 89]
The kingdom of everlasting happiness with God and all the saints.

Hebrews [page 174]
The name given to God's people, the Israelites, when they lived in Egypt.

holiness [page 138]
Life in communion with God.

Holy Orders [page 139]
The Sacrament at the Service of Communion through which a baptized man is consecrated to serve the whole Church as a bishop, a priest, or a deacon.

Holy Spirit [page 40]
The third Person of the Trinity.

Holy Trinity [page 40]
The mystery of one God in three divine Persons—God the Father, God the Son, God the Holy Spirit.

honor [page 190]
To have special respect for someone, to hold someone in high regard.

hope [page 46]
A gift from God that enables us to trust in him and in his promises.

I-J-K-L

incarnation [page 54]
A word meaning "putting on flesh."

Incarnation [page 54]
The mystery of the Son of God, the second Person of the Trinity, becoming truly human while not giving up being divine, or God.

intellect [page 150]
The part of every person that gives us the ability to know God, ourselves, and other people.

Israelites [page 15]
The descendants of Abraham chosen by God to be his people; the Old Testament people to whom God revealed himself and with whom he made the Covenant.

judges of Israel [page 30]
The leaders of the Israelites before they had kings.

kingdom of God [page 48]
The kingdom of mercy and love, peace and justice that will come about when Jesus returns at the end of time and that will last forever.

Last Supper [page 62]
The last meal Jesus celebrated with his disciples at which he gave the Church the gift of his Body and Blood, the Eucharist.

liturgical year [page 100]
The Church's year of seasons and feasts that makes up the Church's year of worship and that celebrates God's great plan of saving love.

liturgy [page 98]
The work of the Church, the Body of Christ, of worshiping God.

Liturgy of the Hours [page 210]
The daily, public, communal prayer of the Church.

Lord's Day [page 182]
The name given to Sunday by Christians, the day of the Lord's Resurrection.

Lord's Prayer [page 226]
A name for the Our Father; the prayer Jesus, our Lord, taught his disciples to pray.

M-N-O

manna [page 114]
The breadlike food the Israelites ate in the desert during the Exodus.

marriage [page 192]
A special kind of friendship in which a man and a woman promise to love and honor each other as husband and wife their whole lives.

Mary [page 54]
The mother of the only Son of God, Jesus.

Matrimony [page 140]
The Sacrament at the Service of Communion through which a baptized man and a baptized woman are united in a lifelong bond of faithful love and become a sign of Christ's love for the Church.

meditation [page 218]
A form of prayer using our imagination that helps us come to know God and how he wants us to live.

Messiah [pages 47 and 48]
The Anointed One who God promised to send to save his people from sin and suffering, Jesus Christ.

miracle [page 56]
A word meaning "wonder, something amazing and marvelous"; the amazing deeds performed by Jesus that are signs of God's love and care for people.

missionaries [page 73]
Christians who travel to places in their own countries and in other countries to live and preach the Gospel.

moral virtues [page 166]
Habits of doing good; the human virtues of prudence, justice, fortitude, and temperance.

mortal sin [page 167]
The free choice of doing or saying something that is known to be gravely evil and against God's will and results in the loss of the gift of sanctifying grace, or holiness.

New Testament [page 24]
The twenty-seven books that make up the second main part of the Bible.

obey [page 190]
To follow the commands of others who have rightful authority in our lives and who are helping us live according to God's laws.

Old Testament [page 23]
The forty-six books that make up the first main part of the Bible.

original sin [page 46]
The sin the first humans committed that lost original holiness not only for themselves but for all human beings.

P-Q

Paschal Mystery [page 98]
The mystery of Jesus passing over from suffering and death to new and glorious life; Christ's work of salvation accomplished by his Passion, death, Resurrection, and Ascension.

Passover [page 62]
The Jewish feast celebrating God's freeing the Israelites from suffering and slavery in Egypt and leading them to freedom in the land he had promised them.

Penance [page 123]
Another name for the sacrament of Reconciliation.

Pentecost [page 70]
The day that the Holy Spirit came to the disciples as Jesus had promised, fifty days after the Resurrection.

People of God [page 86]
A New Testament image for the Church that teaches that God has called together all people in Jesus Christ to be his people.

perjury [page 198]
Lying under oath.

pilgrimage [page 221]
A prayer journey.

pope [pages 87 and 139]
The successor to Saint Peter the Apostle and the bishop of Rome, the shepherd of the whole Church on earth.

pray [page 210]
Raising our minds and hearts to God, who is Father, Son, and Holy Spirit; talking and listening to God.

precepts of the Church [page 185]
Five rules of the Church that help Catholics keep our responsibilities to worship God and grow in our love for God and our neighbor.

prophet [page 47]
A person chosen by God to speak in his name.

public ministry of Jesus [page 54]
The saving work that God the Father sent Jesus to do, beginning with the baptism of Jesus and his announcement of that work in the synagogue in Nazareth.

R-S

Rabbi [page 226]
A Hebrew word meaning "Teacher," a title of honor and respect in the Bible given to someone whom people trusted to help them understand and live the Law of God.

Reconciliation [page 123]
The Sacrament of Healing through which we receive God's forgiveness through the ministry of a bishop or priest.

reparation [page 198]
The work of repairing or making up for harm that we have wrongfully caused.

respect [page 190]
To give someone or something the honor they deserve.

Resurrection [page 64]
The raising of Jesus from the dead by God on the third day after his death.

reveal [page 14]
To unveil, or make known, what is hidden.

sacraments [page 106]
The seven main liturgical signs of the Church, given to us by Jesus Christ, that make us sharers in the saving work of Christ and in the life of the Holy Trinity through the power of the Holy Spirit.

Sacraments of Healing [page 122]
The sacrament of Anointing of the Sick and the sacrament of Reconciliation, or Penance.

Sacraments of Initiation [page 106]
The three sacraments of Baptism, Confirmation, and Eucharist, which are the foundation of the Christian life.

Sacraments at the Service of Communion [page 138] The sacraments of Holy Orders and Matrimony.

Sacred Scripture [page 22]
The holy writings of the people of God, inspired by the Holy Spirit and collected in the Bible.

sacrifice [page 78]
To give up something of value out of love.

sanctifying [page 168]
A word meaning "making holy."

sanctifying grace [page 166]
The gift of God sharing his own life with us, the gift of holiness.

selfishness [page 200]
Wanting and keeping things only for ourselves.

sin [page 122]
Freely choosing to turn away from God's love, and weakening or breaking one's friendship with God and the Church community.

soul [page 150]
The spiritual part of the human person that makes us like God and that lives forever.

stewards [page 39]
People who have been given the responsibility to care for someone or something that belongs to someone else.

synagogue [page 130]
A building in which the Jewish people gather to pray and to read and study the Scriptures and the Law of God and other teachings of the Jewish religion.

T-Z

take in vain [page 183]
To show disrespect for or to dishonor someone or something.

temptation [page 167]
Feelings, people, and things that try to get us to turn away from God's love and not to live a holy life.

Ten Commandments [page 174]
The laws of the Covenant revealed to Moses on Mount Sinai that teach us to love God, others, and ourselves.

theological virtues [page 218]
Faith, hope, and love (or charity); gifts and powers from God that help us keep God at the center of our lives.

triduum [page 100]
A word meaning "three days."

Triduum [page 100]
The center of the liturgical year; the three-day celebration of Jesus' Paschal Mystery beginning on Holy Thursday and continuing on Good Friday through the Easter Vigil/Easter Sunday.

venial sin [page 167]
A sin that does not have the three conditions necessary for a mortal sin, and that weakens our love for God and for one another.

vices [page 167]
Habits of doing what is against God's will.

vocal prayer [page 220]
A form of prayer that uses words that we pray aloud or quietly in our mind and heart.

vocation [page 33]
A call from God to do a special work.

worship [page 182]
To honor and respect above all else; to give adoration and praise to God.

YHWH [page 22]
The four letters of the Hebrew alphabet for the name for God that God revealed to Moses.

Index

Credits

Cover Design: Kristy Howard
Cover Illustration: Amy Freeman

PHOTO CREDITS
Abbreviated as follows: (bkgd) background; (t) top; (b) bottom; (l) left; (r) right; (c) center.

Frontmatter: Page 7, © The Picture Book/PictureQuest; 11 (tl), © The Crosiers/Gene Plaisted, OSC; 11 (tr), © David Duprey/AP/Wide World; 11 (bl), © Myrleen Ferguson Cate/PhotoEdit; 12, © Michele Burgess/Stock, Boston,Inc.

Chapter 1: Page 13, © Martin Heitner/PictureQuest; 14, © Mark Segal/Index Stock; 16, © Scala/Art Resource; 17 (t), © Jim Craigmyle/Masterfile; 17 (bl), © The Crosiers/Gene Plaisted, OSC; 17 (br), © Kathy Ferguson/Photo Edit; 20, © Pete Saloutos/Corbis.

Chapter 2: Page 21,© Myrleen Ferguson Cate/Photo Edit; 24 (t), © The Crosiers/Gene Plaisted, OSC; 24 (b), Artville; 25, © Ed Bock/The StockMarket; 28, © Jeanene Tiner.

Chapter 3: Page 29, © The Crosiers/Gene Plaisted, OSC; 30, © Zev Radovan/Biblical Archaeology Society; 32, © Alinari/Art Resource, NY; 33, © Myrleen Ferguson Cate/Photo Edit; 34, © Donald F. Wristen/RCL; 36, © Bill Bachmann/PictureQuest.

Chapter 4: Page 37, © PictureQuest; 38, © Myrleen Ferguson Cate/Photo Edit; 40, © PictureQuest; 41, © James Lafayette/IndexStock; 44, © Deborah Davis/Photo Edit.

Chapter 5: Page 45, © The Crosiers/Gene Plaisted, OSC; 47, © Paul Harris/Stone; 49 (t), © Marquette University Archives; 49 (b), © Fritz Kaeser; 52, © David Young-Wolff/Photo Edit.

Chapter 6: Page 53, © The Crosiers/Gene Plaisted, OSC; 57, © The Crosiers/Gene Plaisted, OSC; 60, © Corbis.

Chapter 7: Page 61, © Jeanene Tiner; 63 (all), © The Crosiers/Gene Plaisted, OSC; 65 (l), © Alan Oddie/Photo Edit; 65 (r), © The Crosiers/Gene Plaisted, OSC; 68, © Jeff Topping/Reuters/Corbis.

Chapter 8: Page 69, © The Crosiers/Gene Plaisted, OSC; 72, © Michael Newman/Photo Edit; 73 (all), © Sprague/ Maryknoll Fathers & Brothers; 76, © Tony Freeman/Photo Edit.

Chapter 9: Page 77, © Michele Burgess/Stock Boston, Inc.; 81 (t), © Wilfred Ramos/Catholic Relief Services; 81 (cr), © Renee Fischer/Catholic Relief Services; 81 (bl), © CRS Staff/Catholic Relief Services; 81 (br), © Dave Snyder/Catholic Relief Services; 84, © Francisco Cruz/Superstock.

Chapter 10: Page 85, © David Duprey/AP Wide World; 86, © Digital Stock; 89, © The Crosiers/Gene Plaisted, OSC; 92, © Myrleen Ferguson Cate/Photo Edit; 95 (tl), © Robert Daemmrich/Stock, Boston; 95 (tr), © The Crosiers/Gene Plaisted, OSC; 95 (b), © Bill Wittman.

Chapter 11: Page 97, © The Crosiers/Gene Plaisted, OSC; 98, © The Crosiers/Gene Plaisted, OSC; 99, © Anthony Jambor/RCL; 101, © Bob Daemmrich/Photo Edit; 104, © Bill Wittman.

Chapter 12: Page 105, © The Crosiers/Gene Plaisted, OSC; 106, © Sam Martinez/RCL; 107, © Tony Freeman/Photo Edit; 108, © Myrleen Ferguson Cate/Photo Edit; 109 (l), © Tom Fritz/Bread for the World; 109 (r), © Margaret W. Nea/Bread for the World; 112, © Bill Wittman.

Chapter 13: Page 113, © The Crosiers/Gene Plaisted, OSC; 114, © Punchstock; 116, © The Crosiers/Gene Plaisted, OSC; 117 (all), © Catholic Community of St. Elizabeth Ann Seton Love Truck Ministry; 120, © PictureQuest.

Chapter 14: Page 121, © Robert Daemmrich/Stock, Boston; 122 (t), © Merritt A. Vincent/Photo Edit; 122(b), © Steven Frisch/Stock, Boston; 123–124, © The Crosiers/Gene Plaisted, OSC; 125, © Myrleen Ferguson Cate/Photo Edit; 128, © Guy Cali/PictureQuest.

Chapter 15: Page 129, © The Crosiers/Gene Plaisted, OSC; 132 (tr), © Myrleen Ferguson Cate/Photo Edit; 132 (bl), © Alan Oddie/Photo Edit; 132 (br), © Frank Pedrick/Index Stock; 133, © The Crosiers/Gene Plaisted, OSC; 136, © Corbis.

Chapter 16: Page 137, © Peter Christopher/Masterfile; 138, © Bill Wittman; 138 (t), © Tony Freeman/Photo Edit; 139 (b), © The Crosiers/Gene Plaisted, OSC; 140, © Bill Wittman; 141(t), © Myrleen Ferguson Cate/Photo Edit; 141 (b), © Milazzo/Maryknoll; 144, © James L. Shaffer; 147 (tl), © James Shaffer/Photo Edit; 147 (tr), © Michael Newman/Photo Edit; 147 (b), © Joe Gemignan/Corbis.

Chapter 17: Page 149, © Jeffry Myers/Stock, Boston; 150, © Comstock Photography; 152, © Punchstock; 153, © The Crosiers/Gene Plaisted, OSC; 156, © PictureQuest.

Chapter 18: Page 157, © Joe Gemignani/Corbis; 159, © James Shaffer/Photo Edit; 160 (t), © SW Production/Index Stock; 160 (b), © David Young Wolff/Photo Edit; 161, © The Crosiers/Gene Plaisted, OSC; 164, © Thinkstock.

Chapter 19: Page 165, © Michael Newman/Photo Edit; 166 (t), © Jon Feingersh/Corbis; 166 (b), © Myrleen Ferguson Cate/Photo Edit; 169 (all), © Catholic Relief Services; 172, © Steve Skjold/Photo Edit.

Chapter 20: Page 173, © The Crosiers/Gene Plaisted, OSC; 174, © David Harris/Biblical Archaeology Society; 177, © The Crosiers/Gene Plaisted, OSC; 180, © Punchstock.

Chapter 21: Page 181, © Nicholas DeVore/Getty Images; 184 (t), © The Crosiers/Gene Plaisted, OSC; 184 (b), © Dick Luria/ FPG International; 185, © The Crosiers/Gene Plaisted, OSC; 188, © PictureQuest.

Chapter 22: Page 189, © Andy Sacks/Stone; 190, © Kendra Clinett/Stone; 192, © Kent Meireis/The Image Works; 193 (all), © L'Arche USA; 196, © Bill Wittman.

Chapter 23: Page 197, © Don Smetzel/Gettyimages; 198, © Jeffry W. Meyers/Stock, Boston; 201 (all), © Society of St. Andrew; 204, © PictureQuest; 207 (t), © Tony Freeman/Photo Edit; 207 (bl), © Bill Wittman; 207 (br), © Bob Daemmrich/Stock, Boston.

Chapter 24: Page 209, © Robert Cushman Hayes; 210 (all), © Myrleen Ferguson Cate/Photo Edit; 212, © Bill Wittman; 213 (t & bl), © Myrleen Ferguson Cate/ Photo Edit; 213 (br), © Mark Burnett/Stock Boston, Inc.; 215, © Wood River Gallery; 216, © Brand X Pictures.

Chapter 25: Page 217, © Bill Wittman; 218 (t), © Bob Daemmrick/Stock Boston, Inc.; 218 (b), © Myrleen Ferguson Cate/Photo Edit; 220 (t), © Donald F. Wristen/RCL; 220 (bl), © Rommel/Masterfile; 220 (br), © PascalCrapet/Stone; 221 (all), © Richard T. Nowtiz/Corbis; 224, © Punchstock.

Chapter 26: Page 225, © The Crosiers/Gene Plaisted, OSC; 226, © Francene Keery/Stock, Boston; 228 (t), © Photomondo/Gettyimages; 228 (c), © Myrleen Ferguson Cate; 228 (b) © Masterfile; 229 (all), © Darcy Kiefel/Heifer International; 232, © Tony Freeman/Photo Edit.

Liturgical Seasons: Page 235 (all), © Bill Wittman; 237, © Anthony Jambor; 278, © The Crosiers/Gene Plaisted, OSC; 241, © The Crosiers/Gene Plasted, OSC; 243, © Tom Benoit/All Stock; 245, © The Crosiers/Gene Plaisted, OSC; 247, © Karl Holtsnider; 249, © SuperStock, Inc.; 251 (t), © The Crosiers/Gene Plaisted, OSC; 251(b), © Bill Wittman; 292 (t), © Myrleen Ferguson Cate/Photo Edit; 292 (b), © David DeLossy/The Image Bank; 255, © The Crosiers/Gene Plaisted, OSC; 257, © Griffin/The Image Works; 259, © Kirk Condyles/Impact Visuals/PNI; 263, © The Crosiers/Gene Plaisted. OSC; 265 & 267, © Bill Wittman; 269, © Todd Powell/Photo Network; 271, © The Crosiers/Gene Plaisted, OSC; 275, © Don Smetzer/Photo Edit; 277, © Walter Hodges/Stone; 279,281, © The Crosiers/Gene Plaisted. OSC.; 283, © Myrleen Ferguson Cate/Photo Edit; 285, © Masterfile; 286, © Michael Newman/Photo Edit; 287, © Jim Corwin/Stone; 291 & 293, © Eric Williams/RCL; 294, © The Crosiers/Gene Plaisted, OSC; 296,© Myrleen Ferguson Cate/Photo Edit.

ILLUSTRATION CREDITS
Abbreviated as follows: (bkgd) background; (t) top; (b) bottom; (l) left; (r) right; (c) center.

Page 8, 9, 10, Amy Freeman; 22, Eulala Conner; 41, Karen Maizel; 48, Linda Simmons; 50, Karen Maizel; 54, Dynamic Graphics, Inc.; 55, Margaret Lindmark; 56, Amy Freeman; 62, Margaret Lindmark; 70, Margaret Lindmark; 71, © 1996 The Order of St. Benedict, Inc.; 72, Anni Matsick; 79, Jan Palmer; 90, Amy Freeman; 96, Margaret Lindmark; 100, © 1996 The Order of St. Benedict, Inc.; 115, Margaret Lindmark; 131, Margaret Lindmark; 134–135, © 1996 The Order of St. Benedict, Inc.; 148, Mari Goering; 155, © 1996 The Order of St. Benedict, Inc; 168, Amy Freeman; 175, Mari Goering; 203, Jenny Williams; 208, Margaret Lindmark; 222, Bill Alger; 227, Margaret Lindmark; 236, © 1996 The Order of St. Benedict, Inc.; 246, Bob Niles; 250 (t), Chris Schechner; 250 (b), Dynamic Graphics, Inc.; 252, Dynamic Graphics, 261, Jo Arnold; 264, Bob Niles; 266, 270, Dynamic Graphics, Inc.; Renee Daily; 288, Amy Freeman; 289, drawings by Angela Marina Barbieri & Joan Lledõ Vila.